LEXICOGRAPHY, TERMINOLOGY,

AND TRANSLATION

LEXICOGRAPHY, TERMINOLOGY, AND TRANSLATION

Text-based studies in honour of Ingrid Meyer

Edited by

Lynne Bowker

University of Ottawa Press

The University of Ottawa Press gratefully acknowledges the support extended to its publishing programme by the Canada Council for the Arts and the University of Ottawa.

We also acknowledge with gratitude the support of the Government of Canada through its Book Publishing Industry Development Program for our publishing activities.

Library and Archives Canada Cataloguing in Publication

    Lexicography, terminology, and translation : text-based studies in honour of Ingrid Meyer / edited by Lynne Bowker.

(Perspectives on translation)
Includes bibliographical references and index.
ISBN-13: 978-0-7766-0627-9
ISBN-10: 0-7766-0627-1

    1. Terms and phrases. 2. Lexicography. 3. Translating and interpreting. 4. Discourse analysis. I. Meyer, Ingrid II. Bowker, Lynne, 1969- III. Series.

P305.L49 2006   401'.4   C2006-904032-X

All rights reserved. No parts of this publication may be reproduced or transmitted in any form or by any means, electronic or mechanical, including photocopy, recording, or any information storage and retrieval system, without permission in writing from the publisher.

Copy editing: Dallas Harrison
Cover art and design: Kevin Matthews
Typesetting: Brad Horning
Proofreading: Donna Williams

Published by the University of Ottawa Press, 2006
542 King Edward Avenue, Ottawa, Ontario K1N 6N5
press@uottawa.ca / www.uopress.uottawa.ca

Ingrid Meyer
(1957–2004)

TABLE OF CONTENTS

Preface ix

Introduction 1

Part I: Lexicography
    Chapter 1: The Semantic Apparatus of Guy Miège's
    New Dictionary French and English, with Another
    English and French
    Aline Francoeur 13

    Chapter 2: Relevance in Dictionary Making: Sense
    Indicators in the Bilingual Entry
    Beryl T. Sue Atkins and Pierrette Bouillon 25

    Chapter 3: Biased Books by Harmless Drudges:
    How Dictionaries Are Influenced by Social Values
    Kristen Mackintosh 45

Part II: Terminology
    Chapter 4: Terminological Relationships and
    Corpus-Based Methods for Discovering Them:
    An Assessment for Terminographers
    Marie-Claude L'Homme and Elizabeth Marshman 67

    Chapter 5: Semi-automatic Corpus Construction
    from Informative Texts
    Caroline Barrière 81

    Chapter 6: From Terminological Data Banks to
    Knowledge Databases: The Text As the Starting Point
    M. Teresa Cabré Castellví 93

    Chapter 7: Intrinsic Qualities Favouring Term
    Implantation: Verifying the Axioms
    Jean Quirion and Jacynthe Lanthier 107

Part III: Translation

Chapter 8: French Theorists, North American Scholiasts
Barbara Folkart 121

Chapter 9: Consequences of Translation for Legal Terminology during the Middle Ages and Renaissance
Claire-Hélène Lavigne 133

Chapter 10: Sebastian Brant's *Das Narrenschiff* in Early Modern England: A Textual Voyage
Brenda M. Hosington 145

Chapter 11: Criticizing Translations: The Notion of Disparity
Jean Delisle 159

Chapter 12: Translation Memory and "Text"
Lynne Bowker 175

Chapter 13: An Evaluation Methodology for Comparing Two Approaches to Search and Retrieval in Translation Memory Databases
Francie Gow 189

Chapter 14: Corpora and Translation
Roda P. Roberts and Jacqueline Bossé-Andrieu 201

Chapter 15: The Contextual Turn in Learning to Translate
Krista Varantola 215

Chapter 16: Film Translation Research in Spain: The Dubbing of Hollywood Movies into Spanish
José-María Bravo 227

Contributors 239

Select Bibliography of Works by Ingrid Meyer 245

Index 251

PREFACE

LYNNE BOWKER

This volume is intended to pay tribute to Ingrid Meyer, a valued colleague in the fields of lexicography, terminology, and translation. As a professor,[1] Ingrid was unquestionably dedicated to her students and showed a great concern for student welfare. She played a pivotal role in the establishment and ongoing development of a computer lab for translation students in the days before computers were widespread and before the School of Translation and Interpretation had much in the way of a budget to cover such costs. She regularly identified promising students, encouraged them to go on to graduate school, and successfully sought out research grants, which she used primarily as a means of offering financial assistance and research experience to students.

Outside the classroom, Ingrid made numerous contributions to the language community. Not only was she a certified translator fluent in English, French, and German, but she also became an avid student of Spanish. She was a valued member of the advisory board of the journal *Terminology*, and of the reading committee of the translation journal *Meta*, as well as an active member in associations such as the European Association for Lexicography (EURALEX) and the Association for Machine Translation in the Americas (AMTA).

Her research activities are another indicator of the tremendous contribution that Ingrid made to the language community. As can be seen from the select bibliography of her works presented at the end of this volume, Ingrid conducted research in the three interrelated domains of lexicography, terminology, and translation. Within these fields, one of her main interests was technology. Whether it was exploring the potential of electronic dictionaries and corpora or developing tools to represent terminological data or searching for ways to integrate computers into the translation process, much of her research was in some way situated at the intersection of language and computing.

Following from her doctoral dissertation, entitled "Towards a New Type of General Bilingual Dictionary," some of Ingrid's earliest research was in the field of bilingual lexicography, with a particular focus on how dictionaries can be used as tools by both professional and student translators. Early in her career, Ingrid also integrated her role as a translation professor into her research, exploring issues such as selection examinations for student interpreters and the role and nature of computer studies and of specialized writing courses in a translation program.

Undoubtedly, however, Ingrid will be best remembered for the significant contribution that she made to the field of terminology. One of her most notable achievements was her pioneering research into the development of terminological knowledge bases (TKBs). This work was largely carried out in collaboration with her husband and co-researcher Douglas Skuce, a professor of computer science. Together they made a formidable team as they introduced a new way of describing and representing terminological information, taking into account the often complex and multidimensional networks of conceptual relations that exist within specialized fields of knowledge.

Ingrid was also among the first researchers to recognize the value of corpus-based investigations into specialized language. Using specially designed collections of electronic text, which could be interrogated with the help of corpus analysis tools, Ingrid and her collaborators undertook a variety of terminological corpus-based studies. For example, in addition to conducting investigations into phraseology, concept analysis, and metaphor, Ingrid carried out highly original work in the area of de-terminologization—where terms that were once used only in specialized fields become taken up in general language—and in the semi-automatic identification of knowledge-rich contexts via lexical patterns.

Whether acting in her capacity as a skilled language professional, a committed teacher, an expert researcher, or a valued colleague, Ingrid was an excellent role model. Her dedication and optimism shone through in all her undertakings, as can be witnessed from the following extract from a letter of holiday greetings that Ingrid sent to her co-workers at the School of Translation and Interpretation in December 2003:

> I would like to share with you one most unexpected thing about my cancer experience. Before all this happened, if someone had told me that I would get an incurable disease, be on medication indefinitely, and stop working full-time, I would have imagined that there couldn't possibly be much of a life left. But things have turned out so differently. I've learned that the human spirit is incredibly adaptable and that there are bright sides to any situation, if one can learn to see things differently. For example, being able to spend much more time with my kids because I'm not working; getting to know some of the finest people (both patients and health professionals) I have ever had the privilege of meeting at the Cancer Centre; moving my "work" from translation to researching new cancer treatments—and actually trying some of these and finding that they work! It's always thrilling to work on a challenge and meet with success—especially when the challenge is survival.

Throughout her career, Ingrid had an impact on many people. In a profession that can be quite competitive, she was a model of cooperation and collaboration, so it is no surprise that a number of the colleagues with whom she collaborated in various contexts are represented in this volume. Some of the contributors are former professors with whom Ingrid studied when she was a graduate student in translation and linguistics, while others are former students of Ingrid herself who benefited from her guidance while preparing for their own careers. A number of contributors are colleagues who, even though they may not have shared her specific research interests, nevertheless worked in close proximity to her on a daily basis at the School of Translation and Interpretation. Still others are colleagues from a variety of institutions around the world who, though separated geographically from Ingrid, shared her passion for research, who enjoyed meeting up with her at conferences or on research visits, or who engaged in lively e-mail exchanges on topics of shared interest. Although the circumstances of Ingrid's relationship with the various contributors differ, these contributors are united in the sense that they all benefited from having had the opportunity to work with Ingrid in some capacity and thus wish to pay tribute to her memory by participating in this commemorative volume.

The contributors to this volume represent only a small fraction of Ingrid's colleagues and friends. There were many others who, for reasons of timing and circumstance, were unable to submit papers but who nonetheless expressed their support for this project. In fact, in the days following Ingrid's death, as the news spread throughout the language community, messages poured in from colleagues across Canada and around the world. They shared fond memories of collaborating with Ingrid on a particularly fascinating project, of listening to her give an engaging presentation, or of enjoying coffee with her at a conference.

Ingrid was held in such high regard—both professionally and personally—that her death is a great loss not only to the School of Translation and Interpretation and the University of Ottawa but also to the international language community as a whole. This volume is respectfully dedicated to the memory of Ingrid Meyer as a tribute to a woman who was a teacher, colleague, mentor, and friend to so many and an example to us all.

NOTE

1   Ingrid Meyer received a BA in French and German from McMaster University (Canada), followed by an MA in translation and a PhD in linguistics, both from the Université de Montréal. She then went on to work as a professor at the School of Translation and Interpretation at the University of Ottawa—a position that she held from 1983 until the time of her death.

INTRODUCTION

LYNNE BOWKER

In a commemorative volume such as this, it is only natural that the contributors will have different areas of specialization, including dictionary compilation, terminology, literary translation, film translation, translation criticism, translation technology, corpus-based studies, historical studies, and translation practice, among others. Nevertheless, a common theme runs through all the papers in this volume—that of text-based studies. The specific text or type of text under consideration varies from paper to paper, but all report on an issue that is in some way text based.

In accordance with the research interests of Ingrid Meyer, the papers in this volume have been grouped into three main sections: lexicography, terminology, and translation. Given that these fields are interrelated, there is naturally some overlap among the papers, some of which might have found a home in more than one section.

LEXICOGRAPHY

As noted previously, Ingrid Meyer's early research focused on bilingual lexicography, with a particular focus on the usefulness of dictionaries for translators (e.g., Meyer 1985, 1988). The ability of a bilingual dictionary to provide users with information to distinguish between different word senses, and thereby to choose the most appropriate translation for their needs, is a common theme in the first two papers in the "Lexicography" section of this volume.

Aline Francoeur studies this question from a historical perspective, observing that, although the issue of meaning discrimination did not become widely recognized as an important concern in bilingual lexicography until the latter half of the twentieth century, some bilingual dictionaries took semantic features into account at a much earlier date. Based on an analysis of more than 700 entries from Guy Miège's *New Dictionary French and English, with Another English and French,* published in 1677, Francoeur identifies a number of types of direct and indirect semantic information, including definitions, contexts, and field labels, and explains how they were useful to dictionary users for both decoding and encoding purposes.

Leaping ahead to the age of corpus-based lexicography, **Sue Atkins and Pierrette Bouillon** pick up the theme of semantic information and examine it as it pertains to the process of compiling a bilingual dictionary, both in the analysis stage, where lexicographers are seeking facts that are essential to the discovery and recording of how a word behaves, and in the synthesis stage, where lexicographers employ a wider variety of information in order to help guide dictionary users to the appropriate translations. Atkins and Bouillon suggest that the types of information used as "sense indicators" in bilingual dictionaries reflect transfer conditions from source to target language. They present an initial classification of this new type of lexicographically relevant information, which forms the basis of an online database of sense indicators. To date, there has been little research carried out to discover which of the various types of sense indicator employed in current dictionaries are the most effective, and the authors suggest that the Sense Indicator Database presented here may provide a launch pad for such a study.

In the final paper of the "Lexicography" section, **Kristen Mackintosh** considers dictionary entries as a type of text, examining in particular the impact that social values have on both the form and the content of these entries. Using monolingual English and French dictionaries as sources, she explores how social values have affected the form of dictionary entries by examining the phrasing and diction used in definitions as well as the sources used for examples. With regard to content, Mackintosh begins by studying the macrostructure of certain lexicographic works, describing how social values can lead to a type of "censorship" that determines which words get left out of dictionaries. She then moves on to explore the microstructure, examining how both definitions and examples can be ideologically coloured. In her concluding remarks, Mackintosh observes that not only do social values influence dictionaries, but dictionaries can also influence social values, and she presents an interesting discussion about the power that dictionaries have to bring about positive or negative social change as well as some observations about user expectations of dictionaries.

TERMINOLOGY

As previously mentioned, Ingrid Meyer was best known for her research into terminological issues—particularly those that combined some aspect of computers and terminology, such as the use of electronic corpora or the creation of terminological knowledge bases. A number of the themes addressed by Ingrid in her work have been taken up by some of the contributors to this section, while some additional terminology-related themes have also been introduced.

One subject of great interest to Ingrid was the investigation of knowledge patterns, which are generally understood to be linguistic sequences that reveal semantic relations between concepts, such as the "is a kind of" pattern, which indicates a hyperonymic relation, or the "is a part of" pattern, which indicates a meronymic relation. Knowledge patterns and methods for detecting them in corpora are topics also explored by **Marie-Claude L'Homme** and **Elizabeth Marshman.** They begin their paper by explaining some of the different types of semantic relations that exist. This explanation is followed by a thorough review of research carried out to date into different approaches for identifying knowledge patterns in corpora. Some of these approaches are based on linguistic markers—an approach used by Ingrid in her own research (e.g., Meyer 2001, Meyer et al. 1999)—while others rely on formal features of terms or on co-occurrence patterns. L'Homme and Marshman conclude their paper by analyzing the strengths and weaknesses of these different approaches with regard to their usefulness for meeting the needs of terminologists.

A specific application of knowledge patterns is presented in the paper by **Caroline Barrière.** As a precursor to performing terminological research, a terminologist must compile a corpus of texts that will then be mined for terminological data. One of the most challenging tasks facing a terminologist is to determine—as quickly and easily as possible—which texts should be included in the corpus. Ideally, as pointed out by Ingrid in some of her research (e.g., Meyer 1994, 2001), a corpus should be composed of texts that are "knowledge rich," which means that they should contain information about how important concepts in a subject field relate to one another. Barrière explores a method for helping terminologists to automatically construct a useful electronic corpus by using a tool that can compute the knowledge-rich value of a text. The knowledge-rich value is based on the density of knowledge patterns. After presenting an analysis of previous research conducted on knowledge patterns, Barrière introduces a prototype software tool that she is currently developing in order to automatically identify texts that have a high knowledge-rich value. Barrière closes with an evaluation of some of the limitations of the prototype tool and makes some suggestions for future research that will help to overcome these limitations.

Once terminologists have gathered information from specialized corpora, they compile these data into repositories so that they are available in a concise and useful form for other users, such as translators, to consult. As previously mentioned, Ingrid conducted pioneering work in the development of a new type of repository known as a terminological knowledge base or TKB (e.g., Meyer et al. 1992). In her paper, **M. Teresa Cabré Castellví** traces the evolution of linguistic resources from data banks to knowledge databases, describing a number of innovative refinements that have taken place, including the development of thematic resources, the classification of data on the basis of pragmatic and communicative criteria, and the inclusion of explicit grammatical information (e.g., tags). According to Cabré, a specialized knowledge database is a resource that integrates terminological units, conceptual ontologies, and corpora. As an example, Cabré introduces the GENOME project, based at the Institute for Applied Linguistics at the Universitat Pompeu Fabra in Spain, which resulted in the creation of a knowledge database on the specialized subject of the human genome. The contents of and means of interacting with the GENOME knowledge database are described in detail.

It was noted above that Ingrid was an early advocate of corpus-based research (e.g., Meyer and Mackintosh 1996), and the final paper in the "Terminology" section presents a terminological investigation carried out using a specialized corpus. **Jean Quirion** and **Jacynthe Lanthier** present the results of a terminometric study focusing on the implantation of terms. Specifically, this study sets out to verify whether terms that are successfully implanted possess different characteristics than do terms that do not make their way into usage. For many years, researchers have speculated and hypothesized about intrinsic characteristics that would lead to successful implantation; however, the resulting axioms have never been empirically validated. Using a French Canadian-language corpus of written institutional communications taken from the specialized fields of transportation, and retirement and pensions, Quirion and Lanthier present a methodology for assigning an implantation coefficient to every term in the corpus, which gives a precise indication of the proportionate use of the term in comparison to competing terms referring to the same notion. In addition, they investigate the presence or absence of four characteristics—conciseness, absence of competing terms, derivative form capability, and compliance with the rules of the language—in almost 300 terms. All four of the variables tested in the study point to a similar conclusion: they are all more characteristic of terms with an implantation coefficient of 1 (i.e., implanted terms) than of terms that have a coefficient of 0 (i.e., terms that were not accepted into usage). Therefore, what were formerly axioms can now be considered as truths based on the empirical data resulting from this terminometric study.

TRANSLATION

As a professor at the School of Translation and Interpretation, Ingrid Meyer was concerned with many different aspects of translation. She taught a wide range of courses, including courses on translation technology, technical translation, documentation, and grammar and language problems. Although her research interests focused mainly on terminological, lexicographic, and technological applications for translators, she was always interested in expanding her horizons. Some of the subjects treated here overlap with her own research interests, while others bring in new material that she would surely have found stimulating.

The first two papers in this section focus on the translation—or the mistranslation—of specific terms. **Barbara Folkart** conducts a study of lexical collocation using a corpus of academic discourse or "profspeak." Specifically, she investigates the lexical items *interpellate* and *hail*, which first appeared in an English translation of a French-language essay by Louis Althusser. Folkart uncovers unusual collocation patterns for these terms in her corpus and suggests that these malformed patternings, which have become entrenched in the discourse, are often an artifact of (poor) translation. Folkart goes on to offer some suggestions for retranslating these problematic terms and to reflect on translation pathways, terminological pathways, and discursive ruts.

The theme of mistranslation is picked up by **Claire-Hélène Lavigne**, who investigates translation strategies used by four different translators who worked during the Middle Ages and Renaissance to produce Old French translations of a Latin legal text: Book 1, Title 15, of the *Institutes*, which makes up part of the *Corpus Iuris Civilis*. Specifically, Lavigne examines translations of the legal terms *adgnatorum* and *adgnati*. First she provides definitions of the legal concepts represented by these Latin terms; then she analyzes the translations of these terms to evaluate whether or not they captured the correct meaning of the source text. She finds that the translators in question do not appear to share a common strategy when translating legal terminology and that most of their translations of *adgnatorum* and *adgnati* do not succeed in transferring the full meaning of the concept as it is found in the Latin source text. Lavigne concludes that transferring concepts from the Roman legal system to the feudal legal system via translation was extremely challenging and that the translation process had serious consequences for the transfer of legal concepts.

Moving away from the study of specific terms, but staying with historical texts, **Brenda M. Hosington** examines an English translation of Sebastian Brant's *Das Narrenschiff*, a popular satire first published in 1494. The translation in question is *The shyp of folys of the worlde . . . Translated out of Laten, Frenche, and Doche into Englysshe* (1509) by Alexander Barclay. His translation was based primarily on Jacob Locher's *Stultifera Navis* (1497), itself a Latin translation of Brant's text. In her paper, Hosington focuses specifically on the various "domesticating" techniques, including additions, omissions, and modifications to the source text, that Barclay uses to make his translation relevant and significant for his English audience. Hosington analyzes numerous examples of the "englishing" of the text, which include strategies such as referring to England in various ways, naming local places and people in the county in which Barclay was living when he translated the text, effecting cultural shifts in the text, and expressing nationalistic and ideological sentiments different from those of the original author or previous translators. Hosington closes with a discussion of the differing opinions that have been expressed with regard to the extent and success of Barclay's domesticating in *Shyp of Folys*.

This notion of criticism of literary translation is taken up by **Jean Delisle,** who notes that true criticism consists not of inventorying whether each and every element of the original has been transposed but in determining whether the translated work offers the same significance as the original as seen through elements such as literary properties, semantic cohesion, aesthetic qualities, and underlying unity. Delisle notes that this ideal is difficult for translators to achieve and that there is inevitably some "disparity" between source and target texts. It is this notion of disparity that Delisle explores in detail in his paper, beginning with a look at some definitions—in French and in English—of this concept. He then goes on to consider precisely what "disparity" does and does not entail in the context of translation studies, and he provides numerous supporting examples. He likens disparity to "the mark of a bad forgery" and concludes that it affects the aesthetic and literary value of a work judged in the light of contemporary norms. For this reason, Delisle closes by reminding us that standards of acceptability vary from period to period and from genre to genre.

The issue of disparity is also relevant to the paper presented by **Lynne Bowker,** who examines the effect that the use of translation memory tools can have on text. The paper opens with a brief discussion of what is understood by "text" and why text is relevant to translation. This discussion is followed by a description of the basic way in which a translation memory tool works. Bowker then presents a review and discussion of the ways in which this type of technology has had an impact on text and the implications that it has for translation. For instance, the fact that these tools operate primarily on a sentence-based level has prompted some translators to avoid using anaphoric and cataphoric references, which can interfere with the cohesion of the text as a whole. In the concluding section, Bowker stresses that these tools are not inherently "bad," but that care must be taken to apply them in appropriate situations.

Translation memory tools are also the subject of the paper by **Francie Gow,** who presents a methodology for comparing the search-and-retrieval functions used by two different categories of translation memory tool. Gow begins by explaining the underlying differences between tools that use a sentence-based approach and those that use a character-string-within-a-bitext (CSB)-based approach. She then explains how the "usefulness" of the information that each tool retrieves can be defined and measured using a series of scores that take into account the validity of the information retrieved as well as the time that is gained or lost by using the tool. Gow presents the results of a practical experiment conducted using representative tools from each category, and she closes with some observations about the types of text and user that are most suited to each of the two types of translation memory.

Another type of translation technology—an electronic corpus coupled with a corpus analysis tool—is featured in the paper by **Roda P. Roberts** and **Jacqueline Bossé-Andrieu.** They open by providing some different definitions for "corpus" and identifying three different types of corpora that seem to be particularly useful for translators: unilingual corpora, bi-/multilingual translation corpora, and bi-/multilingual comparable corpora. Roberts and Bossé-Andrieu then present a categorization of a number of types of translation difficulties, including source text versus target text-related problems and encyclopedic, linguistic, and textual problems. These general categories of translation problems are then illustrated using a sample English-language source text, and Roberts and Bossé-Andrieu show how a translator can make good use of corpora to resolve translation difficulties when rendering this text into French. The paper concludes with an analysis of the strengths and weaknesses both of specially designed linguistic corpora and of the broader collections of text referred to as general corpora for meeting the needs of translators.

Krista Varantola also considers the value of corpora, along with dictionaries, for providing practical aid to translators. Varantola opens the paper by observing that there have been a number of different "turns" or foci in translation studies in recent decades, including linguistic, cultural, and historical turns, but she notes that there has been surprisingly little attention paid to the practical aspects of translation. She suggests that perhaps the time is right to focus on a "contextual turn in translating," pointing out that recent major developments in the tools of translation, such as dictionaries and corpora, merit this emphasis on the practical aspects because their effect on translators' problem-solving techniques is fundamental and deserves a much more systematic treatment. In her paper, Varantola concentrates on the major changes that have taken place in dictionary making and corpus compilation, and she discusses how these developments and the electronic medium have changed the work of the human translator. She points out, among other things, that, while there has been some convergence between dictionaries and corpora, they still represent very different tools. Following her analysis of what each of these tools has to offer, she concludes by noting that the real challenge is to find out why translators are looking up particular words or lexical items in dictionaries and corpora and what they really want to know in different situations. It is only when this knowledge has been uncovered and incorporated into dictionaries and corpus analysis tools that we will be able to claim that we have really managed to integrate the translators in the contextual turn of translating.

In the final paper of this volume, **José-María Bravo** introduces texts of a different sort: films. Bravo explores the industry of film translation—specifically subtitling and dubbing—as it has developed in Spain. He identifies three main approaches to the study of film translation: an exploration of the impact that the industrial nature of filmmaking has had on film translation, a description of the technical processes involved in the various modes of film translation, and an examination of translation problems in the context of conditions that are specific to audiovisual media. Bravo describes the current state of each of these approaches to film translation in Spain, summarizing the work that has been achieved so far and identifying areas that require further investigation. The last of these three approaches is explored in the most detail in Bravo's paper, and it includes discussions of the subtitling versus dubbing debate, the language of the cinema, general translation problems and core difficulties, and ideology and translation. The paper closes with a discussion of some emerging lines of research in film translation, including investigations into the linguistic characteristics of different film genres, studies of voice-over audio descriptions, and theoretical research into film translation, which has thus far been very limited.

CONCLUDING REMARKS

It has been my privilege, as editor, to bring together these papers, which, though diverse in subject matter, are comparable in terms of the stimulation that they will provide to readers who share Ingrid's passion for lexicography, terminology, and translation. I would like to thank the authors for their contributions, and I hope that they, as well as other readers, will find this collection to be a fitting tribute to Ingrid Meyer.

PART I

LEXICOGRAPHY

CHAPTER 1

THE SEMANTIC APPARATUS OF GUY MIÈGE'S *NEW DICTIONARY FRENCH AND ENGLISH, WITH ANOTHER ENGLISH AND FRENCH*[1]

ALINE FRANCOEUR

INTRODUCTION

Toward the end of the 1950s, James E. Iannucci published an article dealing with a problem that he called "crucial" in bilingual lexicography methodology, that of meaning discrimination (1957, 272). A series of articles followed (Hietsch 1958; Iannucci 1959; Williams 1960), all addressing the same issue and pointing out the fact that "it is necessary to provide meanings as well as words" in bilingual dictionaries (Williams 1960, 121). A quick look at recent editions of the *Grand Dictionnaire Hachette Oxford* and the *Robert et Collins Senior* shows that "semantic indicators and/or typical collocators" (*Grand Dictionnaire* 2001, ix), or "[p]artial definitions or other information which guide the user" (*Robert et Collins* 2002, xx), are included in modern French-English/English-French dictionaries. But as we will see, long before Iannucci and his followers drew the attention of specialists to the issue of meaning discrimination, semantic features were taken into account in bilingual lexicography.

In the following pages, we will look at the work of one specific lexicographer, Guy Miège. Miège's first bilingual dictionary, entitled *A New Dictionary French and English, with Another English and French*,[2] was published in 1677 in London. Its semantic content is particularly rich, especially compared with the dictionaries of Miège's predecessors, Claudius Holyband and Randle Cotgrave. In the course of my study, I analyzed a corpus corresponding to ten percent of the *New Dictionary*, giving a total of 319 entries in the French-English part and 425 entries in the English-French part. Since all the derivatives of a word considered a "primitive" are grouped under the same entry, which acts as the headword,[3] the entries analyzed in the French-English part total 944 headwords and sub-headwords, while those in the English-French part total 1,180 headwords and sub-headwords.[4] The semantic features of the *New Dictionary* will be described in detail in the first part of this text. Their usefulness will then be discussed in the second part.

SEMANTIC FEATURES OF MIÈGE'S *NEW DICTIONARY*

Miège's *New Dictionary* contains semantic features specifying the meanings of both headwords and equivalents. Semantic information relating to headwords is provided in the source language, whereas that relating to equivalents is provided in the target language.[5] Three types of semantic information acknowledged by James E. Iannucci (1957), Edwin B. Williams (1960), Hans-Peder Kromann, Theis Riiber, and Poul Rosbach (1991), Bo Svensén (1993), and Mike Hannay (2003), among others,[6] are represented in the *New Dictionary*. The first type corresponds to partial or complete definitions—that is, to *direct* semantic information: the defining elements relate directly to the meaning of the headword. The second type, consisting of context words or phrases, "discriminates meaning by giving just enough of the context or kind of context in which a word occurs to determine the meaning in question" (Iannucci 1957, 275). The third type takes the form of field labels used to specify the headword's field of knowledge. These two latter categories can be considered as *indirect* semantic information, since they provide information not about the *signifié* of the headword but about its more typical semantic or syntactic environment or the field in which it is most commonly used.

DEFINITIONS

The various forms of definitions used by Miège in the *New Dictionary* are comparable to those used in monolingual dictionaries. The simplest form, the hyperonym, or *genus proximum*, specifies the object class to which the headword or equivalent pertains,[7] as shown in examples (1) to (6).[8]

(1) BRAME (f.) **sorte de poisson,** *a bream,* **a fish so called.**
(2) CHEVRE (f.) **sorte d'animal,** *a she goat.*
(3) EMERAUDE (f.) **sorte de pierre precieuse,** *an emerald,* **a kind**

of precious stone.
(4) GUDGEON, **a fish,** *goujon.*
(5) Ox-eye, *œil de beuf,* ***sorte de plante.***
(6) PHEASANT, **a bird so called,** *un faisan.*

Note that, when a hyperonym follows the equivalent, it is often preceded by an expression such as "a kind of" in English and "sorte de" in French. Such wording "prevent[s] the definition from being taken as a paraphrase" (Svensén 1993, 123).

Synonyms, or synonymous phrases, are also used by Miège as semantic information. They essentially apply to headwords or sub-headwords and, as will be discussed further, generally specify the meaning of polysemous words. Examples (7) and (8) illustrate that feature.

(7) GRACE (f.) **faveur,** *kindness, or favour.*
Grace, **gratitude,** *thanks.*
Grace, **pardon,** *pardon.*
Grace, **affection,** *favour, love, or goodwill.*
Grace, **beauté,** *beauty, or comeliness.*
Grace, **entregent,** *a grace, or decorum.*
(8) Full, or **abounding,** *abondant.*
Full, **large,** or **perfect,** *ample, ou parfait.*
Full, or **full fed,** *saoul, rassasié, plein de viande.*

In other instances, Miège uses morphosemantic definitions, explaining the meanings of derivatives by means of a word from the same family, as shown in examples (9) to (15). This form of definition applies to headwords or equivalents or both.

(9) Chevelu, *hairy, or **full of hair.***
(10) Devoreur (m.) **qui devore,** *a devourer.*
(11) EMBOURSER, **mettre en bourse,** *to put (or lay) up in a purse.*
(12) Gouteux, **qui a la goute,** *gouty, or **troubled with the gout.***
(13) Forked, *fourchu,* ***fait en fourche.***
(14) An INDIVIDUUM, **that cannot be divided,** *un individu.*
(15) Leavy, or **full of leaves,** *feuillu, feuillé,* ***garni de feuilles.***

Note that morphosemantic definitions represent another way to translate the entry word. For instance, the paraphrase *garni de feuilles* would be correct in most, if not all, contexts, though it would be simpler and more concise to use the words *feuillu* and *feuillé* to render the meaning of *leavy* in French.

Finally, Miège uses formal intensional definitions in many cases, providing next to the *genus proximum* features that distinguish the referent from others of the same object class. Intensional definitions apply to headwords, equivalents, or both, as shown in examples (16) to (21).

(16) ENGYSCOPE (m.) **Instrument à voir les petites choses de pres & à les grossir,** *an engyscope, a kind of dioptrick Instrument.*

(17) Point, **marque de distinction, qu'on met à la fin d'une periode ou d'une sentence en écrivant,** *a period, or full point.*

(18) REVULSION (f.) *revulsion,* **a drawing (or forcing) of humours from one part of the body into another.**

(19) EGLANTINE, or sweet brier, *eglantier, petit rosier sauvage à petites feuilles, qui porte des roses fort odoriferantes.*

(20) OXYMEL, **a potion or syrup made of honey, vinegar, and water, in a certain measure sod together,** *oxymel, composition de miel, d'eau, & vinaigre.*

(21) TRAGEDY, **a sort of play that begins prosperously, and ends unfortunately or doubtfully, so that it is quite contrary to a comedy,** *Une Tragedie.*

Four types of definitions have therefore been identified in the *New Dictionary*: hyperonyms, synonyms or synonymous phrases, morphosemantic definitions, and intensional definitions. Indirect semantic information is also present in the dictionary, in the form of context words or phrases and subject fields, as will be discussed in upcoming sections.

CONTEXT WORDS OR PHRASES

Context words or phrases as described by Iannucci (1957) are equivalent to typical collocates used in the recent edition of the *Grand Dictionnaire Hachette Oxford*. They consist of any element specifying the meaning of a word. For instance, the meaning of a verb could be specified by its most usual subject or object, while the meaning of an adjective could be specified by the noun or type of noun that it modifies. Examples given in (22) to (27) illustrate the usage of context words or phrases in Miège's dictionary.

(22) Lit **de bête sauvage,** *the lodge of a Deer, or the like;* Lit **de Riviere,** *the channel of a River.*

(23) Se soûmettre **à son pouvoir, à ses ordres, à son jugement,** *to submit* **to his power, orders, and judgement.**

(24) TRAIRE **le lait,** *to milk a Cow, or the like.*

(25) A forger **of lies**: *forgeur, menteur.*

(26) TO HURRY **a business,** *Precipiter* une affaire.

(27) The mouth **of an oven, or a sack**: *la gueule* **d'un four ou, d'un sac.**

SUBJECT FIELDS

Although not as frequent as definitions or typical collocates, subject fields are part of the semantic apparatus of the *New Dictionary*. They apply to headwords or equivalents, and sometimes to both, as shown in the following examples.

(28) CONTRE-BARRE **(en termes de Blazon)** *Counterbarry,* **in** *Blazon.*

(29) DANCHE **(en termes de Blazon)** dentelé d'un côté, *dancy* **(in** *Blazon)* or indented.

(30) Tranchée (f.) **terme de fortification,** *a Trench.*

(31) Carnation (f.) **terme de Peinture,** *a picture drawn naked, the representation of a naked body in a picture.*

(32) Compositor: *Compositeur* **en Imprimerie.**

(33) A Reach. ***En termes de marine,*** *c'est proprement l'espace qu'il y a entre deux Promontoires, & cela principalement le long des Rivieres, comme, Greenwich-Reach, Lime-house-Reach.*

Subject fields can be combined with other semantic features, as in (29), where a short definition is also given. Unlike other devices previously described, they can also introduce explanatory equivalents, as in (33).

USEFULNESS OF SEMANTIC FEATURES IN THE *NEW DICTIONARY*

Examples (1) to (33) show the richness of the *New Dictionary* in terms of semantic information. A variety of features is used by Miège to provide the user with meaning indications. But how are these indications useful? Are they beneficial to one particular group of users, or do they serve the needs of both francophones and anglophones? These are the questions that we will focus on in the following sections.

SEMANTIC INFORMATION RELATING TO HEADWORDS

As previously mentioned, the elements of definitions provided for headwords are given in the source language—that is, in the language of the headwords — in French in the French-English part of the *New Dictionary* and in English in the English-French part. Therefore, their main function is to help the user to encode a message, "going from the known to the unknown" (Hannay 2003, 146). Suppose that a francophone wants to find the equivalent of the French word *grace* used in the sense of "beauty." Since *grace* is a polysemous French word that can correspond to *grace, charm, favour, mercy, pardon,* or *gift*, there has to be some meaning discrimination device to guide the user in finding the right equivalent. As explained by Veronika Schnorr (1986, 54), "In the case of encoding, the user would need a maximum of help (in his own language) to make it possible for him to select the appropriate equivalent in the other language." In the situation described above, we can obviously talk about *meaning discrimination,* since the main function of the information provided is to help the user distinguish among the various meanings of a polysemous word in order to choose the equivalent that corresponds to the message that he wants to communicate.

Miège makes significant use of meaning discrimination devices. In fact, eighty-three percent of the meanings of polysemous headwords are distinguished in the French-English corpus analyzed and sixty-seven percent in the English-French corpus. In most cases, the device used for meaning discrimination is a synonym. Note that more than one device can be used in the same entry, as in (34) below, where the first instance of meaning discrimination involves a morphosemantic definition, the second a synonym plus a synonymous phrase, and the third a synonym.

(34) RARE, **qui se trouve rarement,** *rare, or scarce.*
Rare, **clair, qui n'est pas épais,** *thin.*
Rare, **precieux,** *rare, precious, excellent.*

There are also several cases where semantic information is associated with monosemous headwords, as in examples (1) to (6). In the corpus studied, forty percent of the monosemous headwords of the French-English section, and twenty-six percent of the monosemous headwords of the English-French section, are in fact defined in some way. As for polysemous words, the semantic information associated with monosemous words is given in the source language and therefore will serve in encoding situations. Since monosemous words do not present any problems in terms of choice of the equivalent, one may wonder about the usefulness of providing semantic information in such cases.

When looking at the monosemous headwords to which Miège associated a definition, one thing is noticeable: many of them are specialized and, as such, are not necessarily part of the common language. For example, there are names of fish (*brame, gudgeon, sprat*), birds (*emerillon, hupe, pheasant*), herbs (*pulmonaire, angelica, calamint, mouse-ear*), plants (*coloquinte, ox-eye*), flowers (*emerocale, martagon, hyacinth*), stars (*hyades*), precious stones (*emeraude, jaiet, ruby*), and illnesses (*hydropisie*). Other words, such as *doloire* (defined as "Instrument de Charpentier"), *ric* (defined as "coupure [ou taille] d'Arbres jusqu'a la racine"), *exsiccate* (defined as "to dry"), and *extirpate* (defined as "pluck up by the roots"), can also be considered as specialized and in some way uncommon.[9]

There is no way to know what specifically motivated Miège to provide semantic information for monosemous words. The preface of the *New Dictionary* does not give any clues about his aim. However, since no general monolingual dictionary had yet been published in either French or English,[10] and since Miège was a language instructor, it seems reasonable to assume that he had a didactic goal in mind. The elements of definition provided for specialized and uncommon words obviously serve to clarify the meanings of these words and thus help the user to understand them better.

SEMANTIC INFORMATION RELATING TO EQUIVALENTS
Since semantic information provided for equivalents in the *New Dictionary* is given in the target language — in English in the French-English section and in French in the English-French section — it serves in decoding situations, or "reception tasks," for the user who "is going from the unknown to the known" (Hannay 2003, 148). Some authors believe that there is no need for semantic information in this particular situation. For instance, Schnorr (1986, 54) explains that "In the case of decoding both users would only need an enumeration of possible equivalents and they would — or at least this has always been assumed — be able to choose the relevant one for their given context, since they 'know' the difference of words in their own language." In Hannay's opinion (2003, 148), "meaning discrimination is in principle irrelevant in a reception dictionary."

Nevertheless, some examples taken from the *New Dictionary* undoubtedly show that meaning discrimination devices associated with equivalents may help to disambiguate their meanings. An interesting example is the subentry *ox-eye*, as seen in (35):

(35) Ox-eye, *œil de beuf*, **sorte de plante.**

In this case, the sole mention of the equivalent *oeil de beuf* may be quite confusing for the francophone because of the proper meaning of the expression: that is, the vision organ of the ox. As stressed by Thomas Szende (2000, 77), lexicographers use semantic information whenever it is necessary to clarify the meaning of an equivalent that they sense is unclear or may be ambiguous. Szende also points out the importance of wording semantic information in such a way that there is no possible confusion with the equivalent. Nowadays, many typographical features are available to help differentiate the equivalent from the rest of the information presented in the entry, as discussed by Alain Duval (2002).

In other cases, such as (36) and (37), Miège might have had a didactic goal in mind when providing definitions for equivalents. Again, the words defined are specialized terms, and Miège might have thought that their meanings would not be well known to the user of his dictionary.

(36) EGLANTINE, or sweet brier, *eglantier, petit rosier sauvage à petites feuilles, qui porte des roses fort odoriferantes.*

(37) REVULSION (f.) *revulsion, a drawing (or forcing) of humours from one part of the body into another.*

CONCLUSION

As we have seen, Guy Miège made use of a rich semantic apparatus in his first dictionary. This is all the more interesting since neither Claudius Holyband nor Randle Cotgrave, Miège's predecessors in producing French-English dictionaries, made systematic use of definitions or other semantic devices in their works. Miège's *New Dictionary* is thus innovative in this regard.[11] The examples shown illustrate the fact that the semantic devices used by Miège assume at least two different functions, depending on whether they accompany a headword or an equivalent. In the first case, they often serve to discriminate the meanings of polysemous entries, thus facilitating the choice of the right equivalent. In the second case, they accompany equivalents and therefore help in the decoding process.

In his preface, Miège does not specify any particular target audience for the *New Dictionary*. Nonetheless, considering that he was, at the time, teaching French to English pupils, and English to Huguenot refugees, we might think that his dictionary was intended for both francophones and anglophones. The fact that there is semantic information given in French and English in both parts of the dictionary tends to confirm such a hypothesis. The *New Dictionary* can presumably be considered as a bifunctional one, each part aiming at both francophones and anglophones. The semantic information contained in the French-English section — in French when relating to entry words and in English when relating to equivalents — serves in fact the two groups of users: it is helpful to the francophone in encoding situations and to the anglophone in decoding situations. The same applies to the English-French section: the information provided in English for the entry words helps anglophones in encoding situations, while the information that appears in French after the equivalents helps francophones in decoding situations. In the continuation of the research, I will analyze other elements of the metalanguage of the *New Dictionary* in order to confirm that it really is a bifunctional dictionary.

NOTES

1 The results presented here are part of a research project financed in 2002–03 by the Fonds québécois de recherche sur la société et la culture. I would like to thank Frédéric Lemelin, who participated in the project as a research assistant, for his help with corpus encoding and analysis. This text is an adapted version of a paper read at the 71ᵉ Congrès de l'Acfas held in Rimouski, Quebec, in May 2003. I would like to thank Bronwyn Burlingham, who corrected the English version of the text.

2 Miège published three other dictionaries: *A Dictionary of Barbarous French* (1679), *A Short Dictionary English and French, with Another French and English* (1684), and *The Great French Dictionary in Two Parts* (1688). See the "References" section for the complete titles of these works.

3 For instance, the words *arbitrage, arbitraire,* and *arbitrairement* are grouped under the headword *arbitre* to form a single entry.

4 In the rest of the text, the term *headword* will be used to refer to both headwords and sub-headwords, since the only difference in the way that they are treated is in the layout: headwords are entirely capitalized, whereas only the first letter of subheadwords is capitalized.

5 I do not consider explanatory equivalents as semantic information, since they are not part of the metalanguage. Furthermore, explanatory equivalents replace equivalents themselves, whereas semantic information, when associated with equivalents, accompanies but does not replace them.

6 These categories are still used today in French-English/English-French dictionaries, as we can see in the *Grand Dictionnaire Hachette Oxford* (2001) and the *Robert et Collins Senior* (2002).

7 In monolingual dictionaries, the *genus proximum* is generally part of an intensional definition, but it can also be used alone, as explained by Svensén (1993, 123): "Information that is not relevant for the ordinary language-user should be omitted. . . . Often the *genus proximum* alone is enough. . . . In many cases, it is even sufficient to give a superordinate concept two or more levels higher in the hierarchy, omitting the intermediate ones. . . ."

8 Note that in the examples given, the words in capitals are headwords, whereas those with only the initial letter capitalized are sub-headwords. Also note that I used a bold typeface to emphasize the semantic information.

9 Interestingly enough, many of the monosemous English words for which Miège provided a definition, for instance *camphire, extenuate, exciccate, extirpate, extoll,* and *exulcerate,* are found in the first hard-word dictionary of English, Robert Cawdrey's *Table Alphabeticall,* published in 1604. This confirms that they were probably uncommon, or learned, words at the time.

10 The first monolingual French dictionary, César-Pierre Richelet's *Dictionnaire François contenant les mots et les choses*, was published in 1680, while the first general monolingual English dictionary, John Kersey's *New English Dictionary*, was published in 1702. English dictionaries published before Kersey's were of the hard-word tradition and, as such, contained mostly learned, specialized, and borrowed words.

11 Miège innovated in many aspects. As James D. Anderson (1978, 41) puts it, "Miège's dictionary has the distinction of being the first bidirectional bilingual French-English dictionary." Originally, Cotgrave's dictionary had only a French-English part, as with Holyband's dictionaries. It is in the 1632 edition of Cotgrave's dictionary that an English-French counterpart was added by Robert Sherwood (Bately 1988, 11). The *New Dictionary* is also different from its predecessors due to Miège's method of grouping derivatives under the same headword, considered the "primitive." Finally, in a research project that I am currently working on, the preliminary results of which were presented in 2003 at the 17th International Congress of Linguists held in Prague, I demonstrated that Miège's *New Dictionary* is innovative in terms of its word list, which is very different from Cotgrave's.

REFERENCES

Anderson, James D. 1978. *The Development of the English-French, French-English Bilingual Dictionary: A Study in Comparative Lexicography.* Supplement to WORD 28 (3). Monograph 6. London: William Clowes and Sons.

Bately, Janet. 1988. "The Old, the New, and the Strange: On Some Dictionaries from the Reign of William and Mary (1688–1702)." In *Words: For Robert Burchfield's Sixty-Fifth Birthday*, ed. E.G. Stanley and T.F. Hoad, 9–36. Cambridge: D.S. Brewer.

Cotgrave, Randle. 1611. *A Dictionarie of the French and English Tongues.* Reproduced [in 1950] from the first edition, with an introduction by William S. Woods. Columbia: University of South Carolina Press.

Duval, Alain. 2002. "Le métalangage, un mal nécessaire du dictionnaire actif." In *Lexicography and Natural Language Processing: A Festschrift in Honour of B.T.S. Atkins*, ed. M.-H. Corréard, 45–48. Grenoble: EURALEX.

Grand Dictionnaire Hachette Oxford français-anglais/anglais-français. 2001. Paris: Hachette; Oxford: Oxford University Press.

Hannay, Mike. 2003. "Types of Bilingual Dictionaries." In *A Practical Guide to Lexicography*, ed. Piet van Sterkenburg, 145–53. Amsterdam: John Benjamins.

Hietsch, Otto. 1958. "Meaning Discrimination in Modern Lexicography." *Modern Language Journal* 42 (5): 232–34.

Holyband, Claudius. 1593. *A Dictionarie French and English: Published for the Benefite of the Studious in That Language*. London: T.O. for Thomas Woodcock.

Iannucci, James E. 1957. "Meaning Discrimination in Bilingual Dictionaries: A New Lexicographical Technique." *Modern Language Journal* 41 (6): 272–81.

———. 1959. "Explanatory Matter in Bilingual Lexicography." *Babel* 5: 195–99.

Kromann, Hans-Peder, Theis Riiber, and Poul Rosbach. 1991. "Principles of Bilingual Lexicography." In *Dictionnaires: Encyclopédie internationale de lexicographie*, tome 3, ed. F.J. Hausmann et al., 2711–28. Berlin: Walter de Gruyter.

Miège, Guy. 1677. *A New Dictionary French and English, with Another English and French According to the Present Use, and Modern Orthography of the French Inrich'd with New Words, Choice Phrases, and Apposite Proverbs; Digested into a Most Accurate Method; and Contrived for the Use both of English and Foreiners*. London: Th. Dawks.

———. 1679. *A Dictionary of Barbarous French: Or, A Collection, by Way of Alphabet, of Obsolete, Provincial, Mis-Spelt, and Made Words in French. Taken out of Cotgrave's Dictionary, with Some Additions. A Work Much Desired, and Now Performed, for the Satisfaction of Such as Read Old French*. London: J.C. for Thomas Basset.

———. 1684. *A Short Dictionary English and French, with Another French and English, According to the Present Use, and Modern Orthography*. London: Thomas Basset.

———. 1688. *The Great French Dictionary in Two Parts. The First, French and English; the Second English and French; According to the Ancient and Modern Orthography. Wherein Each Language Is Set Forth in Its Greatest Latitude: The Various Senses of Words, both Proper and Figurative, Are Orderly Digested; and Illustrated with Apposite Phrases, and Proverbs: The Hard Words Explained; and the Proprieties Adjusted. To Which Are Prefixed the Grounds of Both Languages, in Two Grammatical Discourses; the One English, and the Other French*. London: J. Redmayne for Thomas Basset.

Robert et Collins Senior: Dictionnaire français-anglais/anglais-français. 2002. Paris: Dictionnaires Le Robert; Glasgow: HarperCollins.

Schnorr, Veronika. 1986. "Translational Equivalent and/or Explanation? The Perennial Problem of Equivalence." *Lexicographica* 2: 53–60.

Svensén, Bo. 1993. *Practical Lexicography: Principles and Methods of Dictionary-Making*. New York: Oxford University Press.

Szende, Thomas. 2000. "L'information sémantique en lexicographie bilingue (hongrois-français)." In *Dictionnaires bilingues: Méthodes et contenus*, ed. Thomas Szende, 69–81. Paris: Honoré Champion.

Williams, Edwin B. 1960. "Analysis of the Problem of Meaning Discrimination in Spanish and English Bilingual Lexicography." *Babel* 6: 121–25.

CHAPTER 2

RELEVANCE IN DICTIONARY MAKING: SENSE INDICATORS IN THE BILINGUAL ENTRY[1]

BERYL T. SUE ATKINS AND PIERRETTE BOUILLON

INTRODUCTION

Lexicographic relevance became a hot topic with the development of the text corpus: this is now, for many lexicographers, the principal source of information about their headwords. Gone are the days when you looked at a blank sheet of paper, consulted a meagre card index and a plethora of other dictionaries, and wished for more information. For the common words of the English language, the British National Corpus[2] (from which our examples are taken) offers far more material than anyone can hope to handle in the context of a commercial dictionary—or, indeed, in a lifetime. Faced with screen after screen of key word in context (KWIC) concordances, as illustrated in Figure 1, the lexicographer really is hard put, within the time constraints, to make sense of it all. Some publishing houses offer their dictionary writers a certain amount of formal training; the majority still rely on the new lexicographer learning by trial and error at the wordface. Even after training, discovering and recording the essential facts about a word still depend more on the skill of the individual than on a systematic approach to the data. If the evidence in a corpus is to be exploited to its full potential, not merely by one individual dictionary editor but consistently by the whole editorial team, then a theoretically grounded approach to lexicographic relevance is an essential item in the lexicographer's toolkit.

It is convenient to consider the lexicographic process in two distinct phases (see Atkins 1993 for a fuller account). In the initial stage (*analysis*)

Figure 1: KWIC concordances for *argue*

1. The teachers and medics were	arguing	about who has what of my time.
2. This is a key factor	arguing	against the existence of such a relationship.
3. "You'll stop	arguing	and do as you're damned well told!"
4. We spent most of our time in cafés	arguing	and holding hands.
5. These features	argue	for a local origin.
6. Margaret Mead	argues	for a nurture perspective on behaviour.
7. There was a lot of	arguing	going on between Mom and Dad.
8. Dr. Wilson	argues	that, if ants disappeared, most of....
9. Richard Dawkins has	argued	that it is their genes that survive.
10. This situation	argues	that a serious tax should be levied.
11. The popular press have	argued	the case.
12. The platoon commander was	arguing	with a gang of Christian Phalangists.

of dictionary compiling, when lexicographers are studying the way that the word behaves in the language, they look at the evidence (corpus data, their own notes, etc.), record facts about the headword as they find them (meanings, constructions, collocates, participation in multiword expressions, register, language variety, style, etc.), establish provisional sense distinctions, attempt to order the facts and the exemplifying sentences according to these distinctions, and thus create a rich database entry from which may be extracted the material needed for the particular dictionary on which they are working. The greatest danger at this stage is that, if there is no theoretical basis for the analysis, the collection of facts will be patchy and inconsistent, without any means of ensuring that no important aspect of the word's behaviour has been overlooked.

When editors come to the task of formulating the actual dictionary entry (*synthesis*), in the absence of any theoretical underpinning there is no means of ensuring that their approach to these tasks is consistent from A to Z of the dictionary—a process that may cover a number of years and involve a large team of lexicographers. For every entry and subentry, the major decision is what to put in or, more tantalizingly, what to leave out; obviously, native-speaker intuition informs the selection, but here again objective facts (which normally amount to no more than frequency statistics in the current corpus) are thin on the ground. It is essential that the selection be based on a clear overview of how the word actually behaves, a good counterweight to the salient usages available to native-speaker intuition (see Hanks 2000 for a discussion of social versus cognitive salience). So much for monolingual dictionaries. In the case of bilingual dictionaries, of course, the synthesis stage also includes the "transfer" process, when the source-language items are translated into the target language and the entry crafted to be as helpful as possible to its eventual readers. Here quality depends on good decisions being made at two different points in the process: first, the selection of material to go into the entry and, second, the identification in the target language of the most appropriate equivalent or set of equivalents for the headword in its various uses (see Fillmore and Atkins 2000 for a discussion of this in the context of frame semantics).

RELEVANCE IN THE ANALYSIS STAGE

During the analysis stage, the lexicographer needs both contextual and linguistic information in order to judge what is relevant to the dictionary entry and what is not. Facts about the context from which a citation is drawn allow considered judgments about the status of the citation: whether the usage is typical of the linguistic community whose language is being recorded and/or whether some indicator of language variety, style, register, currency, and so on is required at this point. The types of contextual information normally available in the header of the corpus text include the title of the work, its date of publication, the genre that it belongs to, and its authorship, including probably the sex, age, and regional origin of the author; the header may also include other details such as regional variety, language level, or domain. A different type of contextual information relates to collocation: the significance of the words with which the keyword combines in the corpus citations, the importance allocated to the frequency of the various senses in the corpus, and so on. (Note that frequency statistics have to be read in conjunction with the corpus design criteria before they can be evaluated.) We will not deal with frequency in this paper.

The linguistic information relevant to the analysis stage of dictionary compiling is outlined in Fillmore and Atkins (1998) and developed in Atkins, Fillmore, and Johnson (2003). In brief, this information consists of the semantico-syntactic valence of the keyword reflecting essentially the valence instantiated in the corpus.

This theory of lexicographic relevance based on frame semantics informs the current FrameNet project.[3] Although this project's thorough approach to corpus lexicography is impractical for the professional lexicographer working within specific time and length constraints, a simplified version of this approach has proved helpful. It is useful for lexicographers analyzing word senses to start from the semantic valence, identify its essential components, and note the way in which they are grammatically and lexically realized in the corpus.

The verb *argue*, for which some concordances are shown in Figure 1, will serve as a small case study. Scanning them, the lexicographer begins to feel her way around the word: you argue about something (one sense here—"quarrel"), but you can also argue for and against something—is that the same sense? Or a second one—"make a case, maintain"? Looking at the subjects of the verb in the corpus (critic, economist, proponent, author, feminist, etc.) reinforces the two-sense view, and, just as we are beginning to believe that *argue* can be described in terms of these two senses alone, we notice "This situation argues that a serious tax should be levied," and we are forced to add a third sense to our armoury, that of "be evidence of, indicate," noting that in this sense the subject of *argue* is a fact, event, or situation and

Figure 2: From the Web, *argue* in the "indicate" sense

1.	Cold, hard facts	argue	against the death penalty.
2.	And do not the facts	argue	in favour of the contrary view?
3.	And the law and the facts	argue	strongly for continuation of the lawsuit.
4.	... though the statistics	argue	otherwise.
5.	Women's Caucus statistics	argue	that unfairness does not happen to men. ...
6.	The resulting statistics	argue	that they have orbits with inclinations near 23°.

Relevance in Dictionary Making

not a person. This third sense—rare in the BNC—is absent in many respected dictionaries,[4] yet an ad hoc sweep of the Web produces many instances such as those shown in Figure 2.

The lexicographers would have been less likely to overlook that third sense had they taken a FrameNet approach to the analysis of the corpus data. This approach involves identifying the frame, or conceptual background, to which the lexical unit[5] belongs, then discovering how the various elements in the frame are realized in the corpus sentences. In the case of *argue* (and *argument*), the three relevant frames are as follows.

1. Communication-Conversation (e.g., *She knew better than to argue with him.*)
2. Communication-Arguing (e.g., *He argued that it was unconvincing.*)
3. Reasoning-Evidence (e.g., *Cold, hard facts argue against the death penalty.*)

It is clear that this third sense does not belong to a communication frame, which is described in terms of the frame elements Interlocutor-1, Interlocutor-2, and Topic, inter alia.

It is impossible to do justice to the complexity of the FrameNet approach[6] in the space available to us here, but, taking the "quarrel" sense of argue and argument as an example, we will attempt to show how a cut-down version of it can help day-to-day lexicographic analysis. Figure 3 shows a composed example sentence for the verb, analyzed in this way.

Figure 3: Frame analysis of "quarrel" example

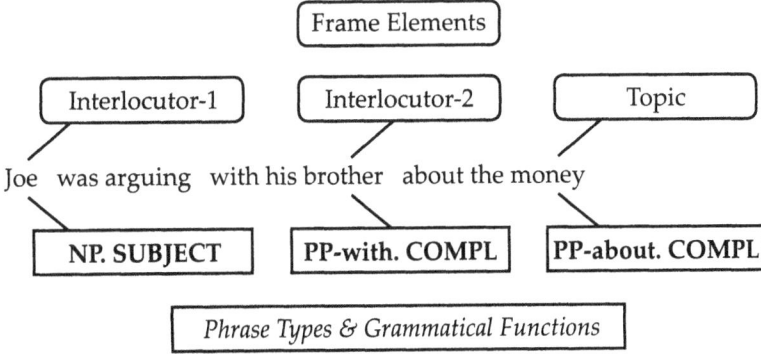

This lexical unit belongs to the Conversation frame, of which three core elements[7] are instantiated in this sentence as follows:

- Interlocutor-1: one of the parties involved in the conversation;
- Interlocutor-2: the other party involved;
- Topic: the subject of conversation—in this case what they are quarrelling about.

These core elements encapsulate the essential grammatical facts that this sentence offers to the lexicographer, identifying the following "chunks" of the sentence as lexicographically relevant:

- Joe: a noun phrase (NP) functioning as the subject of the keyword *argue*;
- with his brother: a prepositional phrase (PP) functioning as the COMPLEMENT of the keyword *argue*; and
- about the money: another prepositional phrase (PP) functioning as the COMPLEMENT of the keyword *argue*.

In FrameNet terms, the frame elements in this sentence and their grammatical instantiation constitute a "valence pattern" for the lexical unit *argue* in the Conversation frame. The set of valence patterns identified in an exhaustive search of corpus data constitutes the valence of this lexical unit. In terms of the needs of the professional lexicographer, the valence identifies all of the facts needed for a full description of the word's corpus behaviour (apart from frequency and collocational data).

Let us look for a moment at what the single sentence *Joe was arguing with his brother about the money* tells us about *argue*: namely, the information shown in Figure 4 as the "contextual features of the keyword." We know from this one sentence that *argue* can occur in a continuous tense, that it can be used with two complements, and that the verb's subjects and its complements can be instantiated by words with the properties detailed in the diagram. All of that—together with the "inherent features" also shown—constitutes lexicographically relevant information. These are facts about the word that must be taken into account by anyone writing a dictionary entry for *argue*, and if the dictionary is destined for encoding language learners, and is of any

Relevance in Dictionary Making

Figure 4: Inherent and contextual features of *argue*

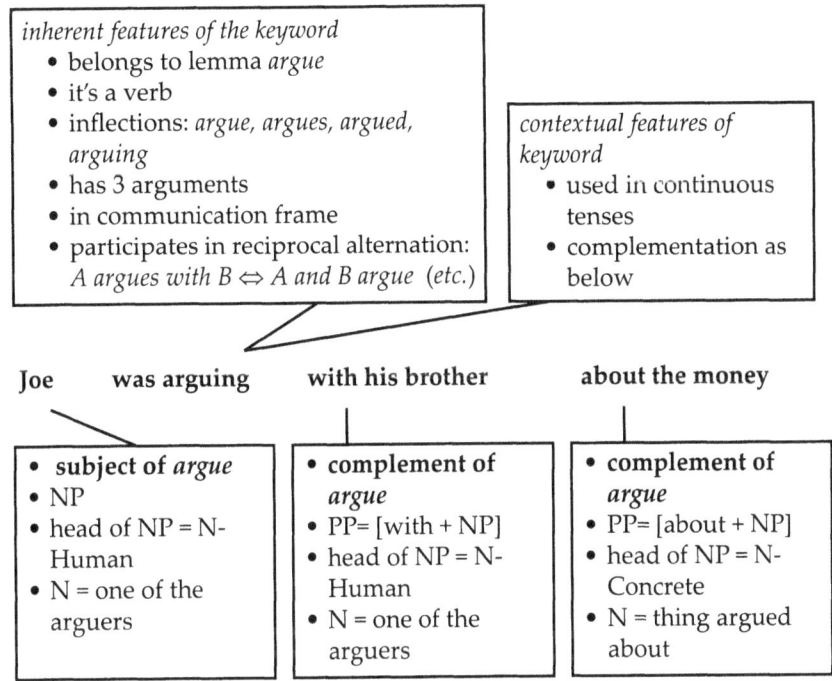

reasonable size, then the contextual features must figure in the entry. If they are not there, then the language learner cannot use the word correctly. If they are not in a bilingual entry, together with their target-language equivalents, then the verb's full potential cannot be expressed in the foreign language.

Figure 5 needs no detailed commentary: we include it to demonstrate the amount of lexicographically relevant information that a single corpus sentence offers about nouns, which tend to be second-class citizens in the world of lexicography.

In summary, the lexicographically relevant information for each word sense, needed by the dictionary editor during the analysis stage of the process, may be described as the inherent features of the keyword itself (e.g., it's a verb, etc.) and the various details of its contextual features.

These contextual features are, for each frame element, expressed in each of the varied corpus contexts:

Figure 5: Inherent and contextual features of *argument*

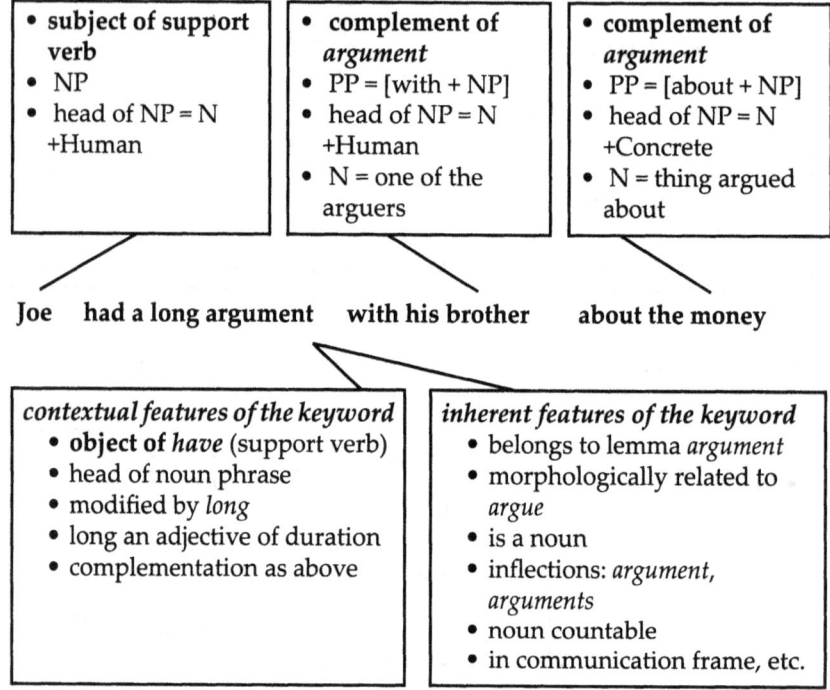

- its semantic role (e.g., one of the arguers);
- its grammatical function (e.g., subject of *argue*);
- its phrase type (e.g., NP); and
- the sortal feature of the head noun of the NP (e.g., "human").

RELEVANCE IN THE SYNTHESIS STAGE

For editors of bilingual, as opposed to monolingual, dictionaries, the synthesis stage is complicated by the fact that it must also contain the "transfer" process, whereby target language equivalents are proposed and evaluated, and selected or rejected, and the structure and content of the entry are subject to changes led by the needs of the users. If the dictionary is destined for use by speakers of both the source and the target languages, then its editors must keep this fact at the forefront of their minds throughout the work of compiling the entry. Indeed, if this is the case, then the dictionary must be two dictionaries rolled into one (and, as such, it will inevitably contain some redundant information for both sets of users). An example of this is given in Figure 6, where alternative entries for the French noun *couche* show how the needs of the encoding francophone override those of the decoding anglophone. Such a dictionary entry is bound to favour the source-language speakers, who need much more help and guidance in formulating sentences in a foreign language than do the target-language speakers. The latter are simply trying to understand an expression in the foreign language and sometimes to find its equivalent in their own. They are unlikely to select an item in their own language that is manifestly at odds with its context.

Figure 6: Entries for *couche* for the francophone (A) and anglophone (B)

A
```
couche¹
  nf (pour bébés) nappy (Brit), diaper (Am).
couche²
  nf 1 (de vernis, peinture, d'apprêt) coat;
     (d'aliments, de poussière) layer.
     2 (strate) stratum, layer.
```

B
```
couche¹
  nf nappy, diaper.
couche²
  nf coat; layer; stratum.
```

The entries in Figure 6 marked (A) would appear in a dictionary prepared for both anglophone and francophone markets; the entries marked (B) show how much of that information the English speakers really need. They know when it is appropriate to select *nappy* or *diaper* and don't need to be told that one is British and one American English. They know when *nappy* is an appropriate choice for their English context and when they should prefer *coat* or *layer* or *stratum*. The French speaker has to be guided to the appropriate English word, by *pour bébés* ("for babies"), or *de vernis, peinture, d'apprêt* ("of varnish, paint, size"), or *d'aliments, de poussière* ("of food, dust"), or *strate* ("stratum").

When it comes to compiling the actual entry, the lexicographer opens a dialogue with the dictionary user and relies on different types of facts in order to help the user understand the entry. In the case of a bilingual dictionary, the entry is rich in indicators (e.g., the italicized material in Figure 7) whose function is to guide the reader to the appropriate foreign-language expression. Most of these indicators, as we have seen, are there to help the source-language speaker. A detailed analysis of items functioning as sense indicators is included in a discussion of the organization of a bilingual dictionary entry in Atkins (1996).

Figure 7: Three types of sense indicators

develop / dI"vel@p / *vi*	**act** / &kt / *n*
(*evolve*) *child, seed, embryo* se développer; *intelligence* s'épanouir; *skills* s'améliorer; *society, country, region* se développer; *plot, play* se développer; . . .	1 (*action, deed*) acte *m*. 2 *Law, Politics* loi *f*; **Act of Parliament/Congress** loi votée par le Parlement/le Congrès; . . .

DATABASE OF SENSE INDICATORS

The classes of indicator shown in Figure 7 all have the same function: to guide the English speaker to the appropriate French equivalent of the headword. The synonyms *evolve* in the *develop* entry and *action, deed* in the *act* entry belong to a class of **hierarchical indicators,** which, as well as synonymy, include instances of antonymy, hyperonymy, hyponymy, and meronymy. The various typical subjects of the verb *develop* (*child, seed, embryo; intelligence; skills; society, country,* etc.) belong to the class of **morphosyntactic indicators,** while the *act* entry offers an example of **language subtype indicators** (*Law, Politics* indicate domain: in legal and political contexts, the equivalent of English *act* is French *loi*). We identify a fourth class of sense indicators that we call **semantico-syntactic indicators**: they are exemplified in Figure 8 by the various synonyms of *set* (*collection, kit, game, pair, group, scenery,* etc.) used to clarify the sense distinctions and lead the anglophone reader to the appropriate translations.

Our work on the database of sense indicators (see Appendix) was carried out under the ISLE project,[8] which had the objective of surveying the semantic content of lexical entries with particular regard to machine-readable dictionaries and proposing a method of standardization; a preliminary account of the work of the Computational Lexicon Working Group is given in Atkins et al. (2002). The set of basic notions needed to describe the multilingual level includes transfer conditions (required by many machine translation systems) that inform the process of translating from source- to target-language text. To define

Figure 8: Synonyms as sense indicators

set /set / I *n*
1   (*collection*) (*of keys, etc.*) **jeu** *m*; ...
2   (*kit, game*) **a chess set** un jeu d'échecs;
3   (*pair*) **a set of sheets** une paire de draps; ...
4   *Sport* (*in tennis*) ...
5   (*television*) ...
6   (*group*) (*social*) monde *m*; (*sports*) milieu *m*; ...
7   (*scenery*) theatre décor *m*; ...
8   *GB school* (*class, group*) groupe *m*; ...
9   (*hair-do*) mise *f* en plis; ...
10   *music* concert *m*;
11   (*position*) (*of sails*) réglage *m*; ...
12   (*direction*) (*of wind*) sens *m*; ... etc., etc., etc.

more precisely what information these transfer conditions should ideally contain, it was decided to compare them with sense indicators to see what kind of information is used to help humans choose correct translations. The ISLE database represents a first attempt to formalize this type of information and to answer this question.

To build the database, we semi-automatically converted one small online dictionary into a suitable format for the database. Thus,

Figure 9: *Collins Gem* entry for *develop*[9]

develop [dI"vel@p] *vt* (*gen*) développer; (*habit*) contracter; (*resources*) mettre en valeur, exploiter // *vi* se développer; (*situation, disease; evolve*) évoluer; (*facts, symptoms: appear*) se manifester, se produire.

for instance, the relevant material from the *develop* entry in Figure 9 is converted into the following representation, which will be taken as input to generate the SQL database:

Headword ¦ headword p.o.s ¦ indicator ¦ indicator p.o.s ¦ indicator type ¦ translation ¦ context

develop | | | | vi | se développer |
develop | Abbr | gen | Lev | vt | développer |
develop | N | habit | Objv | vt | contracter |
develop | N | resources | Objv | vt | mettre en valeur, exploiter |
develop | N | situation, disease; evolve | Subjv | vi | évoluer |
develop | N | symptoms: appear | Subjv | vi | se manifester, se produire |
develop | V | facts, symptoms: appear | Syn | vi | se manifester, se produire |
develop | V | situation, disease; evolve | Syn | vi | évoluer |

Figure 10 shows the current format of the database query screen.

Figure 10: ISLE screen showing some develop data

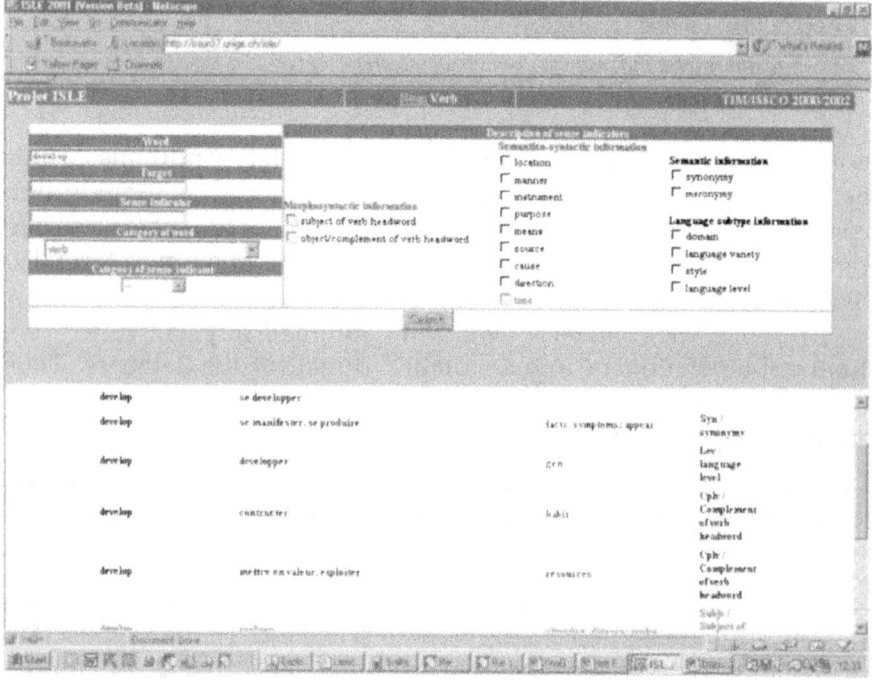

The database can be consulted at http://issun17.unige.ch/isle. It offers the possibility not only of searching for a headword, a target word, or a particular sense indicator (e.g., *person*, CULIN, etc.) but also of extracting all indicators that have a specific syntactic structure (*with N, by N,* etc.) or belong to a particular type (*Loc, Man,* etc.), according to the classification given in the Appendix. The database not only affords interesting statistics about the different types of sense indicators for each syntactic category but also allows a structured study of the way in which these indicators are used, by means of queries such as the following.

1. How is this specific sense indicator used?
2. How is this specific type of indicator used?
3. Which syntactic patterns are used to express a given type of indicator?
4. Which sense indicators are used for specific types of verbs (e.g., pronominal verbs with *se*)?

Note that the database is not complete, and the categories found there are provisional. Nonetheless, it is proving to be an interesting and informative exercise for the computational linguists, machine translation experts, and lexicographers who have contributed to its creation.

LEXICOGRAPHICAL RELEVANCE

We have tried to summarize the various types of information that lexicographers use in the compilation of a bilingual dictionary: first, during the analysis process, the facts essential to the discovery and recording of how a word behaves and, second, the much more varied types of information employed during the synthesis process in order to guide the dictionary user to the appropriate translations. Both types, we believe, are lexicographically relevant, but, while the first is often taught during lexicographer training programs, the second is rarely if ever mentioned. Yet pointing to the appropriate target word in an intelligible, economical, and elegant way is surely one of the skills most needed by bilingual lexicographers. As far as we know, there has been no research carried out to discover which of the various types of sense indicator employed in current dictionaries are the most effective, yet the work reported on in Atkins and Varantola (1997, 1998) shows that this is an area that could benefit from such research. We hope that our Sense Indicator Database may prove to be a launch pad for such a study.

NOTES

1. We would like to thank all of our colleagues in the ISLE Project Computational Lexicon Working Group, especially Nuria Bel, Francesca Bertagna, Nicoletta Calzolari, Alessandro Lenci, Gregor Thurmair, Marta Villegas, and Antonio Zampolli, for their contributions to the discussions that resulted in the SQL database. We are also grateful to Charles Fillmore and colleagues on the FrameNet project for their dedicated scholarly lexicography, which has both inspired and informed us.
2. See http://info.ox.ac.uk/bnc.
3. This research project, of considerable importance to professional lexicographers, is based in the International Computer Science Institute, Berkeley, California, and led by Charles J. Fillmore, whose work in frame semantics and construction grammar informs the lexicography. See http://www.icsi.berkeley.edu/~framenet/.
4. For instance, *Cobuild English Dictionary*, *Oxford Dictionary of English*, *Concise Oxford Dictionary*, among others. We do not pretend that we could have done any better, working under the same constraints.
5. The equivalent of a word in one of its senses.
6. A brief account of the principal aspects of this project is given by the FrameNet team in *International Journal of Lexicography* 16 (3), 2003, an issue devoted to FrameNet and guest-edited by Thierry Fontenelle.
7. A "core" versus "periphery" distinction is established among the frame elements that accompany a frame-bearing word, the former indicating those that are most closely associated with the meaning of the headword, the latter covering expressions of time, place, manner, and so on, that provide modifications of the sort that could be added to almost any situation type. Core frame elements include obligatory objects and complements of the headword; any frame element that, if expressed, would be expressed as direct object of a verb headword or as a PP-of in the case of the corresponding noun; any frame element that, if unexpressed, is interpreted as a case of definite null instantiation (such as the thing that you are blaming John for when you say *I blame John*).
8. International Standards for Language Engineering (ISLE) No. IST-1999-10647. The Computational Lexicon Working Group responsible for this database includes Istituto di Linguistica Computazionale, CNR, Pisa (Project Coordinator); Consorzio Pisa Ricerche; Università di Pisa, Dipartimento di Linguistica; GILCUB (Grup Investigació Lingüística Computacional Universitat Barcelona); Sail Labs, Munich; ISSCO, University of Geneva; ITRI, University of Brighton; New York University; CIS Department, University of Pennsylvania; Psychology Department, Princeton University. See http://www.ilc.pi.cnr.it/EAGLES96/isle/complex/clwg_home_page.htm.

9   This is the actual entry in the *Collins Gem English-French Dictionary,* which populates the database; other entries used as illustrative material in this paper are modelled on those in the larger English-French dictionaries, such as the *Collins-Robert* and the *Oxford-Hachette.*

REFERENCES

Atkins, B.T.S. 1993. "Theoretical Lexicography and Its Relation to Dictionary-Making." In *Dictionaries: The Journal of the Dictionary Society of North America,* ed. W. Frawley, 4–43. Cleveland: DSNA.

———. 1996. "Bilingual Dictionaries: Past, Present, and Future." In *Proceedings of EURALEX '96,* ed. M. Gellerstam, J. Järborg, S.-G. Malmgren, K. Norén, L. Rogström, and C.R. Papmehl, 515–90. Gothenburg: Gothenburg University.

Atkins, B.T.S., N. Bel, F. Bertagna, P. Bouillon, N. Calzolari, C. Fellbaum, R. Grishman, A. Lenci, C. MacLeod, M. Palmer, G. Thurmair, M. Villegas, and A. Zampolli. 2002. "From Resources to Applications: Designing the Multilingual ISLE Lexical Entry." In *Proceedings of the Second International Conference on Language Resources and Evaluation (LREC 2002),* vol. 2, ed. Manuel González Rodríguez and Carmen Paz Suárez Araujo, 687–93. Paris: European Language Resources Association.

Atkins, B.T.S., C.J. Fillmore, and C.R. Johnson. 2003. "Lexicographic Relevance: Selecting Information from Corpus Evidence." *International Journal of Lexicography* 16 (3): 251–80.

Atkins, B.T.S., and K. Varantola. 1997. "Monitoring Dictionary Use." *International Journal of Lexicography* 10 (1): 1–45.

———. 1998. "Language Learners Using Dictionaries: The Final Report of the EURALEX- and AILA-Sponsored Research Project into Dictionary Use." In *Using Dictionaries: Studies of Dictionary Use by Language Learners and Translators,* ed. B.T.S. Atkins, 21–81. Tübingen: Niemeyer.

Fillmore, C.J., and B.T.S. Atkins. 1998. "FrameNet and Lexicographic Relevance." In *Proceedings of the First International Conference on Language Resources and Evaluation (LREC 98),* Granada, Spain, 417–23. Paris: European Language Resources Association.

———. 2000. "Describing Polysemy: The Case of *Crawl.*" In *Polysemy: Linguistic and Computational Approaches,* ed. Y. Ravin and C. Leacock, 91–110. Oxford: Oxford University Press.

Hanks, Patrick. 2000. "Contributions of Lexicography and Corpus Linguistics to a Theory of Language Performance." In *Proceedings of EURALEX 2000,* vol. 1, ed. U. Heid, S. Evert, E. Lehmann, and C. Rohrer, 3–13. Stuttgart: Stuttgart University.

APPENDIX: SENSE INDICATORS IN BILINGUAL DICTIONARIES (WITH EXAMPLES DRAWN FROM AN ENGLISH-FRENCH DICTIONARY)

Morphosyntactic Information (specific part of speech)

Headword	Type	Description of indicator	Headword	Sense indicator	TL equivalent
verb	Subjv	indicator is subject of verb headword	develop	situation, disease	évoluer
verb	Objv	indicator is object of verb headword	develop develop	habit resources	contracter mettre en valeur, exploiter
noun	Subjn	indicator is subject of verb base of noun headword	contortion	of acrobat	contorsion
noun	Argn	indicator is argument of support verb of noun headword	pulse	of heart	battement
noun	Possn	indicator is possessor of noun headword	web	of spider	toile
noun	Adj-Pertn	indicator is pertainym modifying noun headword	bell	electric	sonnerie
noun	Gen	indicator is gender of headword	mousse	feminine masculine	moss cabin boy
adjective	Moda	indicator is noun typically modified by headword	vivid	account	frappant(e)

Semantico-Syntactic Information (specific part of speech)

Headword	Type	Description of indicator	Headword	**Sense indicator**	**TL equivalent**
noun / verb	Loc	indicator is location (typical environment) of headword	promenade	by sea	esplanade, promenade
noun / verb / adjective	Man	indicator is manner of headword	inferior	in rank	subalterne
noun / verb	Inst	indicator is instrument of headword	sign	with hand, etc.	signe
noun / verb/ adjective	Pur	indicator is purpose of headword	bat	for baseball, etc.	batte
noun / verb	Means	indicator is means of headword	passage	by boat	traversée
noun / verb	Sou	indicator is source of headword	deduction	from wage, etc.	prélèvement, retenue
noun / verb	Tim	indicator is time of event of headword	blackout	in wartime	couvre-feu
noun / verb	Dir	indicator is direction of headword	move	forward	avancer
noun / verb / adjective	Cau	indicator is cause of headword	hangover	after drinking	gueule de bois
noun	Coll	indicator is items collected by collective headword n	block shift	of buildings of workers	pâté (de maisons) équipe

Semantico-Syntactic Information (specific part of speech) (continued)

noun	Mass	mass n indicator (of itemizer noun headword)	pinch sheet	of salt, etc. of paper	pincée feuille
noun	Conte	indicator is contents of headword noun container	can	of milk, oil, water	bidon
noun	Conta	indicator is container of headword noun contents	arrow	in quiver	flèche
noun	Des	indicator describes noun headword	bolt lodger ferry	with nut with room and meals small	boulon pensionnaire bac
noun	Mat	indicator is material of which headword is made	moulding	in wood	moulure
noun	Cpln	indicator is complement of noun headword	gallantry	toward ladies	galanterie
noun	Cplna	indicator is complement of an agentive noun headword	trainer	of dogs, etc.	dresseur/euse
verb	Coplv	indicator is complement of verb headword	protect		protéger
adjective	Cpla	indicator is complement of adjective headword	gallant	toward ladies	empressé, galant

Hierarchical Information (any part of speech)

Type	Description of indicator	Headword	Sense indicator	TL equivalent
Syn	indicator is synonym of headword	casual stress	by chance accent	fortuit accent
Ant	indicator is "not" + antonym of headword	wrong	not suitable	qui ne convient pas
Hyper	indicator is hypernym of headword	spinach flying	food activity aviation	épinards aviation
Hypo	indicator is hyponym of headword			
Mer	indicator is the whole; headword is the part	stone butt	in fruit of cigarette	noyau mégot

Language Subtype Information (any part of speech)

Type	Description of indicator	Headword	Sense indicator	TL equivalent
Dom	indicator is domain of headword; e.g., Architecture, Music	grant	Admin	subside, subvention
Lgv	indicator is language variety of headword; e.g., American/British	automobile	US	automobile
Sty	indicator is style of headword; e.g., informal, jargon	aim	fig	viser (à)
Lev	indicator is language level of headword; e.g., general language, technical language, etc.	canvas	gen	toile

CHAPTER 3

BIASED BOOKS BY HARMLESS DRUDGES: HOW DICTIONARIES ARE INFLUENCED BY SOCIAL VALUES

KRISTEN MACKINTOSH

INTRODUCTION

Imagine we opened a dictionary to find the following entry:

> **child abuse** *n* that's what you call smackin' kids around to keep 'em in line. *More child abuse means fewer brats.*

We would undoubtedly be shocked and outraged, for such an entry violates all of our expectations of dictionaries. We may not always know that we bring expectations to dictionaries, and lexicographers might not realize how much they are subject to them, but the above entry makes it clear that certain things cannot be said in dictionaries and that they cannot be said in just any old way. Dictionaries are strongly influenced by social values.

It may seem obvious that dictionaries would be influenced by social values. After all, they examine language, and how can language possibly be free of social influences? The purpose of this paper is therefore not to prove the truthfulness of this phenomenon but to delve into its subtleties. This paper also does not purport to bring vast amounts of new evidence to light, particularly given that the subject has benefited from an increased amount of attention since I conducted my initial research on this topic over a decade ago.[1] Rather, the main goal of this paper is to synthesize findings from a diverse range of sources, including lexicographers, meta-lexicographers, linguists, feminists, and writers, in a concise, and hopefully useful, structure. Those findings, together with my own evidence and analyses, not only cover the impact of social values on the *content* of dictionaries, a topic that has received considerable attention, but also relate to its impact on the *form* of the dictionary, which has been less studied. The paper focuses in particular on the form and content of the definitions in monolingual English and French dictionaries, with brief discussions of how social values also impact the macrostructures and examples of these dictionaries.

As keepers of our language, monolingual dictionaries are important cultural objects and therefore must adhere to certain social rules. Some of those rules can affect the forms of the definitions and of the examples. The form, or style, of dictionary definitions is of particular interest, for that form has developed over the centuries into a whole new type of discourse, sometimes referred to as "lexicographese" or "dictionary-ese." Dictionary-ese is marked in two major ways: a distinctive manner of phrasing, and an elevated level of diction.

THE PHRASING OF DEFINITIONS

Dictionary definitions have not always been written the way that they are today. In the seventeenth century, dictionaries contained more informal, discursive descriptions and explanations, with complete sentences in which many of the purely metalinguistic elements were explicit. Consider, for example, the following excerpt from the definition for *aussi*, in the 1694 edition of the *Dictionnaire de l'Académie françoise:*

> Il se dit souvent pour, De plus....
> Il signifie quelquefois, C'est pourquoi, à cause de cela....
> Il sert quelquefois à marquer la conformité de la proposition qui suit, avec celle qui précède....
> Il sert encore quelquefois à marquer plus fortement la répréhension ou le blâme....
> Il est quelquefois terme de comparaison, et signe. Autant, également, de même, ni plus ni moins....
> (orthography adapted from the Old French of the original entry)

The same dictionary maintained this more discursive style even in its 1932 edition,[2] yet by that time this style of definition was unusual. According to Patrick Hanks (1987, 119), developments in philosophy and logic in the late seventeenth and early eighteenth centuries had made such informality unfashionable, and formalization of the style of dictionary entries began early in the eighteenth century.

Part of that formalization was based on the Leibnizian notion that two expressions are synonymous if one can be substituted for the other and such substitution does not alter the truth. It became the lexicographer's duty to formulate definitions that could be substituted in any context for the word being defined, regardless of the awkward phrasing that resulted. Hanks (1987, 119–20) explains further that the nineteenth century associated two additional principles to the principle of substitutability: (1) reductionism, which implies that the analyst must isolate and describe minimal units, and (2) the "necessary and sufficient" dictum, which requires that a "definiens" (the word[s] used to define another word or expression) should identify all and only the objects or events correctly referred to by the "definiendum" (the word or expression under discussion). Lexicographers' attempts to maintain accuracy while respecting these principles led to an increasingly convoluted style of prose that is still predominant in definitions today.

In modern definitions, full sentences are rare, and purely metalinguistic elements are usually suppressed. Consider, for example, the following excerpt from the entry for *acquit* in the 2003 edition of *Merriam-Webster's Collegiate Dictionary* (hereafter W11).

> **acquit: 3:** to conduct (oneself) usu. satisfactorily esp. under stress

Following the conventions of dictionary-ese, the lexicographer avoids explicitly stating "To *acquit* is . . ." or "*Acquit* means. . . ."[3] The modern dictionary user expects a telegraphic style and would probably be surprised to encounter anything more prosaic.

Other conventions that typify dictionary-ese are abbreviations such as *usu.* or *esp.*, as found in the preceding definition, along with *etc.* and other similar expressions, such as *often, sometimes, some other similar thing,* or *any of various,* which Hanks (1987, 125) refers to as "hedges." These expressions help the lexicographer adhere to the "necessary and sufficient" dictum mentioned above. In addition to using hedges, it has become conventional practice to use parentheses for various purposes, such as to indicate typical objects or subjects, as in the entry for *acquit* above or in the following excerpt from the entry for *bid* in W11.

> ¹**bid 3 b** *past and past part bid* (1) **:** to offer (a price) whether for payment or acceptance (2) **:** to make a bid of or in (a suit at cards)

A practice that takes lexicographese even further from standard prose is that of completely omitting objects or subjects, as in the following excerpt from the same entry.

> ¹bid 1 b : to issue an order to . . . c : to request to come . . . 2 : to give expression to

These conventions and others used in modern dictionary-ese are what we have come to expect in definitions. The style is so typical that we are able to identify dictionary definitions entirely out of context. Because of its distinctive nature, writer Diane Schoemperlen is able to use dictionary-ese to comic effect in her short story "The Antonyms of Fiction." She concocts definitions, such as the following one for *real*, that are instantly recognizable as definitions but, by carrying the conventions of dictionary-ese to an extreme, create humour:

> real is "actually existing as a thing or occurring in fact, objective, genuine, rightly so called, natural, sincere, not merely apparent or nominal or supposed or pretended or artificial or hypocritical or affected." (Schoemperlen 1993, 99)

In her definition, Schoemperlen exaggerates the convention of using synonyms to achieve approximate substitutability. Hanks (1987, 120) calls this technique the "multiple-bite strategy." Schoemperlen also takes the necessary and sufficient dictum to an extreme, for she provides not only an unusually long list of possible correct meanings for *real* but also an extensive list of incorrect meanings. This exaggerated emphasis on conventions aimed at producing substitutable, complete, and precise definientia results in a definition that is too long and unwieldy to be truly acceptable. Yet humour comes from the fact that Schoemperlen's definition nearly meets the criteria for acceptability. Modern dictionary style has reached a point where a definition that borders on incomprehensibility, yet conforms to conventions of dictionary-ese, may be seen as more acceptable than a more comprehensible one written in an informal discursive style.

As William Frawley (1989, 233) points out, acceptability of a text is not a direct consequence of its informativeness. A dictionary definition that reads like prose may be highly informative but considered too "folksy" or "childish" to be acceptable. Yet the primary role of a dictionary definition should be to inform. In the past few decades, there have been attempts to reform the conventional style of dictionary definitions. The reform movement gained impetus with the growing demand for learner's dictionaries for non-native speakers of English.

The dictionary often considered the most revolutionary in terms of definition style is the *Collins Cobuild English Language Dictionary*. It employs a number of techniques that look remarkably similar to ordinary English prose. The style is somewhat informal. The entries consist of paragraphs, usually containing complete grammatical sentences. The definitions actually include the word being defined so that they read more like typical sentences. There is little use of abstract metalanguage. Typical objects and subjects are listed in the place where they would normally be found in an English sentence. The general principle applied was that any definition should, if read aloud, sound like natural spoken English. A typical entry is as follows:

> **catch, catches, catching, caught.** 1. To **catch** an animal, fish, bird, etc means to capture it and stop it from moving freely, usually after chasing it or after using a trap or other weapon. ... 2. If you **catch** a ball or some other object which has been thrown towards you or is moving towards you through the air, you take hold of it when it comes near you. ...

Hanks (1987, 116–17) explains that this simpler system of explanation was introduced as an alternative to lexicographic conventions that are meant to increase precision but that actually create difficulties of interpretation for ordinary dictionary users, particularly the foreign-language learners who make up the majority of the *Collins Cobuild* audience.

Although it may be considered acceptable for learner's dictionaries to be written in an informal simple style, this trend has not spread to native-speaker dictionaries. Perhaps the users of these dictionaries are not ready to change their expectations. Krista Varantola (1993, 255) finds the definitional style of some learner's dictionaries patronizing and condescending for more proficient users. Also, in this fast-paced society, some users may not want to spend time reading longer, more text-like definitions, even if it means an improvement in their comprehension. Frawley, a proponent of seeing dictionary entries as texts and improving their readability, admits that such changes may be too much for some readers. He acknowledges that "Dictionaries come in a tested and culturally expected format" (1989, 246), and he explains that users' expectations may dictate the formal phrasing that gives them their air of authority and objectivity: "Dictionaries speak—or are supposed to speak—much like scientists, and definitions sound like formulas" (1990, 158).

The greatest resistance to change no doubt comes from those who see their language and their dictionaries not merely as means of communication but also as cultural "treasures" to be preserved. The name of the French dictionary *Trésor de la langue française* is no accident. Sidney Landau (1984, 303) has summed up this attitude nicely:

> Although contemporary dictionaries generally disavow any intention to improve or correct anyone's speech, they are nonetheless powerful forces for the preservation and dissemination of a distinctly cultivated form of expression. . . . Dictionaries are not written in informal, chatty style. They employ a sophisticated diction for maximum content in the least amount of space. This use of formal diction is not wholly accounted for by the need for brevity. Although it is considered by dictionary editors to be the style most fitting for a dictionary, there is, however much it may be denied, an element of social judgment in its use.

THE ELEVATED LEVEL OF DICTION

In the above quotation, Landau clarifies that it is not just the phrasing of definitions that is particularly formal but also their level of diction. The famous lexicographer Samuel Johnson gained notoriety not only for the many excellent definitions that he wrote but also for the almost laughable sophisticated level of diction that he occasionally used, as in the following definition of *network*, as mentioned in Landau (1984, 134): "Anything reticulated or deccusated, at equal distances, with interstices between the intersections."

A small survey of my own has revealed that modern-day dictionaries are also guilty of complex diction. Consider the following gems from the 1991 editions of the *Webster's Ninth New Collegiate Dictionary* (hereafter W9) and *Le petit Robert 1*.

    ¹**glass 1 a :** an amorphous inorganic usu. transparent or
        translucent substance consisting of a mixture of silicates

> or sometimes borates or phosphates formed by fusion of silica or of oxides of boron or phosphorus with a flux and a stabilizer into a mass that cools to a rigid condition without crystallization
>
> **1. soie I. 1.** Substance filiforme sécrétée par quelques lépidoptères, essentiellement constituée par deux protéines (séricine et fibroïne), utilisée comme matière textile

These entries are but two among a number of similarly challenging entries that I used in a test conducted in 1994 to determine the difficulties that non-native speakers have with complex definitional metalanguage. The results of this test (reported in Mackintosh 1998) confirmed that complex definitional metalanguage is indeed a major barrier to comprehension for non-native speakers. Other studies (e.g., Quirk 1973 and, more recently, McCreary 2002) have shown that even native speakers frequently struggle with complex diction used in definitions. The informativeness of dictionary definitions decreases proportionately with the amount of unknown information that they contain; the more words in a definition that a user does not understand, the less information the user will derive from that definition. However, the lexicographer's rule of thumb that words used in a definition should not be more complex or less frequent than the word being defined is often broken. Sometimes it is broken out of necessity, as with highly technical concepts, but other times it seems to be broken purely because of intellectual snobbery.

More recent editions of the two dictionaries quoted above show some signs of a move toward slightly simpler definitional metalanguage. The definition of *glass* in *W11* contains fewer technical terms than the *W9* definition, and the long, unpunctuated phrase of the *W9* definition has been broken into smaller, more comprehensible units in *W11*. In the 2003 edition of *Le nouveau petit Robert*, the complex word *lépidoptères* has been replaced with a more generic and presumably slightly more known term, *arthropodes*. However, such efforts still fall short of those made in learner's dictionaries. In *Le Robert méthodique*, for example, the lexicographers avoided a complex genus altogether in the definition for *soie* by replacing *lépidoptères* with *chenilles de papillon*. Some learner's dictionaries even impose strict limitations on the words that can be used in definitions. For example, the *Longman Dictionary of Contemporary English* uses a controlled vocabulary of about 2,000 lexical items and morphemes to describe the meanings of all entries. Some dictionaries have gone further yet to help non-native speakers comprehend the meanings of foreign words by defining words in that speaker's first language. For example, in Fernando de Mello Vianna's *Diccionario inglés for Spanish Speakers,* English headwords are defined in Spanish as well as in English.

The fact that there are so few dictionaries following de Mello Vianna's technique may attest to its lack of acceptability. Even controlled vocabularies have met with violent opposition from many people. Some have greeted them with about as much warmth as fervent Bible traditionalists greeted Nida's *Good News Bible*—I choose this comparison because dictionary traditionalists seem to think that controlled vocabularies propagate the same kind of "sacrilege." Controlled vocabularies have rarely been used outside of English-language learner's dictionaries. To the best of my knowledge, Georges Gougenheim's *Dictionnaire fondamental de la langue française* is the only French-language dictionary to use such a technique. This could be a reflection of the more purist attitude perpetuated by institutions such as the Académie française, as opposed to the emphasis on propagation of the English language among institutions in English-speaking countries.

It sometimes seems that, the more hermetic the language of the dictionary, the more the dictionary is revered. Robert Galisson (1983, 84) claims that the more mysterious a dictionary is to its users, the more they seem to admire it as a cultural object; they accept its complexity and hermeticism as part of its richness. He is probably right, for despite the complex language often used in the *Robert* dictionaries, they are among the most successful French-language dictionaries. Similarly, despite its complex diction, the *Oxford English Dictionary* is probably the most revered of all English-language dictionaries. The desire to maintain a certain level of intellectualism in dictionaries by means of sophisticated diction can probably be attributed to the social values of the dominant class.

HOW SOCIAL VALUES AFFECT THE FORM OF EXAMPLES

The same social values that affect dictionary definitions also affect dictionary examples. It is generally expected that the examples in monolingual dictionary entries will be taken primarily from classical authors. Lexicographer-composed examples and even citations from nonclassical authors or other types of writers are often looked down on for a supposed lack of sophistication in their form. The language of the classical authors is considered to be the language that dictionaries should uphold.

Rey-Debove (1971, 271–72) explains that although such restrictions can sometimes result in outdated examples and can eliminate many good sources for examples, French lexicographers cannot escape the social constraints of "le bon usage." Lexicographers compiling English learner's dictionaries have managed to break free from such social constraints. They were among the first to draw their examples from corpora consisting of a variety of literary and nonliterary sources. The fact that large electronic corpora with nonliterary sources were at first more readily available in English than in other languages largely explains the progressive English approach. However, the discrepancy between the English and French approaches could also perhaps be attributed in part to a greater emphasis on "le bon usage" in French than in English (a claim that die-hard proponents of "the Queen's English" might dispute). It could also perhaps be explained by the fact that examples are generally less frequent in English dictionaries, and there has therefore been less material on which to impose traditional social values.

One other reason that traditional social values reign over dictionary form is that there is a type of intertextuality involved in lexicography. Frawley (1985, 14) claims that "A dictionary is an intertext in the discursive space called 'lexicography.' There is no such thing as an autonomous dictionary. Because lexicography is a discursive practice, every dictionary calls up its relation to every other dictionary." It is hard to see such a relation between a dictionary of Parisian argot and a dictionary of Inuktitut, but a monolingual dictionary of a given language is certainly related to all other monolingual dictionaries of that language. The relation is especially obvious when one considers the common, albeit unofficial, lexicographic practice of drawing examples and parts of definitions from previous dictionaries. Like a gene that is passed from relative to relative, certain social values are perpetuated by the intertextual relations that exist between dictionaries. The practice of "borrowing" from previous dictionaries not only maintains the form dictated by traditional social values but can also perpetuate what the social norm considers to be acceptable in terms of content. The impact of social values on dictionary content is the focus of the next section.

HOW SOCIAL VALUES AFFECT THE CONTENT OF MONOLINGUAL DICTIONARIES

The content of dictionaries is affected by social values even more markedly than is the form. The impact on dictionary content is seen primarily in the macrostructure, definitions, and examples. The most obvious impact is on the macrostructure, so I begin with it.

THE CONTENT OF THE MACROSTRUCTURE

The dictionary macrostructure is a target for censorship. Dictionaries must be acceptable to the society that uses them, and lexicographers and dictionary editors must therefore cater to that society. Furthermore, as they too are part of that society, lexicographers and editors undoubtedly impose their own personal brand of censorship on the choice of entries. Such censorship generally applies to words considered to be "taboo," to terms of insult, and to anglicisms, gallicisms, and other borrowings or neologisms.

The taboo topic par excellence is sex, and many sexual terms are therefore omitted from dictionaries. Gradually, lexicographers are being forced to adapt to our more sexually open society, but the most contentious sexual topics continue to be overlooked. Feminists such as Susanne de Lotbinière-Harwood (1991, 59) lament the failure to include in dictionaries certain female sexual realities, such as *cyprine*, which designates the sexual secretions of women. In 1993, I also noted the lack of an entry for the term *yeast infection* in that year's edition of *Merriam-Webster's Collegiate Dictionary* (10th edition, hereafter W10), even though this female sexual reality was being discussed ad nauseam in television commercials at the time with the advent of over-the-counter treatments for it. Perhaps the influence of the media prevailed, for shortly thereafter *yeast infection* finally entered the realm of lexicographic acceptability, in revised editions of W10, some thirty years after the term was coined. Henri Béjoint (2000, 127) claims that there is a move toward greater liberalism in the inclusion of taboo terms in general-purpose dictionaries. Yet, as Robert Wachal (2002, 201) specifies, for certain topics, dictionaries lag behind the mass media.

One topic that is very hot in today's media, but that is evidently too contentious for the lexicographers of the latest edition of W11, is that of *gay marriage* or *same-sex marriage*.[4] Neither term appears in the wordlist. Even more surprisingly, W11 does not have an entry for the term that I used in the introduction to this paper, *child abuse*. One might argue that it is impossible to cover all compounds, but if *green peach aphid* makes the list, then surely *child abuse* should.

In addition to taboo words, dictionary editors must also decide if terms of insult, whether they denigrate a nationality or a race, such as *Newfie* or *nigger*, a profession, such as *cop* or *pig*, or a gender, such as *skank* or *skirt*, should be included. Ethnic slurs seem to be the most controversial. Jonathon Green (2004, 111) indicates that society now deems them less acceptable than sexual taboo terms, and Wachal (2002, 201) indicates that "ethnic slur terms have been getting more tabooed in dictionaries, as in our culture." Even with increasingly socially conscious usage labelling, editors may fear that the mere inclusion of taboo words somehow validates their use.

For similar reasons, purists may resist the inclusion of borrowings and neologisms in dictionaries. Yet, when an English neologism such as *Web* becomes a prevalent reality in French society, even the Académie française has no choice but to relent to the prevailing social context.

When social values do not censor items from the dictionary macrostructure, there may be censorship of these items at the microstructural level, in both the definitions and the examples.

THE CONTENT OF THE DEFINITIONS
Censorship in the microstructure can result in ideologically coloured definitions. As in the macrostructure, the terms affected often concern sexuality. When anatomical, physiological, and pathological terms are included in the dictionary, social values can affect the way in which such items are defined. Their definitions can be prudish, evasive, overly general, or so scientific as to be nearly incomprehensible to most users. Consider, for example, the definitions of *penis* and *vagina* in W9.

> **penis** a male organ of copulation
> **vagina 1** a canal in a female mammal that leads from the uterus to the external orifice of the genital canal

These definitions will probably not be very enlightening for the user who does not know what a *penis* and a *vagina* are in the first place. It is not for their overall lack of informativeness, however, that these and similar definitions have raised ire; rather, they are controversial for what they do and do not include. Virginia Braun and Celia Kitzinger

(2001) bemoan the fact that most dictionary definitions of *vagina* neglect to mention that the vagina has a sexual function, while this information is virtually always given for *penis*, and in some cases, as in the W9 definition, it is the *only* information given.[5] Although the above definitions were probably written by different lexicographers, and parallelism therefore cannot be fully expected, the definitions nevertheless reflect an undeniably patriarchal point of view. Such a viewpoint is further exaggerated in the following definition of *clitoris* (also from W9 but similar to those in many other dictionaries).

> **clitoris** a small organ at the anterior or ventral part of the vulva homologous to the penis

Like the definition of *vagina*, this definition does not clarify the sexual role of the clitoris, which, as emphasized by Béjoint (2000, 128) and Braun and Kitzinger (2001, 220), is a particularly glaring omission given that the only purpose of the clitoris is to give sexual pleasure. Yet what is most shocking about this definition is the comparison to the penis. Biologically speaking, there are similarities, but is this comparison really essential to the definition? Furthermore, without expecting total symmetry between definitions of related words within a dictionary, it is still hard to ignore the fact that the lexicographer who defined *penis* in W9 did not feel obliged to mention its homology to the clitoris. These definitions may be a reflection of sexism in our society.

Feminist linguist Jane Mills has studied sexism in dictionaries in great depth. In her dictionary, *Womanwords: A Vocabulary of Culture and Patriarchal Society*, she examines many words, including *clitoris*, that have been defined in a clearly sexist manner. For example, Mills (1989, 54) compares the definitions for *coquette* and *male flirt* in the *Oxford English Dictionary*. *Coquette* is defined as

> A woman (more or less young) who uses arts to gain the admiration and affection of men, merely for the gratification of vanity or from a desire of conquest, and without any intention of responding to the feelings aroused: a woman who habitually trifles with the affection of men: a flirt.

The *male flirt*, on the other hand, is simply defined as "one who plays at courtship." You don't have to be a feminist to recognize the double standards at play here. Mills's criticism of patriarchal attitudes in dictionary definitions echoes that of other feminists (e.g., Miller and Swift 1976, 58–60; Yaguello 1979). Such feminist condemnation is expressed particularly strongly in the following words of de Lotbinière-Harwood (1991, 131):

> Like the rest of patriarchal discourse, dictionaries work to block women's voices. They contain male lexicographers' word selections, definitions and usages, as well as organization of ideas, gathered from a male-authored intertext, composed with male readers and users in mind. Their sexist, classist, racist, ageist and homophobic definitions pass themselves off as the norm while perpetuating white male heterosexist supremacy.

De Lotbinière-Harwood's criticism of male lexicographers seems to be undeservedly harsh. They may not always be the "harmless drudges" that Samuel Johnson portrayed them to be, but they are also generally not evil racists or sexists who deliberately write prejudiced definitions. Much of the time, lexicographers are probably not even conscious of the social values that influence their writing. Consider, for example, the following definition of *aphrodisiaque,* taken from *Le Petit Robert 1,* which is often considered one of the more liberal French dictionaries:

> **aphrodisiaque 1** Propre (ou supposé tel) à exciter le désir sexuel, à faciliter l'acte sexuel. . . .

The lexicographer who constructed this definition was probably not even aware that in writing it he or she was adhering to the status quo. As a member of a society in which the power of aphrodisiacs is generally considered dubious, it would seem only normal to add the comment "ou supposé tel." Most Western users would not bat an eye at such a definition, for they entertain the same doubts about aphrodisiacs. Yet, to an Asian from a culture where the power of aphrodisiacs is a near-sacred belief, this definition would seem to be heavily biased and insulting. Béjoint (2000, 131–33) and Tom Dickins (2000) have identified similar biases, often subconscious, in definitions of words used to describe political concepts. Prejudice is frequently in the eye of the beholder, and lexicographers simply see things through the same eyes as most other members of their society. According to Marina Yaguello

(1979, 167), they cannot escape from cultural stereotypes and social constraints when defining certain concepts, for they are victims of their own prejudiced society, subject to its taboos, its prohibitions, and its models, both conscious and subconscious.

Although subconscious prejudices are often hard to identify, there appears to be some concerted effort of late to eliminate socially unacceptable definitions. Consider, for example, the *Collins Cobuild* definition of *clitoris* (as mentioned in Béjoint 2000, 128):

> A woman's clitoris is the small sensitive lump above her vagina which, when touched, causes pleasant sexual feelings that can lead to an orgasm.

This definition clearly reflects a shift away from traditional ideological tendencies seen in other definitions of this word. A progressive attitude is typical of the *Cobuild*, however. Such changes are perhaps less common in more conservative dictionaries. *W11*, for example, has retained almost exactly the same definition of *clitoris* as in previous editions. Generally, however, I have noted minor improvements in the female lot in dictionaries over the past decade. The clitoris is suffering from less penis envy, and the vagina occasionally gets credit for its sexual function, at least in some French dictionaries. The change that I found most surprising was that, unlike all other dictionaries that I consulted, the *New Shorter Oxford English Dictionary* and its Canadian cousin, the *Canadian Oxford Dictionary*, now omit all explicit references to copulation in their entries for *penis*. In these entries, the penis has been somewhat desexed; instead of copulating, it simply "carries the duct for the emission of sperm." Have the female editors of these two dictionaries reversed an ideological stance that traditionally saved sexless definitions for the vagina?

Dictionary entries, like all texts, can never be free from ideological stance. However, there is a new ideological stance influencing much of our society, including our dictionaries, a politically correct stance in which sexist and ideologically coloured definitions are unacceptable. The task of making dictionaries more politically correct should be facilitated not only by the recent increase in the number of female lexicographers but also by the fact that women and minority groups are writing more and more. As lexicographers rely heavily on the written word as sources for their work, a range of social values that goes beyond the status quo should consequently be reflected in dictionary definitions and examples.

THE CONTENT OF THE EXAMPLES
The elements of dictionaries that are probably most telling of the society that produced them are the examples. A study of the examples in an older dictionary will often reveal shifts in social values that have occurred in the time between its publication and the present day. Landau (1985) has gathered together an extensive list of dictionary examples from the 1968 and 1983 editions of the *Thorndike Barnhart Beginning Dictionary* to show how the content had to be changed to acknowledge the shift in gender-related attitudes that occurred in the intervening years. One such example follows.

> 1968: "He was *sandwiched* between two large fat women."
> 1983: "I was *sandwiched* between two large boxes in the backseat of the car."

The changes to this example obviously reflect a modern sensitivity to the problem of obesity in addition to a greater awareness of sexism.

That is not to say that today's dictionaries are free of sexist examples. Élisabeth Campbell (2004) has found many examples of a subtle and seemingly unconscious sexism in bilingual dictionary examples. A more overt and seemingly deliberate form of sexism can be found in the following example, from the entry for *souris* in the *Trésor de la langue française*.

> En amour, l'homme est la souris
> Pour qui toute femme est la chatte.
> Le sot ne voit pas l'ongle gris
> Sous le doux velours de la patte.
> Rollinat, *Névroses*,
> 1883, p. 119

One cannot help but wonder if this example was selected for reasons other than the renown of its author; it may have been deliberately chosen to perpetuate sexist values. Dictionaries have the power to propagate harmful social trends and preserve undesirable traditions. It is true that social values influence dictionaries, but dictionaries can also influence social values.

DISCUSSION: THE INFLUENCE OF DICTIONARIES ON SOCIAL VALUES

Throughout this paper, I have often referred to *the* dictionary, much in the same way that people refer to *the* Bible. This usage is common, and it is a clear indication of the status of the dictionary. In the minds of some, a dictionary parallels the Bible in terms of authority. Beryl T. Sue Atkins (1985, 23) claims that dictionaries are "endowed with the numinous quality of Moses' tablets." Frawley (1990, 143) states that "Most literate households have at least one dictionary. . . . No other book I know of, except perhaps the Bible, has such a sense of necessity about it."

With such authority and necessity comes great power. Landau (1985, 269) claims that, by recognizing one particular set of values over another, dictionaries give those values stability and authority. Furthermore, by representing more progressive values, they can help to further social change. Alma Graham (1975) comes to essentially the same conclusion. It is interesting that both Landau and Graham came to this conclusion in their work with children's dictionaries. Such dictionaries may be the most powerful of all dictionaries, for not only do their users tend to be less biased, but children also tend to read definitions more carefully than adult dictionary users. Children's dictionaries could therefore be instrumental in bringing about positive social change, but they might also have the power for negative influence on the minds of children. Yaguello is one author who sees the possibility for negative influence. In a book chapter entitled "Faut-il brûler les dictionnaires?" she indicates her feelings on this topic:

> The dictionary is an ideological creation. It is a mirror of society and of the dominant ideology. As an indisputable authority and a cultural tool, the dictionary plays a part in establishing and preserving not only language, but also attitudes and ideology. As Hugo used to say, every revolution should be accompanied by dictionary reform. (1979, 165)[6]

Dictionaries are indeed ideological creations that reflect social values as well as propagate and preserve them. As both product and protector of our social values, they are invaluable documents: invaluable yet not infallible. Béjoint (2000, 139) claims that we seem to be less and less naïve in our expectations of dictionaries, which is a good thing. If we are realistic in what we expect of dictionaries, then we need not consider burning them, as Yaguello implies. We simply need to be more careful about how we read them and write them.

NOTES

1   This paper is a revised and updated version of a term paper that I submitted in 1993 as an MA student at the University of Ottawa. I am grateful for the insightful comments given to me then by Dr. Annie Brisset and Dr. Ingrid Meyer and for their encouragement to publish the paper. Although I did not heed their encouragement at the time, it ultimately inspired me to resurrect my work for publication in this memorial volume.
2   A comparison of the 1694 and 1932 definitions for *aussi* reveals only a few very minor word changes.
3   Cf. Josette Rey-Debove (1989, 309–10) for further explanation of the ellipsis of metalinguistic verbs in dictionary entries.
4   I would like to thank Dr. Lynne Bowker of the University of Ottawa for suggesting these terms.
5   The omission of any reference to the urinary function of the penis in the *W9* definition is in itself quite shocking and was rectified in subsequent editions of the *Merriam-Webster's Collegiate Dictionary*.
6   My translation. The original reads as follows:
> Le dictionnaire est une création idéologique. Il reflète la société et l'idéologie dominante. En tant qu'autorité indiscutable, en tant qu'outil culturel, le dictionnaire joue un rôle de fixation et de conservation, non seulement de la langue mais aussi des mentalités et de l'idéologie. Toute révolution devrait s'accompagner d'une réforme du dictionnaire, comme le disait Hugo.

REFERENCES

Atkins, Beryl T. 1985. "Monolingual and Bilingual Learner's Dictionaries: A Comparison." In *Dictionaries, Lexicography, and Language Learning*, ed. Robert Ilson, 15–24. Oxford: Pergamon.

Béjoint, Henri. 2000. *Modern Lexicography: An Introduction*. New York: Oxford University Press.

Braun, Virginia, and Celia Kitzinger. 2001. "Telling It Straight? Dictionary Definitions of Women's Genitals." *Journal of Sociolinguistics* 5 (2): 214–32.

Campbell, Élisabeth. 2004. "La représentation des femmes dans les dictionnaires bilingues." *French Studies* 58 (1): 61–76.

The Canadian Oxford Dictionary. 1998. Don Mills, ON: Oxford University Press.

Collins Cobuild English Language Dictionary. 1987. London: Collins.

de Lotbinière-Harwood, Susanne. 1991. *Re-belle et infidèle/The Body Bilingual.* Montréal: Les éditions du remue-ménage; Toronto: Women's Press.

de Mello Vianna, Fernando. 1982. *Diccionario inglés for Spanish speakers.* Skokie: National Textbook.

Dickins, Tom. 2000. "Changing Ideological Directions: A Study of the Czech Dictionary *Slovník jazyka českého* (1937–1952)." *Slavonica* 6 (1): 24–74.

Dictionnaire de l'Académie française. 1932. 8th ed. Paris: Hachette.

Dictionnaire de l'Académie françoise. 1694. Paris: Vve de J.B. Coignard et al.

Frawley, William. 1985. "Intertextuality and the Dictionary: Toward a Deconstructionist Account of Lexicography." *Dictionaries* 7: 1–20.

———. 1989. "The Dictionary As Text." *International Journal of Lexicography* 2 (3): 232–48.

———. 1990. "Reading the Dictionary." *Lexicographica* 6: 141–59.

Galisson, Robert. 1983. "Image et usage du dictionnaire." *Études de linguistique appliquée* 49: 5–88.

Gougenheim, Georges. 1958. *Dictionnaire fondamental de la langue française.* Paris: Didier.

Graham, Alma. 1975. "The Making of a Non-Sexist Dictionary." In *Language and Sex: Difference and Dominance,* ed. Barrie Thorne and Nancy Henley, 57–63. Rowley, MA: Newbury House.

Green, Jonathon. 2004. "Language: Wash Your Mouth Out." *Critical Quarterly* 46 (1): 107–11.

Hanks, Patrick. 1987. "Definitions and Explanations." In *Looking Up: An Account of the COBUILD Project in Lexical Computing and the Development of the Collins Cobuild English Language Dictionary,* ed. J.M. Sinclair, 116–35. London: Collins.

Landau, Sidney I. 1984. *Dictionaries: The Art and Craft of Lexicography.* New York: Charles Scribner's Sons.

———. 1985. "The Expression of Changing Social Values in Dictionaries." *Dictionaries* 7: 261–69.

Longman Dictionary of Contemporary English. 1995. Harlow: Longman.

Mackintosh, Kristen. 1998. "An Empirical Study of Dictionary Use in L2-L1 Translation." In *Using Dictionaries: Studies of Dictionary Use by Language Learners and Translators,* ed. B.T.S. Atkins, 123–50. Tübingen: Max Niemeyer.

McCreary, Don R. 2002. "American Freshmen and English Dictionaries: 'I Had *Aspersions* of Becoming an English Teacher.'" *International Journal of Lexicography* 15 (3): 181–205.

Merriam-Webster's Collegiate Dictionary. 1993. 10th ed. Springfield, MA: Merriam-Webster.

———. 2003. 11th ed. Springfield, MA.: Merriam-Webster.

Miller, Casey, and Kate Swift. 1976. *Words and Women: New Language in New Times.* Garden City, NY: Doubleday.

Mills, Jane. 1989. *Womanwords: A Vocabulary of Culture and Patriarchal Society.* Harlow: Longman.
The New Shorter Oxford English Dictionary: On Historical Principles. 1993. Oxford: Clarendon Press.
Le nouveau petit Robert: Dictionnaire alphabétique et analogique de la langue française, nouvelle édition du petit Robert. 2003. Paris: Le Robert.
Le petit Robert 1: Dictionnaire alphabétique et analogique de la langue française. 1991. Paris: Le Robert.
Quirk, Randolph. 1973. "The Social Impact of Dictionaries in the U.K." In *Lexicography in English,* ed. R.I. McDavid and A.R. Duckert, 76–88. New York: New York Academy of Sciences.
Rey-Debove, Josette. 1971. *Étude linguistique et sémiotique des dictionnaires français contemporains.* Paris: Mouton.
———. 1989. "La métalangue lexicographique: Formes et fonctions en lexicographie monolingue." In *Dictionaries: An International Encyclopedia of Lexicography,* vol. 1, ed. Franz Josef Hausmann et al., 305–12. Berlin: Walter de Gruyter.
Le Robert méthodique: Dictionnaire méthodique du français actuel. 1988. Paris: Le Robert.
Schoemperlen, Diane. 1993. "The Antonyms of Fiction." In *Parallel Voices/ Voix parallèles,* ed. Matt Cohen and André Carpentier, 97–101. Kingston: Quarry; Montreal: XYZ.
Trésor de la langue française: Dictionnaire de la langue du XIXe et du XXe siècle (1789–1960). 1971–85. Nancy: Éditions du Centre national de la recherche scientifique.
Varantola, Krista. 1993. "Technical Vocabulary and Learner's Dictionaries." In *English Far and Wide: A Festschrift for Inna Koskenniemi,* ed. R. Hiltunen et al., 249–60. Annales Universitatis Turkuensis B:197. Turku: Turun Yliopisto.
Wachal, Robert S. 2002. "Taboo or Not Taboo: That Is the Question." *American Speech* 77 (2): 195–206.
Webster's Ninth New Collegiate Dictionary. 1991. Springfield, MA: Merriam-Webster.
Yaguello, Marina. 1979. *Les mots et les femmes.* Paris: Payot.

PART II

TERMINOLOGY

CHAPTER 4

TERMINOLOGICAL RELATIONSHIPS AND CORPUS-BASED METHODS FOR DISCOVERING THEM: AN ASSESSMENT FOR TERMINOGRAPHERS

*MARIE-CLAUDE L'HOMME
AND ELIZABETH MARSHMAN*

INTRODUCTION

Recent work in terminology shows an increasing interest in a large variety of relationships between terms (qualified by authors as *semantic, terminological,* or *conceptual*). Hyperonymy and meronymy remain central in most terminological descriptions, but other non-hierarchical and lexical relationships are being considered by terminographers and other specialists using specialized corpora.

During the past decade, researchers with different backgrounds and motivations have developed methods for discovering these relationships either automatically or semi-automatically in specialized corpora. Among these are terminographers who seek information about terms in order to describe them in dictionaries or term banks. Other applications include information retrieval and knowledge representation. These methods all rely on formal properties displayed by terms or by the text in which they appear but differ in other ways (e.g., the relationships that they capture or the technique used to capture them).

In this paper, we will review some of these methods and show how they can assist terminographers in their work, for example in compiling specialized dictionaries. We will first present a list of typical relationships that terminographers consider when describing terms. We will then describe methods for identifying these relationships in corpora. In examining the first, based on linguistic markers, we will review important concepts introduced by Ingrid Meyer, one of the first researchers to consider this issue from a terminological perspective. Then we will present other methods that reveal interesting semantic aspects of terms that are not captured by linguistic markers. We will conclude with a discussion of the advantages and limitations of each set of methods for terminological work.

RELEVANT TERMINOLOGICAL RELATIONSHIPS

When analyzing the meanings of terms that form the lexical structure in a field of knowledge, terminographers may be interested in various types of relationships. Any or all of these relationships may be pertinent in a given domain, and understanding them is fundamental to concept analysis and the construction of domain knowledge structures.

It is widely recognized that the most important relationship is that of hyperonymy (e.g., *peripheral* is the hyperonym of *mouse*). This relationship has generally been considered as the fundamental one for developing knowledge structures since it allows for the construction of hierarchies linking generic domain concepts and their specifics. In addition, the generic is a key part of the classical Aristotelian definition, making its identification particularly important for terminographers.

While not always considered to be as fundamental as hyperonymy, meronymy (e.g., *central processing unit* is a meronym of *computer*) is nevertheless of great value in classifying and structuring some types of concepts. As noted by Morton Winston, Roger Chaffin, and Douglas Herrmann (1987), among others, the relationship of meronymy actually includes several different relational subtypes (e.g., physical parts versus temporal parts).

Two additional, non-hierarchical conceptual relationships—that is, the relationships between an entity and its function (e.g., *data entry* is the function of a *keyboard*) and between a cause and an effect (e.g., an *error* is the cause of a *crash*)—had typically been set aside in favour of hyperonymy and meronymy but have begun to be explored in recent years. As underlined by Meyer and her colleagues, such relationships may be critical for the development of concept analysis, and these links should be preserved in terminological resources (e.g., Meyer et al. 1992). The function relationship is of course critical for the description of artefacts but can also be observed in many other contexts. The cause-effect relationship, one of the most fundamental in human perception, has been identified as central in many domains, especially science and medicine.

Other relationships are also important in terminological analysis and description even though they have not often been studied in terminology. Some of these relationships are listed below:

- antonymy (e.g., *install, uninstall; accuse, defend; compatible, incompatible*);
- synonymy (e.g., *screen, monitor; press, hit [key]*);
- predicates and arguments: predicate-agent (e.g., *infects, virus*); predicate-instrument (e.g., *print, printer*) (some of these were investigated by Judit Feliu [2004]);
- different parts of speech with the same meaning: nouns and adjectives (e.g., *virus, viral*) or nouns and verbs (e.g., *processing, process*); and
- co-occurrents and collocations: typical function associated with an entity (e.g., *computer, process [data]*), the typical use of an entity (e.g., *surf the Internet*), a property associated with an entity (e.g., *program, user-friendly*).

All of the relationships listed in this section are expressed in one way or another in specialized corpora. In the following sections, we will see how they can be discovered using computational methods.

KNOWLEDGE-RICH CONTEXTS AND KNOWLEDGE PATTERNS

At the beginning of the 1990s, Meyer and other researchers working with specialized corpora in electronic form started devising methods for exploiting them in a more efficient way in terminological work. One general question held their attention: how can terminographers locate informative contexts (i.e., contexts that can be used to analyze the meanings of terms) and ignore others, using computer applications such as concordancers or more sophisticated programs?

In 1994, Meyer introduced the concept of the "knowledge-rich context" (KRC) and the possibilities that lie in "exploiting the many regularities in the way that 'linguistic patterns' found in specialized texts encode conceptual information" (8).[1] At this time, Meyer defined knowledge-rich contexts as "free (i.e., non-collocational) language combinations that frequently identify a particular conceptual relation or attribute" (8).[2] A precise definition of "knowledge-rich context" was provided by Meyer in 2001: "By knowledge-rich context, we designate a context indicating at least one item of domain knowledge that could be useful for conceptual analysis. In other words, the context should indicate at least one conceptual characteristic, whether it be an attribute or a relation" (281).

Applications of KRCs in terminological work are numerous and varied. Some "high-quality" knowledge-rich contexts can be used directly in term records, for example in definitions. Contexts that are not appropriate for formulating definitions—because they do not indicate a given relationship or for other reasons—may still assist in the process of concept analysis, helping the terminographer to gain a better picture of how the concept fits into the knowledge structure of the domain. Meyer et al. referred to these contexts as "good noise" (1999, 261).[3]

KRCs often contain knowledge patterns, linguistic sequences that indicate conceptual characteristics.[4] These patterns should be "predictable" and "recurring in text" and "manifest the relations in which the terminologist is interested" (Meyer et al. 1999, 257). Formally, knowledge patterns can be classified into three types:

> 1) *Lexical patterns* involve specific lexical items and can convey all types of relations. For example ... HYPERONYMY patterns include *is the, is a, such as, and other* and *known as*. 2) *Grammatical patterns* apply to a small number of relations. The pattern NOUN + VERB (with some verbs excluded), for example, is highly productive for indicating the FUNCTION relation. 3) *Paralinguistic patterns* include punctuation, as well as various elements of the general structure of a text. The phrase "placenta previa (a placenta abnormally located in the lower part of the uterus)," for example, illustrates how parentheses may indicate HYPERONYMY. (Meyer et al. 1999, 257–58)

Most work on knowledge patterns has been based on lexical patterns, since very few grammatical patterns are predictable (they can vary from one corpus to another), and paralinguistic patterns are highly ambiguous.

METHODS FOR DISCOVERING KNOWLEDGE PATTERNS

Meyer (2001), in line with other researchers carrying out similar work (e.g., Pearson 1998; Condamines and Rebeyrolle 2001), described a term-oriented approach to locating knowledge-rich contexts, beginning with a set of terms to be described. In the approach as described by Meyer, the terminographer searches the corpus using a search tool, specifying a term and the relationship of interest (often hyperonymy initially, in search of defining contexts, followed by others such as meronymy, function, or cause-effect). This relationship is associated with a set of knowledge patterns that are used in combination with the term to search for potential KRCs. The retrieved contexts can then be displayed by the tool (e.g., in a concordancer-inspired KWIC format), for evaluation by the terminographer.

Ideally, KRCs should be located with simple methods. Knowledge patterns may be expressed with character strings, possibly combined with linguistic information such as morphosyntactic tags. As in Khurshid Ahmad and Heather Fulford's (1992) model, Meyer and her colleagues (1999, 258) believed that identification of KRCs should be interactive, semi-automatic:

> we feel that conceptual sampling is not likely to be fully automated in the near future: rather, it will be a semi-automatic, *terminographer-assisted* technology. Terminographers will need to examine the output of sampling tools critically to eliminate errors (i.e., "noise"). Furthermore, even when the output is correct, they will want to bring their world knowledge to bear on it, in order to maximize its value.

They viewed the development of tools for KRC extraction as an iterative process involving the gradual development and refinement of pattern sets for each conceptual relationship to be handled by the tool. The goal, as with most NLP tools, was to balance the often conflicting measures of recall and precision.

This process has been extended by researchers aiming to discover knowledge patterns automatically (e.g., Morin 1999; Séguéla 1999). Automatic discovery methods are based on the hypothesis that each corpus is different (Condamines 2002) and that patterns will thus differ from one corpus to another. For each new corpus, patterns are discovered using pairs of terms for which a relationship has already been identified. The system looks for contexts in which these pairs appear and identifies a potential pattern. The patterns discovered are then used to find new term pairs, and so on.

RELATIONSHIPS EXPRESSED BY KNOWLEDGE PATTERNS

Knowledge patterns have been studied mostly for discovering the hierarchical conceptual relationships of hyperonymy and meronymy. The relationship of hyperonymy can be identified using knowledge patterns such as *X is a kind of Y, an X is a Y,* and *As include Bs, Cs, and Ds* (Meyer 1994, 8). In addition to the identification of generic-specific pairs, KRCs may identify a series of coordinate concepts, co-hyponyms of a generic. This is the case, for example, in structures such as *As include Bs, Cs, and Ds,* in which the generic is also introduced, and *X, Y, and Z* and *X as well as Y* (Meyer 1994, 8), which do not explicitly introduce the generic but may indicate co-hyponymy alone. Knowledge patterns such as *is a part of* and *contains* can indicate meronymy (Meyer 2001, 290).

Among non-hierarchical conceptual relationships, function patterns have been studied by Meyer et al. (1999) as well as Elizabeth Marshman, Tricia Morgan, and Ingrid Meyer (2002) and include *needed for, serve as,* and *designed for.* The function relationship is also often associated with grammatical knowledge patterns, for instance the combination of noun + verb (Meyer et al. 1999, 257). Cause-effect patterns have been studied by a number of researchers (e.g., Garcia 1997; Barrière 2001; Marshman 2002; and Feliu 2004) and include *X causes Y, X results in Y,* and *X results from Y* (Meyer et al. 1999, 260).

In addition to those expressing the four conceptual relationships above, other knowledge patterns have received some attention. Meyer (2001) stressed the importance of taking into account what she referred to as *attributes,* characteristics of the concept in isolation. They may include, for example, the colour, height, and weight of the object represented by the concept. While not as widely studied as the relationships between concepts, the link between a concept and its attributes is valuable for concept analysis (e.g., shared attributes may be the basis for establishing hyperonymic relationships, while differing attributes may be the basis for differentiating between co-hyponyms). Patterns indicating attributes include grammatical patterns composed of a noun and an adjective as well as lexical patterns such as *X is characterized by Y* and *the features of an X include Y and Z* (Meyer 1994, 8).

Some researchers have been interested in another category of patterns, called *metalinguistic patterns,* such as *X is defined as Y, X is called Y,* which do not introduce a conceptual relationship as such but provide information on the term viewed as a lexical unit (Pearson 1998, in English corpora; Rebeyrolle 2000, in French corpora; Malaisé, Zweigenbaum, and Bachimont 2004, in medical corpora, using automatic pattern identification).

METHODS FOR FINDING OTHER RELATIONSHIPS

Although extremely useful, knowledge patterns do not reveal all the semantic relationships between terms that are expressed in corpora. Hyperonyms and hyponyms, synonyms, predicates, and arguments, as well as typical co-occurrents, can appear in corpora without a pattern indicating the relationships that exist between them.

Other researchers have adopted a different approach to the problem of finding semantic information about terms in corpora. To discover some of these relationships automatically or semi-automatically, they rely on the formal properties of terms and/or on lexical units found in the vicinity of terms. We present these methods briefly below.

FINDING RELATIONSHIPS BETWEEN TERMS BASED ON THEIR FORMAL PROPERTIES

Some methods assume that terms in a specific domain that share formal properties also share semantic components. This may be the case for multiword terms (MWTs) (e.g., *data processing, information processing*) or for single-word terms (e.g., terms with the suffix *-itis* in the field of medicine refer to an inflammation).

One technique exploits the similarities between MWTs. Terms that share the same head (e.g., *laser printer, ink jet printer, impact printer*) or the same modifier (e.g., *Web page, Web browser, Web site*) are assumed to be semantically related and are grouped together. Some applications simply base their analysis on similar character strings; others identify the syntactic relationships between the constituents (Bourigault 1994) and then look for constituents that share the same syntactic function (e.g., terms with the head *printer* or with the modifier *printer*). In these methods, groups of terms are submitted to the user (often a terminographer) who will decide which candidates are relevant for the task at hand, for example

- *printer* (head): *dot matrix ~, ink jet ~, laser ~, portable ~, shared ~*
- *printer* (modifier): *~ market, ~ output, ~ option, ~ wizard.*

The semantic relationship between candidates that belong to a series is not formally identified. However, most terms will share relationships such as hyperonymy, co-hyponymy, synonymy, or antonymy.

A second method that also applies to MWTs tries to identify terms that share semantic components based on morphological features. Béatrice Daille (2001, 152) proposed a strategy for relating terms with noun modifiers and terms with relational adjective modifiers, such as *expérimentation animale* (Engl. *animal testing*) or *expérimentation sur les animaux* (Engl. *testing on animals*). Lexical features, including morphological resemblance, have also been exploited by Natalia Grabar and Pierre Zweigenbaum (2004) to identify semantic relationships between terms, including single-word terms (SWTs). Even though this latter work was not carried out on corpora, it shows that the formal properties of terms can be exploited to a certain extent for identifying semantic relationships.[5] Here again, unless an external resource is used, these techniques are able to build series of terms but do not formally identify the semantic relationship between them (with the exception of the method developed by Daille [2001], which assumes that pairs identified are synonyms). However, relationships are most likely to be hyperonymy, co-hyponymy, synonymy, and antonymy if the series contain noun terms.

FINDING RELATIONSHIPS BETWEEN TERMS BASED ON THEIR CO-OCCURRENTS

Other methods assume that, if two lexical units (and, more specifically, two terms) share a significant number of co-occurrents, then they must be semantically related. For example, *program, application, editor,* and *word processor* can all combine with *launch, install, quit,* and *powerful*; hence, they are most likely to be semantically related.

These methods are based on distributional analysis, introduced by Zellig Harris (1968). The idea is to build automatically series of similar terms based on a significant number of shared contexts (e.g., Habert, Naulleau, and Nazarenko 1996; Nazarenko et al. 2001). The relevant contexts are identified according to the lexical units that appear in the vicinity of terms. In some methods, statistical techniques are applied to simple character strings. In others, a specific syntactic relationship is identified (e.g., noun + modifier in adjective form, noun + modifier in the form of a prepositional phrase); then frequency or statistical measures are added to filter the candidates. As with the method based on the formal properties of MWTs, distributional analysis will produce series of related terms that users will need to analyze in order to find relevant relationships. These series are likely to contain synonyms, hyperonyms, and co-hyponyms. The co-occurrents themselves can yield interesting clues about typical functions and causes as well as properties associated with noun terms. Finally, considering both terms and co-occurrents can reveal important predicate-argument relationships.

DISCUSSION

Linguistic markers have several advantages from the point of view of terminographers. Hearst (1992, 544) pointed out that such an approach has an advantage over statistical discovery of links between lexical items because it is capable of locating single occurrences of pairs in a corpus. Also unlike approaches based on statistical measures of co-occurrence, knowledge patterns often allow the user to identify a particular relationship and to label it (e.g., *is a type of* is associated with hyperonymy, *is a result of* is associated with cause-effect). Moreover, knowledge-pattern discovery seems to be the most compatible approach with traditional terminological methods for analyzing corpora.

Identification of KRCs based on knowledge patterns, as noted by Khurshid Ahmad and Margaret Rogers (2001, 750), can theoretically be applied in many languages, requiring only a new language-specific set of knowledge patterns. Once a method of automatic discovery of knowledge patterns has been developed and refined, it could allow such a list to be created relatively quickly.

However, a knowledge-pattern-based approach also has its drawbacks, several of which were noted and analyzed by Meyer and her colleagues. Many of these are recurrent and can be very difficult to overcome computationally. Probably the most widespread and problematic of these is the ambiguity of many knowledge patterns: patterns may not clearly show the orientation of a relationship, may potentially indicate more than one relationship, or in some contexts may not indicate a relationship (or attribute) at all. Other difficulties include pattern form variation, domain- or corpus-specific patterns (which are thus not reusable for analyzing other corpora in other domains), and problems in resolution of anaphoric reference. There may also be difficulties in evaluating the validity of KRCs retrieved (e.g., patterns may link terms that are only distantly or subjectively related, and contexts may contain attenuating phrases, modal verbs, or negation). Finally, there are inherent limitations of the approach. As noted above, not all KRCs include knowledge patterns; rather, a relationship can be stated or implied without using linguistic markers (Meyer et al. 1999, 261). Many important semantic relationships (e.g., predicate-argument relations, collocations, co-occurrents) are not generally indicated by knowledge patterns at all.

Methods based on formal features of terms or on co-occurrence allow users to find series of terms that are likely to share a semantic relationship that is not expressed with a knowledge pattern. While not vulnerable to knowledge-pattern-linked problems such as pattern ambiguity or variation in pattern form, an approach to identifying semantically related items that relies on lexical items' form also encounters a number of pitfalls. On the one hand, many related terms may not be similar in form (e.g., *program, virus, worm* [hyperonymy]; *infects, virus* [predicate-agent]); on the other, many similar forms are not semantically related (e.g., homonyms or polysemous items and their derivatives, which have been observed to be far more common in specialized language than some had previously believed [e.g., *reprogrammable*, derived from *program* in one of its senses, and *programmer*, derived from another sense]).

Finally, an approach based on co-occurrence (i.e., distributional analysis) is interesting because it can associate terms that do not necessarily share formal properties. However, it cannot identify the specific relationships between the terms and thus requires significant interpretation by the terminographer before the information retrieved can be used. In addition, this approach requires large amounts of data for the calculation of the associations between terms.

CONCLUSIONS

Research on the automatic and semi-automatic extraction of terminological relationships from text corpora has played a particularly important role in the study of conceptual and semantic analysis for terminology. The knowledge-pattern approach, studied by Meyer and other researchers cited in this article, can be extremely valuable alone or as a complement to other formal, morphological, or statistical techniques for identifying relationships between terms. The latter methods have received significant attention in computational circles but much less in the field of terminology, which usually focuses on the conceptual relationships expressed by knowledge patterns. However, with a good understanding of all of these techniques, as well as their strengths and weaknesses, a terminographer can more easily and accurately plan strategies for building an understanding of a subject field and its terminological and conceptual structures. Work carried out by Ingrid Meyer and other researchers on the possibilities of exploiting the formal expression of specialized knowledge in corpora not only improves practical terminological research but also raises a number of fundamental questions about terminology as a discipline.

NOTES

1. Other researchers in terminology were carrying out related work (Ahmad and Fulford 1992; Pearson 1998; Condamines and Rebeyrolle 2001). Also, pioneering work had been conducted for other applications (Hearst 1992; Bowden, Halstead, and Rose 1996).
2. Readers may note that at the time "knowledge-rich context" and "knowledge pattern" were not explicitly differentiated.
3. Meyer, in the context of her research in terminology, often drew parallels between terminological work—and more specifically concept analysis—and knowledge engineering (e.g., Meyer 1994, 6). This view was at the root of her projects on the development of the terminological knowledge base (TKB), which links a knowledge structure with a term base in a particular domain. In her work on the use of knowledge-rich contexts for concept analysis, Meyer identified various types of information that could be useful for the terminographer and several ways in which this information could be integrated into terminology records or the TKB.
4. While the terms used to designate linguistic markers of conceptual characteristics (generally relations) have varied, including *knowledge probes* (Ahmad and Fulford 1992), *defining expositives* (Pearson 1998, 1999), *marqueurs de relations sémantiques* (Séguéla 1999), and of course *knowledge patterns,* proposed by Meyer (1994, 2001), the basis of the object of study has remained largely consistent.
5. Although it was not developed for this purpose, this technique could be used to identify morphological series containing verbs and adjectives (e.g., *program, reprogram, programmable, reprogrammable*).

REFERENCES

Ahmad, Khurshid, and Heather Fulford. 1992. *Knowledge Processing: 4. Semantic Relations and Their Use in Elaborating Terminology*. Computing Sciences Report CS-92-07. Guildford: University of Surrey.

Ahmad, Khurshid, and Margaret Rogers. 2001. "Corpus Linguistics and Terminology Extraction." In *Handbook of Terminology Management*, vol. 2, ed. Sue Ellen Wright and Gerhard Budin, 725–60. Amsterdam: John Benjamins.

Barrière, Caroline. 2001. "Investigating the Causal Relation in Informative Texts." *Terminology* 7 (2): 135–54.

Bourigault, Didier. 1994. "LEXTER, un logiciel d'EXtraction de TERminologie: Application à l'acquisition de connaissances à partir de textes. " PhD diss., École des Hautes Études en Sciences Sociales, Paris.

Bowden, Paul R., Peter Halstead, and Tony G. Rose. 1996. "Extracting Conceptual Knowledge from Text Using Explicit Relation Markers." In *Advances in Knowledge Acquisition: Proceedings of the 9th European Knowledge Acquisition Workshop (EKAW '96)*, ed. N. Shadbolt, K. O'Hara, and G. Schreiber, 147–62. Berlin: Springer-Verlag.

Condamines, Anne. 2002. "Corpus Analysis and Conceptual Relation Patterns." *Terminology* 8 (1): 141–62.

Condamines, Anne, and Josette Rebeyrolle. 2001. "Searching for and Identifying Conceptual Relationships via a Corpus-Based Approach to a Terminological Knowledge Base (CTKB): Method and Results." In *Recent Advances in Computational Terminology*, ed. Didier Bourigault, Christian Jacquemin, and Marie-Claude L'Homme, 127–48. Amsterdam: John Benjamins.

Daille, Béatrice. 2001. "Qualitative Terminology Extraction: Identifying Relational Adjectives." In *Recent Advances in Computational Terminology*, ed. Didier Bourigault, Christian Jacquemin, and Marie-Claude L'Homme, 149–66. Amsterdam: John Benjamins.

Feliu, Judit. 2004. "Relacions conceptuals i terminologia: Anàlisi i proposta de detecció semiautomàtica." PhD diss., Universitat Pompeu Fabra, Barcelona.

Garcia, Daniela. 1997. "Structuration du lexique de la causalité et réalisation d'un outil d'aide au repérage de l'action dans les textes." In *Actes des deuxièmes rencontres: Terminologie et Intelligence Artificielle (TIA '97)*, 7–26. Toulouse: Équipe de Recherche en Syntaxe et Sémantique.

Grabar, Natalia, and Pierre Zweigenbaum. 2004. "Lexically-Based Terminology Structuring." *Terminology* 10 (1): 23–53.

Habert, Benoît, Émile Naulleau, and Adeline Nazarenko. 1996. "Symbolic Word Clustering for Medium-Size Corpora." In *Proceedings of the 16th*

International Conference on Computational Linguistics (COLING '96), Copenhagen, vol. 1, 490–95.

Harris, Zellig. 1968. *Mathematical Structures of Language.* New York: Interscience Publishers; John Wiley and Sons.

Hearst, Marti. 1992. "Automatic Acquisition of Hyponyms from Large Text Corpora." In *Proceedings of the 14th International Conference on Computational Linguistics (COLING '92),* Nantes, 539–45.

Malaisé, Véronique, Pierre Zweigenbaum, and Bruno Bachimont. 2004. "Detecting Semantic Relations between Terms in Definitions." In *Proceedings of 3rd Workshop on Computational Terminology (Computerm 2004),* Geneva, ed. Sophia Ananiadou and Pierre Zwiegenbaum, 55–62. http://acl.ldc.upenn.edu/coling2004/W7/pdf/proceedings.pdf.

Marshman, Elizabeth. 2002. "The Cause Relation in Biopharmaceutical Texts: Some English Knowledge Patterns." In *Proceedings of Terminology and Knowledge Engineering (TKE '02),* Nancy, ed. Alan Melby, 89–94. Le Chesnay, France: Inria.

Marshman, Elizabeth, Tricia Morgan, and Ingrid Meyer. 2002. "French Patterns for Expressing Concept Relations." *Terminology* 8 (1): 1–29.

Meyer, Ingrid. 1994. "Linguistic Strategies and Computer Aids for Knowledge Engineering in Terminology." *L'actualité terminologique/Terminology Update* 27 (4): 6–10.

———. 2001. "Extracting Knowledge-Rich Contexts for Terminography: A Conceptual and Methodological Framework." In *Recent Advances in Computational Terminology,* ed. Didier Bourigault, Christian Jacquemin, and Marie-Claude L'Homme, 279–302. Amsterdam: John Benjamins.

Meyer, Ingrid, Kristen Mackintosh, Caroline Barrière, and Tricia Morgan. 1999. "Conceptual Sampling for Terminographical Corpus Analysis." In *Proceedings of Terminology and Knowledge Engineering (TKE '99),* Innsbruck, ed. Peter Sandrini, 256–67. Würzburg: Ergon-Verlag.

Meyer, Ingrid, Douglas Skuce, Lynne Bowker, and Karen Eck. 1992. "Towards a New Generation of Terminological Resources: An Experiment in Building a Terminological Knowledge Base." In *Proceedings of the 14th International Conference on Computational Linguistics (COLING '92),* Nantes, 956–60.

Morin, Emmanuel. 1999. "Extraction de liens sémantiques entre termes à partir de corpus de textes techniques." PhD diss., Institut de Recherche en Informatique (IRIN), Université de Nantes.

Nazarenko, Adeline, Pierre Zweigenbaum, Benoît Habert, and Jacques Bouaud. 2001. "Qualitative Terminology Extraction: Identifying Relational Adjectives." In *Recent Advances in Computational Terminology,* ed. Didier Bourigault, Christian Jacquemin, and Marie-Claude L'Homme, 327–51. Amsterdam: John Benjamins.

Pearson, Jennifer. 1998. *Terms in Context.* Amsterdam: John Benjamins.

———. 1999. "Comment accéder aux éléments définitoires dans les textes spécialisés?" *Terminologies nouvelles* 19: 21–28.

Rebeyrolle, Josette. 2000. "Utilisation de contexts définitoires pour l'acquisition de connaissances à partir de textes." In *Actes Journées Francophones d'Ingénierie des Connaissances, IC 2000,* Toulouse, 105–14.

Séguéla, Patrick. 1999. "Adaptation semi-automatique d'une base de marqueurs de relations sémantiques sur des corpus spécialisés." *Terminologies nouvelles* 19: 52–60.

Winston, Morton E., Roger Chaffin, and Douglas Herrmann. 1987. "A Taxonomy of Part-Whole Relations." *Cognitive Science* 11 (4): 417–44.

CHAPTER 5

SEMI-AUTOMATIC CORPUS CONSTRUCTION FROM INFORMATIVE TEXTS[1]

CAROLINE BARRIÈRE

INTRODUCTION

Constructing a corpus is the first step in the process of building a *terminological knowledge base* (TKB). To do so, terminologists face the difficult task of finding informative domain-specific texts by searching through scientific journals, monographs, technical reports, user guides, and so on. In recent years, they have also begun to search on the Internet, which has presented itself as an invaluable source of text-based information in electronic form. Once the domain-specific corpus is available, further analysis can be performed to extract important terms and semantic relationships between them. These two components, terms and semantic relationships, are at the core of a TKB, a notion first introduced in Meyer et al. (1992) and now commonly used within the field of computational terminology. The idea is to move away from conventional term records and closer to semantic networks as used in *artificial intelligence* (AI). Although in AI such networks are often manually built, much research in computational terminology looks at how to create the TKB semi-automatically, investigating ways to search for terms as well as the surface expressions of semantic relationships through *knowledge patterns*. Meyer (2001) defined *knowledge-rich contexts* as sentences that are of interest to terminologists because they contain important terms and knowledge patterns. For example, the knowledge-rich context "an air embolism is another kind of decompression illness" can be found in text via the knowledge pattern "is another kind of," which is indicative of a hyperonymic relationship between the terms "air embolism" and "decompression illness."

What is not included in the semi-automatic process of TKB building is domain-specific corpus construction, quite a complex and somewhat subjective task. Of course, search tools such as search engines and Web site crawling tools are available to retrieve domain-specific texts, but these tools are not specifically aimed at terminologists who must decide, based on specific guidelines, which texts to keep. These guidelines, as can be found in L'Homme (2004, 126ff.), are aimed at human users and are expressed as criteria to be qualitatively measured about a text, such as how much it is within the specialized domain of interest, its language, its level of specialization, its type, its date, et cetera.

As a first step in moving from qualitative to quantitative evaluation of text selection criteria, I suggest a quantitative notion of a text's *knowledge-rich value* via the density of knowledge patterns that it contains. This proposal is simple and does not specifically address any of the criteria given in L'Homme (2004), although my aim is to explore indirectly the specialization level and text type criteria. As knowledge patterns indicate the presence of knowledge-rich contexts that the terminologist is looking for, my proposal is to make use of them at the time of corpus construction. As I develop a corpus-building tool, I wish to allow a terminologist to perform a document search about a particular domain, and present the retrieved texts in decreasing order of knowledge-rich value, reducing the browsing process time and therefore helping in the task of corpus construction. I am aware that this corpus-building tool should eventually include many additional criteria on which the terminologist could sort the results, but this article focuses on a single one, the criterion of knowledge-rich value.

First I briefly discuss the notion of knowledge patterns, their value in information searches, and their definitions. Then I look at the task of corpus building and how it is defined from a terminological perspective. I then present an original idea of using knowledge patterns as criteria for determining a text's knowledge-rich value. This idea is explored through the construction of a software tool for corpus building that is currently in development. Finally, I offer some concluding remarks and look at future work.

KNOWLEDGE PATTERNS

Creation of a TKB must go through three main steps: corpus construction, term extraction, and semantic relation extraction. Much work has been done at the term extraction level, and I refer the reader to Cabré Castellví, Bagot, and Palatresi (2001) for an excellent review of different term extraction systems. A considerable amount of work has also been done at the level of semantic relation extraction, as can be shown by the work of Bowden, Halstead, and Rose (1996); Biebow and Szulman (1999); Barrière and Copeck (2001); and Condamines and Rebeyrolle (2001), to name just a few. This nonexhaustive list presents some different flavours of the research undertaken in this area, which most people would agree started with the early work by Hearst (1992) and her exploration of the expression of the hyperonym relationship in text via lexico-syntactic patterns.

Meyer et al. (1999) have labelled these as knowledge patterns, and this work provides much insight into their definitions and their uses within a terminological context. Following in that direction, Barrière (2004) presents an extensive study of knowledge patterns, looking at their presence in corpora as well as in electronic dictionaries.

Before providing examples, let me abbreviate verb, adjective, determinant, noun, and preposition as V, A, D, N, and P respectively. Knowledge patterns are lexico-syntactic patterns that could look like "is D A kind of" (hyperonymy relation), "is D tool P" (function relation), "is D N who" (agent relation). The part-of-speech component of each pattern usually allows for limited variation. The first pattern above could see "is *a specific* kind of," "is *an interesting* kind of," "is *an important* kind of" as different variations.

The software SeRT (Semantic Relations in Text) shown in Figure 1 can perform searches on such lexico-syntactic knowledge patterns. The software allows a KWIC (keyword-in-context) view as well as an extended view (Barrière and Copeck 2001).

Knowledge patterns do not all perform equally. Meyer et al. (1999) present an interesting qualitative study on the difficulty of extracting such patterns from text and on their noise variation, which impacts their value as indicators of semantic relationships. In addition to noise, which determines how well a pattern reliably indicates a semantic relationship and not other linguistic phenomena, Barrière (2004) defines the notion of a pattern's productivity as its relative effectiveness among a set of patterns. As a good strategy, the most productive patterns should be used first to direct the terminologist to valuable sentences (i.e., sentences that have knowledge-rich contexts containing information about the relationship between terms). Terms and semantic relationships become

Figure 1: Knowledge pattern search in SeRT software

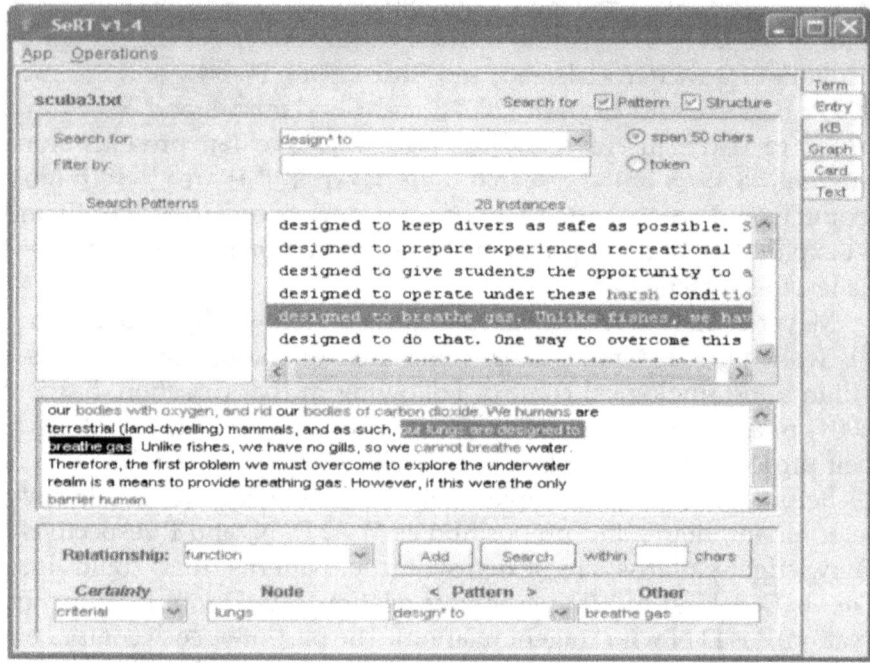

the building blocks of a TKB, which can be visualized graphically as shown in Figure 2.

DOMAIN-SPECIFIC CORPUS CONSTRUCTION FOR TERMINOLOGICAL USE

Most terminological work assumes a manually created corpus before involving the use of any tool to help the terminologist toward the construction of a TKB. The corpus construction step is a critical one since the terminologist must retrieve domain-specific texts from different sources. These texts should not be just any old texts. In Meyer et al. (1999), the preferred type of text for TKB building is the semi-technical text. Pearson (1998, 60–61) defines criteria of factuality, technicality, and audience type for deciding whether or not to include a text in a corpus. The types of texts that tend to give explanations of terms and to identify the relationships that terms have to each other assume

Semi-automatic Corpus Construction

Figure 2: Visualization of a term in a TKB as presented in SeRT

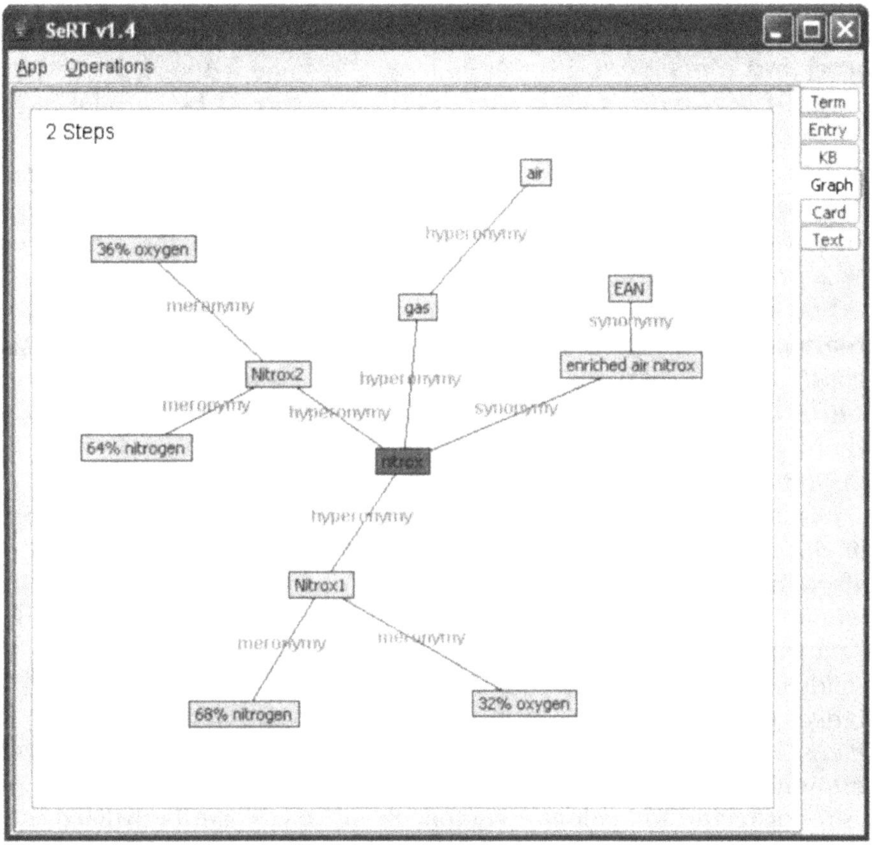

an expert-to-novice communicative goal as opposed to an expert-to-expert communication in which much information can remain implicit (Pearson 1998). An expert-to-novice text will tend to render all new notions explicit to ensure that they are understood by the reader.

In Barrière (2001), the notion of informativeness of a text is briefly explored and set in relation to the work of Jacobson (1966), who defined informative texts as having the goal of communicating facts and informing the reader, such as is typically done by newspapers, scientific journals, information leaflets, and the like. From a discourse analysis point of view, Jacobson contrasted informative texts with incitative, expressive, poetic, or ludic texts. From a language-learning point of view, Kintsch and Van Dijk (1978) contrast informative texts with narrative texts. In this research, I prefer to take a purely terminological view and talk about a text's knowledge-rich value. As terminologists look for texts from which they will eventually extract terms and semantic relationships found in knowledge-rich contexts, I suggest that a text's knowledge-rich value should be defined as its density of knowledge patterns.

In a manual evaluation by a terminologist of the value of a text, many other criteria can be examined (e.g., see L'Homme 2004), although no quantitative measures have been suggested, and the evaluation relies on the terminologist's experience. Some criteria, such as a text's author, date, or language, could be determined automatically. Other criteria, such as type of document (advertisement, user guide, thesis, report, article, catalogue), are less easy to determine. Research in natural language processing has barely looked into text genre analysis, where genre is defined as the combination of a text's type and its communicative purpose.

As terminologists make increasing use of the Web to search for documents, they will be faced with an extremely rich source of information but also a very noisy one. All search engines allow for domain searches, but the reader is left to decide on the quality of what is returned. Austermühl (2001) suggests a few elements to look for to decide on the authoritative value of a document, such as whether it is signed, contains a bibliography, has other trusted sites point to it, et cetera. Some of these criteria could be automated, and this avenue will certainly be investigated in future research. However, for the moment, I am not trying to evaluate whether or not a site can be trusted, nor am I suggesting quantitative evaluation of text genre or level of specialization. At this stage, I am proposing a first attempt at exploring a text's knowledge-rich value in terms of density of knowledge patterns once the domain relevancy of the text has been established. Note, however, that it would also be possible to establish domain relevancy automatically if a known list of domain-specific terms is made available beforehand.

LOOKING FOR A TEXT'S KNOWLEDGE-RICH VALUE

Although researchers seem to agree on basic semantic relationships and associated knowledge patterns, there is still much debate about the universality of semantic relationships across domains. Barrière (2002)

Semi-automatic Corpus Construction

discusses such issues of knowledge-pattern specificity. At this early stage of my exploration into the evaluation of a text's knowledge-rich value, I decided to build a software tool that would provide as much flexibility as possible, allowing a user to decide which relationships to look for. As a starting point, I provide the user with a basic list of semantic relations and an associated list of basic patterns that I have collected through manual exploration of different corpora.[2] Working in different domains, users can add their own patterns.

Figure 3 shows the interface as designed so far. We can see the list of semantic relationships and knowledge patterns as presented to a user, both with selection capability. I mentioned earlier how these patterns are usually defined in a lexico-syntactic manner. It is not problematic to use such definitions to perform searches on a specific corpus (as is done in SeRT), but it is problematic in the present context since, hundreds of documents must be browsed through, and searching through texts using syntactic tags is quite time consuming. Therefore, I opted for purely lexical patterns and do not allow for any syntactic components. Future research will look into this problem.

As previously mentioned, the productivity of patterns varies considerably, as does the amount of noise associated with them. When

Figure 3: Selecting knowledge patterns for calculating a text's knowledge-rich value

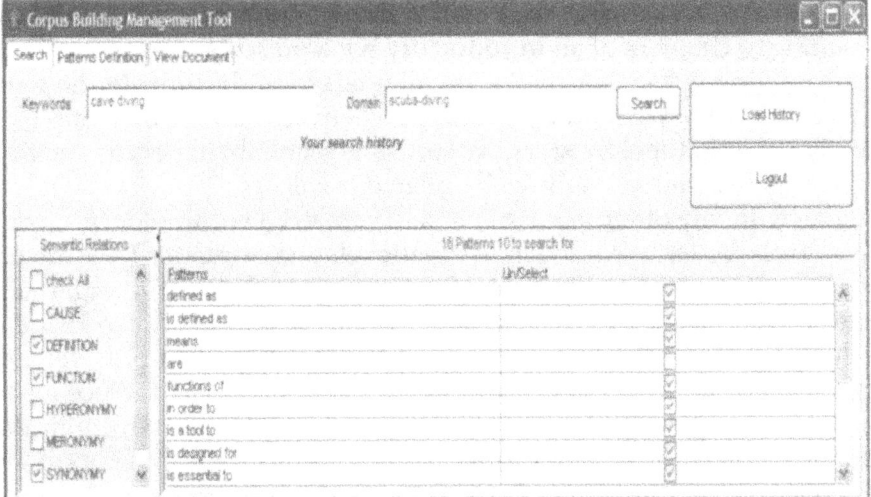

measuring knowledge-rich value, we should opt for patterns that are productive and not noisy. Noise is an important factor since it will render the evaluation totally unreliable. One can imagine the pattern *is a/an* that can definitely express hyperonymy, as in "A dog is an animal," but can be present in so many other contexts that are totally unrelated to semantic relations, such as "There is a chance that . . . ," "It is a good opportunity . . . ," "It is a bit late . . . ," and so on, which would artificially inflate the pattern density with these erroneous counts. As an example, Figure 3 shows semantic relationships of definition, function, and synonymy selected for a search, and among the available patterns *are* has not been selected since it is considered too noisy.

As can be seen at the top of Figure 3, the corpus being built is part of a specific domain, in this case scuba diving. For each domain explored so far, a keyword history is maintained so that the terminologist has a record of all keywords already explored.

As a new search is initiated, the software retrieves a certain number of documents (as specified by the user) and, for each one, establishes the density of knowledge patterns. Although a document search could be done on specific sites with the help of some crawling methods to follow all the internal links, so far in this prototype we have performed our searches via a search engine, retrieving only the entry page of each site.

Figure 4 presents some results, with the possibility for the user to sort them in decreasing order of pattern count or pattern density. An examination of the results of a search on the term *scuba diving* as part of the domain of *scuba-diving* reveals that, among the first five documents, there is one about "What You Need to Know about Scuba Diving," one pointing to chapters of an introductory book on scuba diving, and one scuba diving newsletter. These are all interesting documents showing this expert-to-novice communicative goal. In contrast, at the bottom of the list, we find mostly stores advertising scuba diving equipment or travel agencies advertising scuba-related travel.

As with any other tool that aims to support a terminologist's work (e.g., tools for term extraction, semantic relation extraction), we intend for the terminologist to have the final say as to whether the suggested sites should be accepted or rejected. The tool includes a way to visit the actual Web site (first column in Figure 4) or to view a text-only version of the Web site with the knowledge patterns highlighted. Once a site has been accepted (last column in Figure 4), its content (which for the moment consists only of the entry page of the site) becomes part of the corpus.

Semi-automatic Corpus Construction

Figure 4: Retrieving Web pages with their knowledge-rich value indicated as pattern density

URL	Title	Pattern Count	TotalWord	Pattern De...	Un/Select
http://www.divekauai.com/	DIVE KAUAI SCUBA CENTER - Come	14	965	0,015	
http://www.ntsinai.org/pulmonary/		24	1824	0,013	✓
http://www.divertalertnetwork.org	Divers Alert Network - Scuba	8	885	0,009	✓
http://www.ntsinai.org/pulmonary/	Scuba Diving Explained - Lawrence	8	1058	0,008	
http://www.3rdules.com/	Scuba Diving Directory	5	740	0,007	✓
http://diver.ocean.washington.edu/	SCUBA page!	3	553	0,005	✓
http://scuba.about.com/	Scuba Diving - What You Need to	5	940	0,005	✓
http://www.simplyscuba.co.uk/	Scuba	3	638	0,005	✓
http://www.phuket-scuba-club.co	Diving Phuket Scuba Club Thailand -	2	566	0,004	
http://www.abyss.com.au/	Scuba Diving Sydney - Padi Scuba	2	625	0,003	
http://www.scubadivemaui.com/	Diving Maui -DIVE On Maui - Scuba	1	785	0,001	
http://www.naui.org/	Divers	1	814	0,001	
http://www.naui.org/index-side.ht	Divers	1	2470	0	
http://www.divernet.com/	Diver Magazine on line ... and much	0	9	0	
http://www.mauiscuba.com/	Scuba Diving and Ed Robinson's	0	289	0	
http://www.skin-diver.com/	Scuba Diving Equipment, Scuba	0	110	0	
http://www.scubaspots.com/	Scuba Spots - Scuba Diving	0	38	0	
http://www.diveguide.com/	Dive Thailand Caribbean Scuba	0	26	0	
http://www.oneamp.ca/~adb/ontdi	Diving in Ontario	0	265	0	✓

The purpose of the tool is to facilitate document browsing by the terminologist, and we assume that the knowledge-rich value of a document as determined by knowledge-pattern density will be useful. To confirm this intuition, further formal evaluation should be done within an environment in which we collect the positive and negative selections of a user.

CONCLUDING REMARKS AND DIRECTIONS FOR FUTURE WORK

In this paper, I have presented some work on corpus construction within a terminological context, an important first step toward the construction of a terminological knowledge base. I have taken inspiration from Ingrid Meyer's work on knowledge patterns and have reviewed their original role as surface patterns that reveal underlying semantic relationships. I now give them a further role at the beginning of the chain for the evaluation of the knowledge-rich value of a text. Given that there has been relatively little work done in the area of semi-automatic corpus construction, the research presented here represents an interesting first step in exploring that subject. I have developed a tool that can help terminologists to select appropriate texts by having access to a quantitative account of the knowledge-pattern density of those texts. Search engines, as we know them today, are domain oriented. Keywords are entered, and the search engine looks for texts containing these words. Further processing, as suggested here, is becoming necessary in many applications to filter the immense number of documents retrieved.

For future research, I will look into speed issues to allow reasonably fast searches to be conducted not only on lexical patterns but also on lexico-syntactic patterns. I will also perform density calculations not only on the entry page of a Web site but on a limited depth level of the site as well. An important next step will be the integration of the corpus-building tool with SeRT, which already includes term extraction, semantic relation extraction, and visualization features, in order to move toward the creation of an integrated TKB construction tool. Yet another direction for future research is to expand the tool into a Web interface platform to allow different terminologists to build their own corpora through a multi-user corpus management tool.

NOTES

1   I would like to thank Terry Copeck for the software development of SeRT, from 1999 to 2002, and Akakpo Agbago for the recent software development (2004) of the Corpus Building Management Tool.
2   From 1998 to 2003, while at the School of Information Technology and Engineering of the University of Ottawa, I worked with four specialized corpora, all of which were provided by Ingrid Meyer and collected by her students at the School of Translation and Interpretation, University of Ottawa. I have used these corpora extensively in my research on computational terminology and published work based on their contents. They treat the domains of scuba diving, composting, computing, and childbirth. I am extremely grateful for Ingrid Meyer's generosity in allowing me to use them.

REFERENCES

Austermühl, F. 2001. *Electronic Tools for Translators*. Manchester: St. Jerome Publishing.
Barrière, C. 2001. "Investigating the Causal Relation in Informative Texts." *Terminology* 7 (2): 135–54.

———. 2002. "Hierarchical Refinement and Representation of the Causal Relation." *Terminology* 8 (1): 91–111.
———. 2004. "Knowledge-Rich Contexts Discovery." In *Canadian AI 2004, LNAI 3060*, ed. A.Y. Tawfik and S.D. Goodwin, 187–201. Berlin: Springer-Verlag.
Barrière, C., and T. Copeck. 2001. "Building a Domain Model from Specialized Texts." In *Proceedings of Terminologie et Intelligence Artificielle (TIA 2001)*, Nancy, 109–18.
Biebow, B., and S. Szulman. 1999. "TERMINAE: A Linguistics-Based Tool for the Building of a Domain Ontology." In *11th European Workshop on Knowledge Acquisition, Modeling, and Management (EKAW '99)*, Dagstuhl Castle, Germany, ed. Dieter Fensel and Rudi Studer, 49–66. Berlin: Springer-Verlag.
Bowden, P.R., P. Halstead, and T.G. Rose. 1996. "Extracting Conceptual Knowledge from Text Using Explicit Relation Markers." In *Proceedings of the 9th European Knowledge Acquisition Workshop (EKAW '96)*, Nottingham, ed. N. Shadbolt, K. O'Hara, and G. Schreiber, 147–62. Berlin: Springer-Verlag.
Cabré Castellví, M.T., R.E. Bagot, and J.V. Palatresi. 2001. "Automatic Term Detection: A Review of Current Systems." In *Recent Advances in Computational Terminology*, ed. D. Bourigault, C. Jacquemin, and M.-C. L'Homme, 53–87. Amsterdam: John Benjamins.
Condamines, Anne, and Josette Rebeyrolle. 2001. "Searching for and Identifying Conceptual Relationships via a Corpus-Based Approach to a Terminological Knowledge Base (CTKB): Method and Results." In *Recent Advances in Computational Terminology*, ed. Didier Bourigault, Christian Jacquemin, and Marie-Claude L'Homme, 127–48. Amsterdam: John Benjamins.
Hearst, M. 1992. "Automatic Acquisition of Hyponyms from Large Text Corpora." In *Proceedings of the 14th International Conference on Computational Linguistics (COLING '92)*, Nantes, 539–45.
Jacobson, R. 1966. *Essais de linguistique générale*. Paris: Éditions de Minuit.
Kintsch, W., and T.A. Van Dijk. 1978. "Toward a Model of Text Comprehension and Production." *Psychological Review* 85 (5): 363–94.
L'Homme, M.-C. 2004. *La terminologie: Principes et techniques*. Montréal: Les Presses de l'Université de Montréal.
Meyer, I. 2001. "Extracting Knowledge-Rich Contexts for Terminography: A Conceptual and Methodological Framework." In *Recent Advances in Computational Terminology*, ed. D. Bourigault, C. Jacquemin, and M.-C. L'Homme, 279–302. Amsterdam: John Benjamins.
Meyer, I., K. Mackintosh, C. Barrière, and T. Morgan. 1999. "Conceptual Sampling for Terminographical Corpus Analysis." In *Terminology and*

Knowledge Engineering (TKE '99), Innsbruck, ed. Peter Sandrini, 256–67. Würzburg: Ergon-Verlag.

Meyer, I., D. Skuce, L. Bowker, and K. Eck. 1992. "Towards a New Generation of Terminological Resources: An Experiment in Building a Terminological Knowledge Base." In *Proceedings of the 14th International Conference on Computational Linguistics (COLING '92)*, Nantes, 956–60.

Pearson, J. 1998. *Terms in Context*. Amsterdam: John Benjamins.

CHAPTER 6

FROM TERMINOLOGICAL DATA BANKS TO KNOWLEDGE DATABASES: THE TEXT AS THE STARTING POINT[1]

M. TERESA CABRÉ CASTELLVÍ

INTRODUCTION

Nowadays, linguistic technologies and resources contribute greatly to translation, not only as a means of finding information but also as tools that can aid in the translation process itself. Translators use tools to search for linguistic and conceptual information and to locate new resources that can help them in the translation process. They also use translation technology to increase their productivity and to achieve a greater degree of consistency in the translated texts. Tools used in this fashion include translation memories and their associated terminology managers. Not only do such technologies facilitate an automated reuse of previously translated segments and ensure the consistent use of the same terminological units for a given lexical item in the source text, but they also make it possible to accumulate a significant number of terms in a database format.

EVOLUTION OF ELECTRONIC LINGUISTIC RESOURCES

The design of electronic linguistic resources, the suitable storage and selection of information that meets the needs of applied linguists (a generic term that I will use to refer to all language professionals), and the design of data search techniques have evolved over time.

In the early days of electronic linguistic resources, terminological and lexical data banks were the most typical type of resources available from which the nomenclature of thematic glossaries and dictionaries could be extracted. They were also the resources that applied linguists turned to in order to find solutions to linguistic queries in both translation and standardization contexts.

The data contained in these resources had a database record format in which each lexical or terminological entry was associated with various types of information organized into different fields. Typical fields found in most term banks included, for example, grammatical information, domain, definition, and, in the case of multilingual banks, equivalents in other languages. Sources for all types of information were also provided. Each record corresponded to a terminological unit. This unit appeared in a decontextualized form, and only sometimes was it accompanied by an example, usually in the form of a single context in which it had been found. These resources served primarily as repositories for lexical or terminological data, and their value increased as the number of entries in the data bank grew.

Text banks represent the second stage in the evolution of resources that have become useful to translators. Text banks display data in multiple nonfragmented authentic contexts—as many contexts as there are occurrences of a given lexical unit in the texts. With the help of search engines, translators can directly access all occurrences of a unit in the texts, which means that translators can view documented uses of this unit. Furthermore, text banks become test beds adapted for the description of the units in discourse.

Another significant development that took place during this second stage of evolution was the compilation of large monolingual corpora, often referred to as *reference corpora*. The texts included in this kind of corpus are selected based on the criteria of representativeness and balance. The most historically representative example is the COBUILD corpus (Bank of English), developed at the University of Birmingham (UK) to assist with the compilation of the Collins dictionaries. An example of a reference corpus in Spanish is the Corpus de Referencia del Español Actual (CREA), compiled by the Real Academia Española. CREA contains about 140 million words in Spanish texts that date from 1975 to the present.

Other examples of reference corpora include all the corpora compiled as part of the LE-PAROLE Project,[2] financed by the European Union (EU) under the auspices of the 4th Framework Programme. This project aimed to develop linguistic resources, corpora, and electronic lexicons for all the languages of the EU to be used directly in language-engineering applications. It also endeavoured to provide a reference corpus in each of the official languages, as well as in two additional languages (Catalan and Danish), which could be used as a resource for the development of computational tools aimed at the automatic processing of these languages. The PAROLE Project also resulted in the production of lexica containing 10,000 entries per language, which were based on data extracted from the PAROLE corpora.

Although textual corpora represent an advance in the development of linguistic resources in electronic form, until recently such resources have been used primarily for the creation of dictionaries. Researcher Manuel Sanchez Ron, speaking in reference to the above-mentioned CREA corpus, stated that "Thanks to CREA it is possible to extract information to study words, their meaning[s], and contexts."[3]

However, linguistic resources are continuing to evolve. We have now moved on from the construction of large-scale, multimillion-word, general-language corpora to the compilation of smaller corpora with more focused content, which brings us to the third stage in the evolution of linguistic resources.

INNOVATIVE REFINEMENTS OF LINGUISTIC RESOURCES

I have identified three ways in which text banks have been refined to meet the data query and extraction needs of applied linguists.

- a) Text banks have been constructed based on specific themes or specialized subjects, which offer more selective information and permit more efficacious retrieval.
- b) Text banks have been classified according to pragmatic and communicative criteria, which allow users to automatically retrieve and generate the format and typical features of different types of documents.
- c) Grammatically tagged banks have been created, which makes it possible for users to retrieve information on the basis of strict linguistic criteria.

TEXT BANKS ON SPECIALIZED SUBJECTS

Given the importance that specialized knowledge has acquired in our society, text banks focusing on specific subject fields have become one of the most valuable types of resource available for investigating specialized communication.

With the help of information technology, it is possible to store, update, and access the data in a targeted, user-friendly, and efficient way. The exponential growth of science and technology, as well as the development and transfer of technology and services, have resulted in the creation of a considerable number of concepts, and standardized terminology is required in order to designate them, not only in national but also in international communication. Applied terminology is also playing an increasingly important role in fields that deal with multilingualism, such as translation and the teaching of language for specific purposes, as well as in the development of technologies for automatic language processing.[4]

Specialized text banks have also become fundamental resources for developing tools such as systems that can automatically identify and extract candidate terms, as well as those that can automatically generate text summaries or extract information for constructing terminological data banks and ontologies.

TEXT BANKS CLASSIFIED BY PRAGMATIC AND COMMUNICATIVE CRITERIA

A second way in which text banks have been improved is through the creation of banks that are classified by genre or that provide explicit access to genre and text-type information about each text. This access facilitates the descriptive linguistic analysis of specialized texts and makes it possible to compare them based on the selection and frequency of the different grammatical devices being used.[5]

TAGGED BANKS

A third innovative way in which text banks have been refined is through annotation or tagging. In other words, the banks have been enriched by the addition of information to the various linguistic units that form the texts. The type of information that can be encoded in a tag can be morphological, syntactic, semantic, or pragmatic in nature. Among the most common type of tagged banks are ones that contain morphological information, usually in the form of part-of-speech tags, which makes it possible, for example, to group related grammatical forms under the same lemma or to identify all the forms belonging to a given lemma.

Morphological or part-of-speech tagging, like most forms of tagging, is carried out with the help of tools that are generally known as taggers. To automatically process data on the basis of linguistic criteria, and not simply on the basis of the superficial recognition of character strings (e.g., as done by tools such as TACT or WordSmith), it is necessary to have part-of-speech tags. This type of tagging is useful when searching for syntactic patterns prior to identifying units that could be term candidates as well as rejecting those combinations that could never form a multiword terminological unit. It is also useful for identifying some types of phraseology, such as deverbal nouns and their complements.[6]

A less commonly used type of tagging is the sort that breaks each lexical unit down into its constituent morphemes. Doing so makes it possible to retrieve groups of units that have the same morphological configuration or that have the same number of morphemes. In addition, it would be possible to automatically generate complete lexical units from morphemes provided that the tagger is accompanied by a set of grammatical rules and restrictions.

It is becoming more common to have parsed text banks. A parser uses part-of-speech tags to identify the syntactic relationships that words have with one another. It assigns basic syntactic functions to the groups of words appearing to the left and right of given part-of-speech categories, whether they are simple (e.g., verb, noun, adjective) or complex (e.g., verb phrase, noun phrase, adjective phrase). For example, the presence of the verb *poner* (*to put*) in the corpus will activate a search by the parser to its right for a noun or noun phrase (NP) that acts as direct complement or internal complement and to its left for another noun or NP that will act as external complement or subject. Moreover, if a prepositional phrase appears, it is likely that *en* is the preposition at the head of this phrase in Spanish.

In fact, these tools that are used to attribute basic syntactic functions to the complements of predicative units are not actually full parsers, which are necessary for applications such as machine translation; rather, they are partial parsers or "chunkers" able to recognize when a certain combination constitutes a given structure.

If its dictionary contains a predicate with a description of the type (i.e., obligatory or optional), number, and structure of its complements, then a natural language processing system can recognize the predicate and identify its complements, assigning a grammatical tag to them. If, in addition to grammatical information, each complement is associated with an argument role such as *topic, object, agent,* or *locative,* and each argument is specified as belonging to a specific semantic class, then the system will try to tag each unit with the semantic tag that corresponds to the description of each unit in the dictionary.

This type of tagging is necessary for advanced automatic language processing and for the selective extraction of data. Nevertheless, very few corpora are semantically tagged. There are, however, a number of tools that have been developed for Spanish and Catalan that would facilitate this type of tagging. Some of these tools, such as the WordNet system[7] and the dictionary developed as part of the SIMPLE Project[8] (an extension of the PAROLE Project), have been developed using public funds and are therefore freely available.

It is even rarer to find general or specialized corpora that have been annotated with pragmatic information. A few very small corpora containing pragmatic tags have been compiled for very specific studies.

Given the challenges, time, and cost involved in creating tagged corpora, it is imperative that members of the scientific community work together to develop useful electronic resources for the study of language. The more grammatical information that can be incorporated into a corpus, the more useful it will be for descriptive and applied research.

AN INTEGRATED DIGITAL RESOURCE: SPECIALIZED KNOWLEDGE DATABASES

A knowledge database is a resource that attempts to bring together grammatical, textual, terminological, documentary, and semantic information. Although developing such a resource is an expensive and labour-intensive process, the resulting information is of great value for teaching languages and translation.

THE CONCEPT OF KNOWLEDGE DATABASES

Knowledge databases have been defined as knowledge repositories represented in a formal language that can be accessed by users via an expert system based on terminological units, which are organized into a conceptual network containing various types of relations. The *FOLDOC* dictionary[9] provides the following definitions.

knowledge base: A collection of knowledge expressed using some formal knowledge representation language. A knowledge base (KB) forms part of a knowledge-based system (KBS).

knowledge-based system <artificial intelligence> (KBS): A program for extending and/or querying a knowledge base. The related term expert system is normally used to refer to a highly domain-specific type of KBS used for a specialised purpose such as medical diagnosis.

Knowledge databases are superior to terminological data banks for several reasons. Not only do they offer the possibility of retrieving all the contexts in which a unit appears, but they also provide semantic knowledge. This is provided both through texts, from which it is possible to retrieve the distinctive contexts of each unit, and through ontologies, since each term is linked to a concept located in a knowledge structure that connects it to other concepts in the same field by means of different relations (hyperonymy, hyponymy, meronymy, causality, etc.). Thus, the "content" of a term corresponds to the set of relations that the concept linked to this term establishes with other concepts in the specialized field.

Unlike lexical classifications such as WordNet (Fellbaum 1998; Vossen 1998), the ontologies in a knowledge database are knowledge based rather than lexically based. In other words, the representation of a concept includes the set of relations that this concept establishes in the ontology, and it is represented by means of a character string that acts as a functional tag. In some cases, this character string may be the same as the lexical unit used to formally designate a concept, but it does not necessarily have to be so. In contrast, lexical classifications are structures of lexical units because of their content.

Knowledge databases can be useful to members of various professions involved in the communication of specialized knowledge. For instance, they can be used by translators and interpreters to find answers to linguistic and conceptual queries. Terminologists and lexicographers can use them to facilitate the elaboration of general and specialized dictionaries, while documentation professionals can use them to elaborate thesauri and classifications, to index documents, and to facilitate information retrieval. Technical writers can use knowledge databases as an information resource, while professors and subject specialists, as well as teachers of language for special purposes, can use them as a teaching resource and a source of course material. Finally, scientific journalists can consult knowledge databases when they are preparing to popularize specialized knowledge.

THE GENOME PROJECT

At the Institute of Applied Linguistics (IULA) at Pompeu Fabra University, our research group,[10] working in the context of the TEXTERM Project,[11] has developed a knowledge bank on the Human Genome Project (Cabré et al. 2004).

Within this project, a specialized knowledge database has been defined as an integration of the following four types of resource into a single platform:

a) a text bank that contains relevant texts dealing with the specialized field under investigation;
b) a documentary bank that contains bibliographic information as well as other relevant information (e.g., word count) about the texts;
c) a terminological bank that contains the term records for the terminological units belonging to the field; and
d) an ontology that represents the concept structure of the field.

The structure of the GENOME knowledge database is illustrated in Figure 1. In this figure, we can observe how the three modules come together, each one corresponding to a bank of information (i.e., text, documentary, and terminological). In addition, we can see how the terminological bank is in turn linked to an ontology in which each term is connected to a concept represented by a functional tag that brings together the set of relations that this concept has with other concepts in the field. The relations belong to a closed list described in detail by Feliu (2004) and summarized below.

(A) *Similarity*
- positive [be similar to]
- negative [be different from]

Figure 1: Structure of the GENOME Knowledge Database

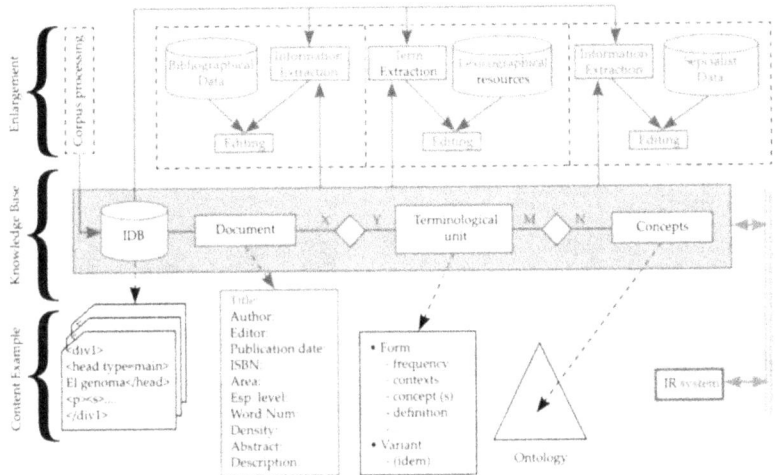

- (B) *Inclusion*
  - class inclusion or hyponymy [to be (a kind of)/is a]
- (C) *Sequentiality*
  - place [to be in/in front of/behind, to go from x to y]
  - time [to be simultaneous/previous/later]
- (D) *Causality*
  - causal [to cause/to be the cause of/to be the effect of/produce/make]
- (E) *Instrument* [to be useful for/to use/to be done with]
- (F) *Meronymy* [to be part/element of; have + SN, to be constituted of; to include]
- (G) *Association*
  - general [to be related to/to show]
  - specialized [to manifest/to determine]

The documentary bank, which in our project corresponds to the GENDOFAC database, was developed using MS-Access 2000, and it contains all the bibliographical references of the texts contained in the text bank and of the sources from which the contexts contained on the term records in the terminological bank were taken. It comprises monographs, magazines, journal articles, and theses, which have been classified according to the structure designed by a subject expert. This

classification has the following sections or subfields in the Human Genome Project:
- Internal structure
- Genetic engineering
- Diseases
- Genetic research
- Differentiation
- Immunology
- Biotechnology
- Phylogeny
- Neuroscience
- Pharmacogenomics
- Eugenics

The text bank includes a set of texts on the human genome thematically arranged into the categories described above. The texts, in Catalan, Spanish, and English, have different levels of specialization, though all have been produced by specialists.

Using software available at IULA, researchers have morphologically tagged the texts, which makes it possible to search for information using character strings, forms, lemmas (headwords), grammatical categories, or any combination of these. Searches are carried out using the previously mentioned BwanaNet tool, which has been integrated directly into GENOME.

The terminological bank was developed in parallel with the ontology, rather than being developed after the ontology was complete, which has been the case in some other systems. It was developed in accordance with the theoretical framework of the communicative theory of terminology (CTT) described in Cabré (1999, 2003). The only way to access concepts is through the terminological units that designate them. Therefore, for each term, there will be an associated concept in the ontology, which can be accessed via the corresponding term.

The system used to develop the ontological module is the OntoTerm system, developed using the Mikrokosmos ontology by Professor Antonio Moreno of the University of Malaga. OntoTerm is composed of an ontology editor, a terminology editor, a browser, and an HTML code generator (Moreno and Pérez 2001; Pérez 2002).

ACCESSING INFORMATION IN GENOME

The contents of GENOME can be queried using one of three types of search:
a)   simple search;
b)   complex search; and
c)   combined search (still under development).

By means of a simple search, one can query information about a unit (form or lemma) or about a character string in the text bank or in the terminological bank. Once the search has been defined and the unit recognized, users can obtain associated information, whether from the text bank, the documentary bank, the terminological bank, or the ontology. Types of information that could be retrieved for a given term include:

- its frequency in a corpus of texts or previously selected subcorpus;
- its occurrences in the corpus or subcorpus presented with concordances;
- its occurrences in a predefined grammatical or lexical environment;
- the documentary sources in which the unit appears;
- its record in the terminological bank; and
- its conceptual value in the ontology.

By searching in the terminological bank, we can obtain information about a unit's category and subcategories, definition, contexts, variants (if any exist), and equivalents in other languages, as well as information from the ontology about all the conceptual relations that the unit has with other concepts in the same field.

A complex search allows users to obtain lists of units that meet certain conditions in one or more fields, combined using Boolean operators.

Finally, the combined search, still under development, will allow users to define a search in one module for all units that meet a given set of criteria and then to take the results of this search and apply them to progressive searches in other modules.

Once users have provided basic registration information, multilingual access to GENOME is free. It can be accessed via the IULA resource site (http://www.iula.upf.edu).

CONCLUDING REMARKS

There is no doubt that information technologies have significantly affected the way in which translators work. Searches in printed dictionaries are nowadays complemented by queries in electronic dictionaries as well as by online searches for information about the concepts in question or for translation equivalents.

However, alongside the development of powerful search engines and of more refined filters, language engineering has been exploring the design of applications suited to meet the specific needs of language professionals. Specialized knowledge databases are one such resource.

Conceptually organized terminology resources, in other words term banks with an associated ontology, have already been applied to the management of knowledge in complex organizations. This concept should be extended even further. Accordingly, the GENOME project team has designed a specialized knowledge database that can act as a linguistic resource that integrates, into a single platform, terminological units, their conceptual structure, authentic texts containing this terminology, and the bibliographic details of these texts. All this information is organized into a series of interrelated databases. We hope that such a resource will prove useful for meeting the needs of translators.

NOTES

1. An initial translation of this paper from Spanish was done by Mercedes Suárez from the Autonoma University of Manizales (Colombia). Lynne Bowker edited the final version. I would like to thank Mercedes Suárez and Lynne Bowker for this work.
2. LE-PAROLE Project (LE2-4017): http://www.ub.es/gilcub/SIMPLE/simple.html.
3. This statement was delivered during a seminar entitled Spanish As a Scientific Language, organized by the Foundation of Science and Technology of the Spanish government in December 2003.
4. An example of a multilingual specialized text bank is the one created at the Applied Linguistics Institute (IULA) of Pompeu Fabra University, which contains texts in Spanish, Catalan, English, French, and German (note that there is a different number of texts in each language). The text bank contains material on five main subjects: informatics, medicine (including human genomics), environment, law, and economics. See http://www.iula.upf.edu.

5   One example, within the Spanish context, is the genre-based text bank compiled at the Faculty of Translation and Interpretation at the Universitat Jaume I located in Castelló (García Izquierdo and Monzó Nebot 2002). It has resulted in the creation of an electronic encyclopedia of specialized genres for translation.
6   An example of a tool that makes use of inflectional morphological tags is BwanaNet, developed at the Applied Linguistics Institute (IULA) of Pompeu Fabra University to explore textual corpora. BwanaNet allows searching on combinations of units expressed as character strings or as categories. For more information, see http://www.iula.upf.edu in the resource site of IULA.
7   See http://www.cogsci.princeton.edu/~wn/index.shtml.
8   See http://www.ub.es/gilcub/SIMPLE/simple.html.
9   A number of general and specialized online dictionaries, including the *Free On-Line Dictionary of Computing (FOLDOC)*, can be accessed through a common interface at the following site: http://dict.die.net/.
10 The following people have collaborated in the development of the GENOME project: M. Teresa Cabré (project director), C. Bach, J. Feliu, G. Martínez, and J. Vivaldi. In addition, J.J. Giraldo and V. Vidal participated as researchers for the terminological module.
11 Specialized texts and terminology: selection and automatic retrieval of information, BFF2000-0841.

REFERENCES

Cabré, M.T. 1999. *La terminología: Representación y comunicación*. Barcelona: Institut Universitari de Lingüística Applicada, Universitat Pompeu Fabra.
——. 2003. "Theories of Terminology: Their Description, Prescription, and Explanation." *Terminology* 9 (2): 163–99.
Cabré, M.T., C. Bach, R. Estopà, J. Feliu, G. Martínez, and J. Vivaldi. 2004. "The GENOMA-KB Project: Towards the Integration of Concepts, Terms, Textual Corpora, and Entities." In *Proceedings of the Fourth International Conference on European Language Resources and Evaluation (LREC 2004)*, Lisbon, 87–90.
Feliu, J. 2004. "Relacions conceptuals i terminologia: Anàlisi i proposta de detecció semiautomàtica." PhD diss., Universitat Pompeu Fabra, Spain. http://www.tdx.cesca.es/TDX-0520104-111213/ (consulted October 11, 2004).
Fellbaum, C., ed. 1998. *WordNet: An Electronic Lexical Database*. Cambridge, MA: MIT Press.
García Izquierdo, I., and E. Monzó Nebot. 2002. *La traducción científico-técnica y la terminología en la sociedad de la información*. Castelló de la Plana: Universitat Jaume I.

Moreno, A., and C. Pérez. 2001. "From Text to Ontology: Extraction and Representation of Conceptual Information." In *Actes des quatrièmes rencontres "Terminologie et Intelligence Artificielle" (TIA 2001)*, Nancy, 233–42.

Pérez, C. 2002. "Explotación de los córpora textuales informatizados para la creación de bases de datos terminológicas basadas en el conocimiento." PhD diss., Málaga University, Spain. http://elies.rediris.es/elies18/ (consulted October 11, 2004).

Vossen, P., ed. 1998. *EuroWordNet: A Multilingual Database with Lexical Semantic Networks*. Dordrecht: Kluwer Academic Publishers.

CHAPTER 7

INTRINSIC QUALITIES FAVOURING TERM IMPLANTATION: VERIFYING THE AXIOMS

JEAN QUIRION AND JACYNTHE LANTHIER

INTRODUCTION

All nations have a linguistic policy whether they state it explicitly or not. Linguistic policies that are explicitly stated more often than not involve language and terminology planning programs aimed at managing the relationship between different languages sharing the same territory. Over the years, terminologists have formulated a series of principles and methods to help them attain these objectives. The development of the principles and methods in use now began with the first large-scale research studies carried out in terminology back in the mid-1970s, some thirty years ago. At that time, terminology planning was broken down into various phases ranging from actual terminological research to the updating of terminologies. No matter how they are dissected, terminology planning efforts, like any management process, always include an evaluation and control phase. This phase is an opportune time to take a critical look at the overall planning process. The critical examination described in this paper will be limited to principles regarding the choice of terms to be recommended for usage. To be more precise, our discussion is focused on the verification of axioms, which the *Gage Canadian Dictionary*, for example, defines as "statements seen to be true without proof." The postulates examined in the following pages concern factors that have an influence on terminology implantation.

Even though several of the principles underlying term selection are unproven, many nations invest huge amounts of human and financial resources to eradicate terms considered to be undesirable and to promote usages that correspond to their criteria of linguistic acceptability. In spite of these efforts, a good number of the terms recommended by official sources are not accepted into usage; it seems important, therefore, to identify the factors governing the acceptance or the rejection of a recommended term or terminology. If such factors can be determined, then terminologists and language planners will be better able to propose terms that have a greater chance of successfully taking hold.

To successfully identify factors influencing term acceptance, we must begin by looking for differences between terms that successfully take root and those that do not. Are there differences between the two groups, and if so what is the nature of these differences? Several authors have expressed their opinions on this matter and enumerated, in all, dozens of factors that could have a bearing on terminology implantation. However, without a scientific measurement of terminology implantation, these factors are founded solely on supposition. Only through a rigorous scientific measurement process and the terminometric analysis that it provides will researchers be able to verify if successfully implanted terms possess certain characteristics that favour their implantation and if, in corollary, terms that do not take hold are lacking these characteristics. Terminometric data can therefore open up an entire new field of research.

The ability to gather precise data on terminology implantation enables us to reexamine the initial criteria used for term selection. The terminometric study of lexical items at opposite ends of the implantation spectrum (terms fully implanted and terms not at all implanted) affords researchers a rigorous means for determining if there are factors that foster or impede the acceptance of a term into usage. Terminology-planning decisions could then be based on precise criteria rather than on intuition. To our knowledge, this is the first study verifying the validity of some of the factors that have been suggested by various researchers over the years as having an influence on implantation.

METHODOLOGY

Having established the necessity of terminometric research, it was essential to develop a terminometric protocol that would enable researchers measuring implantation to obtain similar results over different fields of study. One such protocol was developed in 2000 and recently published (Quirion 2003); it has been applied to two areas of specialization in Quebec: namely, the field of transportation in 1996, and the field of retirement and pension plans in 2003. The terminometric tool proposed entails the synchronous measurement of written institutional communications. These communications are broken down into four major groups according to the classification designed by Jean-Claude Corbeil (1980): administration, economy, education, and media. An implantation coefficient is assigned to every term in the corpus; it gives a precise indication of the proportionate use of the term in comparison to competing terms referring to the same notion.

The terminological data banks TERMIUM and *Grand dictionnaire terminologique* were interrogated to draw up the list of all the terms referring to a notion. Then the number of occurrences of each term was compiled from a corpus made up of texts from the four major groups defined by Corbeil. Only occurrences designating the notion under study were counted; for example, an occurrence of the lexical item *bénéficiaire* (beneficiary) in reference to pension plans was included, whereas an occurrence of the same lexical item used in the adjectival form to mean "qui a rapport aux bénéfices" (pertaining to income) was not included in the study.

Figure 1 below gives an example of the implantation data provided by the terminometric protocol. The example shown is from the field of pension plans. Eight terms are used to designate the notion *régime de retraite* (pension plan); four of the eight terms are from the French language: namely, *plan de retraite, régime de pension, régime de rente*, and *régime de retraite;* and four of the terms are from the English language: namely, *pension plan, retirement pension plan, retirement plan*, and *superannuation plan*. From the diagram, we see that the corpus contains 8,092 occurrences of the term *régime de retraite* in reference to the notion being considered. Competing terms, on the other hand, are used relatively infrequently: sixty-one occurrences of *régime de pension*, thirty-three occurrences of *plan de retraite*, two occurrences of *régime de rente*, and no occurrences of any one of the four English terms. From this information, it can be determined that Quebec institutions involved in the field of retirement and pension plans used the term *régime de retraite* 99 times out of 100 to designate the notion "plan set up to provide a retirement pension to its participants" (our translation) as defined by the *Grand dictionnaire terminologique* of the Office québécois de la langue française. The term *régime de retraite* therefore has an implantation coefficient of 0.99; the three other expressions used in the corpus have a cumulative implantation coefficient of 0.01.

Figure 1: Terminometric data — notion *régime de retraite*

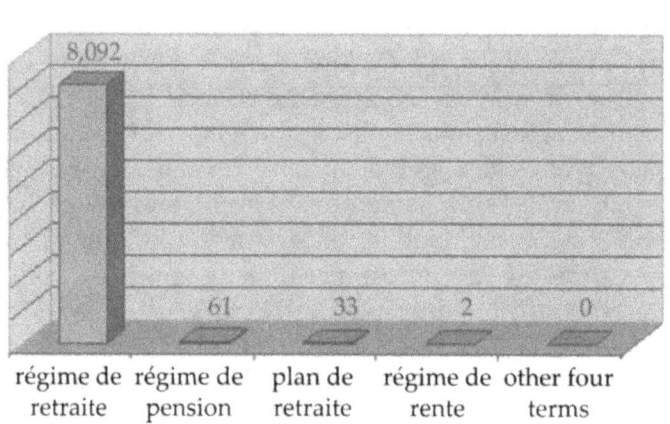

The study presented in this paper is based on the implantation coefficients yielded by the terminometric protocol described above.

In addition to the terminometric measurement of implantation coefficients, research was carried out to identify factors that are generally considered to favour implantation. To this end, the main manuals, treatises, monographs, and articles in the field of terminology were studied. This step identified several dozen factors. It quickly became apparent that the variables suggested were not all similar in nature. Therefore, three categories were created for classifying the factors favouring terminology implantation: terminological factors, socioterminological factors, and procedural factors.

Let us begin by describing the last two. Socioterminological factors concern the social aspects of terminology or of a given field of study; examples could be linguistic attitude, role of the speaker, or resistance to change. Procedural factors concern the conditions in which the descriptive process was carried out; examples could be the method of compilation, the period of time covered, and inclusion of the terminology in reference material. Terminological factors, the focus of this study, concern the intrinsic characteristics of the terms. Four intrinsic characteristics were considered for our study: conciseness, absence of competing terms, derivative form capability, and compliance with the rules of the language. These particular factors of implantation were selected for the study because they are the most frequently identified by researchers as having an influence on implantation. In fact, the various terminological factors noted can be separated into two groups according to their frequency and distribution. The other factors—namely, the absence of pleonasm, the degree of homophony and homography with other elements, the degree of lexicalization and monosemy—are much less frequently mentioned by authors; they were therefore excluded from the study.

It is important to note that the reference material consulted gave only brief explanations of the variables included in the study. The variables are sometimes simply mentioned without any further discussion; only in a few rare cases is there a brief one- or two-line explanation to be found. Lack of detailed explanations makes interpretation more difficult; this will be discussed further on in the paper.

To validate the variables considered in the study, terms at opposite ends of the implantation spectrum were selected. At one end of the spectrum were the terms that were totally implanted. They are lexical items used to the exclusion of all others to designate a notion; these terms have an implantation coefficient of 1. There are eighty-eight such terms included in the study. At the opposite end of the spectrum were 183 terms not implanted at all. Although they refer to a notion in use, they are supplanted by one or several competing terms and are therefore totally absent from the corpus in reference to the notion under study. In all, 271 terms from the fields of transportation and pension and retirement plans were included in the study. Here are some examples of the terms considered:

- fully implanted terms (implantation coefficient of 1): *administrateur provisoire, cotisant, courant de circulation, déficit actuariel de modification, traversier, viaduc*
- terms not implanted at all (implantation coefficient of 0): *bande, bretelle de raccordement, fiducie principale, halte-repos, régime cotisable, régime de retraite à double volet*

At first glance, there are no particular characteristics that distinguish the two groups from one another. The working hypothesis consisted in verifying whether totally implanted terms possess the intrinsic characteristics most frequently identified as favouring implantation and whether the terms that are not accepted into usage are devoid of these characteristics. The two groups of terms were therefore compared with one another to determine if there were any notable features distinguishing them. Each of the 271 terms was evaluated according to the four intrinsic characteristics or variables most often mentioned in the reference documents: namely, conciseness, absence of competing terms, derivative form capability, and compliance with the rules of the language.

CONCISENESS

As mentioned previously, the reference material provided only very brief explanations of the implantation variables. The following excerpts show to what extent the descriptions are brief.

> [T]erms should be concise and not contain unnecessary information. (Sager 1990, 89)

> Since the beginnings of terminology research, many **appreciation criteria** have been developed. . . . **Phonetically and graphically**, written and spoken language forms can be evaluated on the basis of their length, which can be judged as acceptable or not. This is referred to as brevity or term conciseness [our translation]. (Kocourek 1991, 224)

> Brevity. Conciseness is a property of language. Intuitively, one tries to say the most with the fewest words. Given this fact, a term that is concise has an advantage over competing terms [our translation]. (Dubuc 2002, 130)

To determine whether a term was concise or not, it was necessary to devise criteria for measuring conciseness. The number of letters, syllables, and typographical words making up the term were all calculated. The results obtained are presented in Table 1.

It is noticeable that, whatever the means of measurement used, implanted terms are systematically more concise than terms that are not implanted. The average number of typographical words making

Table 1: Statistics on term conciseness

	Terms fully implanted	Terms excluded from usage
Number of words/term	2.4	3
Number of syllables/term	6.7	7
Number of letters/term	16.5	18.1

up the eighty-eight implanted terms is twenty-five percent lower than that of terms that are not implanted. Implanted terms have ten percent fewer letters than do terms that are not implanted. As for the number of syllables, the difference is negligible. We should mention that the calculation of the number of syllables was based on spoken language and therefore probably had uncertain influence on the terms selected by the authors of written communications. From the findings presented here, it can be concluded that terms that are fully implanted are more concise than terms that are not implanted.

NUMBER OF COMPETING TERMS

After examining the variable *conciseness,* the researchers calculated the number of competing terms for each of the expressions included in the study. Only competing French terms were counted. This was because the implantation factors mentioned in the reference material apply to terminologies within the sphere of influence of terminology intervention efforts. Terminologists have no influence on the number of competing terms in other languages; the only influence that they can have—and it is an uncertain one at that—is on the number of terms in the language considered. First of all, terminologists can attempt to restrain the number of French terms put into circulation (if we take the language intervention efforts in Quebec as an example) by giving preference to one particular form. Inversely, they can put several terminological propositions into circulation, each of which could become implanted. Such a solution could be preferred if the terminologist wanted to let usage be the judge. We must remember as well that language-planning efforts have much less of an influence on the number of competing terms if these terms are already in use. In such cases, they do not have the power to exclude certain terms but only to promote one of the terms in use. Of the four implantation variables considered, the number of competing terms is the one upon which terminologists have the least influence.

Pierre Auger and Louis-Jean Rousseau (1977, 58) explain the importance of the competing term factor in the following fashion:

> A neologism that is suggested for usage will not be able to compete with other terms, whether the other terms are neologisms or not. For that reason, the new term should generally be the only one that is used to designate a notion. Proposing too many French terms aimed at supplanting a borrowed term will, on the contrary, only serve to favour the continued use of the borrowed term [our translation].

The absence of competing terms is a criterion also mentioned by Tina Célestin, Gilles Godbout, and Pierrette Vachon-L'Heureux (1984, 64), who note that "the term that is created should be the only term used to express the notion so as to respect the principle of a single referent, which is the objective in terminology" (our translation), and by Juan Sager (1990, 89), who observes that "There should be no synonyms whether absolute, relative or apparent."

Table 2 indicates the average number of competing French terms for each term.

Table 2: Number of competing French terms per term

	Terms fully implanted	Terms excluded from usage
Number of competing French terms/term	0.98	5.8

The difference in the number of competing French terms between terms that are implanted and terms that are not is quite significant. Terms that were successfully implanted generally had a single competing French term; terms that were not accepted into use faced severe competition, six French terms on average. We can conclude that an absence of competition is definitely a factor that favours terminology implantation. However, it is worth repeating that this is also the variable upon which the terminologist has the least amount of influence, all other things being equal.

DERIVATIVE FORM CAPABILITY

The third factor considered in the study is the capability of derivative form creation. Louis Guilbert (1965, 137) explains this criterion more precisely:

> The inventor . . . seeks to ensure a place for his invention . . . by proposing all the linguistic forms that could possibly correspond to the various expressions of his idea. That is why he will try to create a diversified term stemming from a master term and . . . look for a "radical that can produce an entire family of derivative forms" [our translation].

Guy Rondeau (1984, 135) also proposes a definition of derivative form capability or derivability: "Criteria for neonym selection. . . . Derivative creation. Derivative form capability is defined as the capacity of a neonym to show up in various grammatical categories through the adjunction of a prefix or of a suffix" (our translation).

To evaluate the influence of this implantation variable, two categories were created: terms allowing for the creation of at least one morphological derivative, and sterile terms or, in other words, terms offering no possibility of derivation. The results are summed up in Table 3.

Table 3: Number of derivatives per term

	Terms fully implanted	Terms excluded from usage
Number of derivatives/ term	0.33	0.18

The results show that, of all terms that are successfully implanted, one in three allows for the creation of derivative forms. As for terms that do not become successfully implanted, only one in five or six lends itself to the creation of derivative forms. We can conclude from these findings that derivative form capability increases the likelihood of a term being successfully implanted. In other words, a term that lends itself to the formation of derivatives has a greater chance of being implanted than a term that does not have derivative form capabilities.

COMPLIANCE WITH THE RULES OF THE LANGUAGE

The final implantation variable evaluated in this study is compliance with the rules of the language. Heribert Picht and Jennifer Draskau (1985, 115) explain that "The formation of the term must be in accordance with the syntactic rules of the language." Sager (1990, 89) also discusses this factor: "A term should conform to the morphology, spelling and pronunciation conventions of the language for which it is intended." Picht and Draskau limit compliance to syntax, but Sager extends the concept to include other aspects of language. Different aspects of compliance have also been discussed by other authors. We have therefore chosen to highlight terms that, for one reason or another, demonstrate some form of linguistic non-compliance with the French language. The results are displayed in Table 4.

Table 4: Number of instances of non-compliance per term

	Terms fully implanted	Terms excluded from usage
Number of examples of non-compliance/term	0	0.04

The data shown in the table indicate that, whether the terms are implanted or not, it is rare that they do not respect the rules of the language. Among the terms that are successfully implanted, there are no cases of non-compliance with the rules of the language; among the nonimplanted terms, there are only seven instances of non-compliance. All seven of these cases of non-compliance involve terms that are borrowed from the English language and whose pronunciations do not correspond to the phonetics of the French language. With regard to compliance with the linguistic rules of language, there is no significant difference between terms with an implantation coefficient of 1 and terms that are not accepted into usage.

CONCLUSIONS

The validity of the intrinsic characteristics that researchers have traditionally attributed to implanted terms has, to our knowledge, never been proven or even questioned. The objective of this study was to verify if terms that are successfully implanted possess different characteristics than do terms that do not make their way into usage. The study was based on almost 300 terms from two different fields of study and covered the province of Quebec. All four of the variables tested in the study point to a similar conclusion: they are all more characteristic of terms with an implantation coefficient of 1 than of terms that are not accepted into usage.

Certain precisions must be mentioned with respect to the presumed influence of each of the four variables studied. The variable that most distinguishes the two groups of terms examined is the number of competing terms. Implanted terms have six times fewer competing terms than do terms that do not enter into usage. It must be remembered as well that terminologists have only partial influence over this variable.

The second most important variable for terminology implantation is derivative form capability. The study showed that terms rejected from usage have approximately half as many derivative forms as do the other lexical items in the study.

The third variable in order of importance is conciseness. Concise terms are on the average better implanted than those that are less concise. The degree to which fully implanted terms are more concise varies between ten percent and twenty-five percent depending on whether the calculation is based on the number of letters or the number of typographic words.

The variable that has the least significant effect on implantation is compliance with the rules of the language. None of the implanted terms was grammatically non-compliant, and only a small portion (four percent) of all the terms studied presented some form of linguistic non-compliance.

The data obtained in this study show that successfully implanted terms do indeed possess the characteristics traditionally considered necessary for implantation. Hypotheses concerning the influence of certain terminological variables on implantation can now be statistically confirmed. Conciseness, absence of competing terms, derivative form capability, and compliance with the rules of the language are indeed factors that can contribute to the acceptance of a term into usage. What was previously an axiom can now be considered as fact.

Terminometric studies open up new possibilities for research on the importance of socioterminological and procedural factors on term implantation. If it is assumed that implantation is influenced by terminological factors alone, how can we explain the feminization of titles, which is so widespread in Canada but slow to take hold in France? Terminological variables cannot be the sole factors having an influence on implantation. Socioterminological factors and their influence on terminology acceptance constitute an avenue for future research.

REFERENCES

Auger, Pierre, and Louis-Jean Rousseau. 1977. *Méthodologie de la recherche terminologique*. Québec: Éditeur officiel du Québec.

Célestin, Tina, Gilles Godbout, and Pierrette Vachon-L'Heureux. 1984. *Méthodologie de la recherche terminologique ponctuelle: Essai de définition*. Coll. Études, recherches, et documentation. Québec: Office de la langue française.

Corbeil, Jean-Claude. 1980. *L'aménagement linguistique du Québec*. Coll. Langue et société 3. Montréal: Guérin.

Dubuc, Robert. 2002. *Manuel pratique de terminologie*. 4e éd. Brossard, QC: Linguatech.

Gage Canadian Dictionary. 1983. Toronto: Gage Publishing.

Guilbert, Louis. 1965. *La formation du vocabulaire de l'aviation*. Paris: Larousse.

Kocourek, Rostislav. 1991. *La langue française de la technique et de la science: Vers une linguistique de la langue savante*. 2e éd. Wiesbaden: Brandstetter.

Office québécois de la langue française. *Grand dictionnaire terminologique*. www.granddictionnaire.com (consulted October 7, 2004).

Picht, Heribert, and Jennifer Draskau. 1985. *Terminology: An Introduction*. Guildford: University of Surrey.

Quirion, Jean. 2003. *La mesure de l'implantation terminologique: Proposition d'un protocole. Étude terminométrique du domaine des transports au Québec*. Coll. Langues et sociétés 40. Montréal: Office québécois de la langue française.

Rondeau, Guy. 1984. *Introduction à la terminologie*. 2e éd. Chicoutimi: Gaëtan Morin.

Sager, Juan C. 1990. *A Practical Course in Terminology Processing*. Amsterdam: John Benjamins.

PART III

TRANSLATION

CHAPTER 8

FRENCH THEORISTS, NORTH AMERICAN SCHOLIASTS

BARBARA FOLKART

Anyone familiar with contemporary North American academic discourse has the sense that certain lexical items—*gaze, recuperate* (for "retrieve"), *interpellate,* to name just a few—occur with a much higher frequency in academic writing than "in the general population." What's more, the combinatorial range of these items can differ markedly, in academic discourse, from the patterns of "ordinary," garden-variety English: certain items appear in co-texts that are well outside their etymologically determined range of collocation or frankly incompatible with their core meanings.

To be sure, *gaze, recuperate,* and *interpellate* are all bona fide lexical items. But their atypical frequencies and collocational ranges in academic writing give them the status of register markers. Their immediate French counterparts, on the other hand (*regard, récupérer, interpeller*), are perfectly ordinary words that continue to be used routinely in everyday discourse—even as some of them have become central to the writings of people such as Jacques Lacan and Louis Althusser.

One plausible explanation for the increased frequency and skewed collocational range of such items might well be that the vast majority of North American academics seem to have accessed "The Parisians"—Baudrillard, Derrida, Lacan, Foucault, Althusser, et cetera—uniquely through translations (and through each other's scholia of *morceaux choisis* from these translations). While increases in frequency and narrowing of collocational range are typical of terminological formation, there may well be (at least in the humanities) a difference in kind between "home-grown" terminologies—those that emerge from direct, hands-on involvement—and those cobbled together *après coup* by academics turned translators. The very fact that these lexical oddities can all be traced back to items that are widely and idiomatically used in the writings of French theorists (Lacan's *regard*, Althusser's *interpeller*, etc.) would seem to point to the heavy hand of translation.

I propose, in this short paper, to examine one particularly flagrant case, *interpellate* and its fellow traveller *hail*, both of which owe their current visibility on the North American academic scene to one specific translation of an essay by Louis Althusser. Examples of Althusser's assimilation into the Academy abound. The discourse of postcolonialism, in particular, seems to be rife with *hailing*s and *interpellation*s, often in co-texts that violate the semantic constraints governing the usual patterns of collocation: "to call or 'hail' or 'interpellate' the indigenous peoples of a colony 'savages' is to subjectify them as wild, uncivilized, irrational, etc." (Robinson 1997, 23); "the Indians were 'interpellated' or 'hailed' as mystical, primitive, unreliable, mendacious, etc. by the British colonizers" (119).

The collocational pattern *to hail X as Y* normally demands that Y be a noun phrase, determiner + N, where N has positive denotations: it is quite idiomatic to speak of *a bystander hailed as a heroine*, or *leaders hailed as Ø men of great vision*, or *a discovery hailed as a major breakthrough*, but strings such as **they were hailed as unreliable and mendacious* are both grammatically and lexically anomalous. It turns out, as we will see, that the malformed patternings of what I refer to as "profspeak" are often an artifact of translation—that they bear witness, indeed, to the process through which less than competent translation entrenches itself in and ultimately informs academic discourse.

Much, if not all, of this discourse claims descendence from the following snippet of Althusser, as Englished by Ben Brewster (1971, 174):

> I shall then suggest that ideology "acts" or "functions" in such a way that it "recruits" subjects among the individuals (it recruits them all), or "transforms" the individuals into subjects (it transforms them all) by that very precise operation which I have called *interpellation* or hailing, and which can be imagined along the lines of the most commonplace everyday police (or other) hailing: "Hey, you there!"

It is time now that we had a look at the source text that spawned such a cumbersome and tenacious terminology in academic English.

ALTHUSSER'S ESSAY: CONTENT, ETHOS, AND STYLISTICS

Althusser's "Idéologie et appareils idéologiques d'État: Notes pour une recherche" was first published in 1970, then reprised, in 1976, in *Positions (1964–1975)*, a collection of Althusser's essays. The material evidence alone points to the canonical status of this essay: the University of Ottawa's copy of *Positions* has been in constant circulation (and invariably put on reserve) since at least March 1, 1981. And it is this essay that has borne the brunt of the attention: while the remainder of the volume has escaped undue notice, these pages bear the marks of the undergraduates for whom they have been required reading, year in, year out (underlining, annotations, stains left by coffee, midnight oil, sweat, and God knows what else). The physical evidence is much the same on the English side: the Althusser sampler *Lenin and Philosophy and Other Essays,* while distinctly less sebaceous, has been circulating year in, year out, since February 10, 1991, with the essay of interest to us capturing the lion's share of the annotations.

Althusser's "notes pour une recherche" are just that: jottings, even fragments (see the lacuna at the bottom of page 76 and the "P.-S." that starts on page 122), written loosely and at times hastily.[1] This is earnestly didactic writing, writing that has the ring of catechism to it, spells things out for the working class (see 75n5), and reads as if it may have been intended to impart some badly needed elements of "political culture" at a Marxist night school (e.g., 73–74). Yet the ponderous writing is redeemed by the depth of the analyses, the sudden flashes of humour, and the startlingly reverent allusions to Pascal (108) and Saint Paul (111) cheek by jowl with positively Célinien outbursts of religious burlesque (117): decidedly, the man was not all of a piece.

Althusser draws heavily on *Das Kapital* (or the authorized French translation thereof). His purpose is to provide a rigorous "scientific" basis (back in the 1960s and 1970s, it was not uncommon to use "scientific" in such contexts) for Marx's account of things. At the same time, he is ever so careful to avoid anything that smacks of heresy or revisionism. His is a reverential, quasi-hagiographic text, one that treads lightly indeed when it comes to adding to, criticizing, or (God forbid!) revising the great received texts: "Nous devons ici avancer avec prudence dans un terrain où, en fait, les classiques du marxisme nous ont depuis longtemps précédés, mais sans avoir systématisé, sous une forme théorique, les progrès décisifs que leurs expériences et leurs démarches impliquent" (81). One senses on the back of his neck (and ours) the glacial breath of that most rigid, reactionary, and repressive of instances, the French PC (Parti communiste) of the 1960s.

Althusser's thesis, to put it simply, is that the state, through an array of (mainly private [84]) ideological "apparatuses" (church, media, family, law, education system, cultural entities, political parties, labour unions ... [83]), shapes the subjectivity of its members, co-opting its citizens into seeing themselves as the kinds of subjects that best serve its purposes. "L'idéologie interpelle les individus en sujets" (110)—patriotic, God fearing or atheistic as required, salt-of-the-earth yeoman, Stakhanovite or factory owner, captain of industry or e-commerce entrepreneur, "settler" with a birthright from Jehovah, or "martyr" with his sights set on paradise.... And this is where the passage that has granddaddied all those *hailings* and *interpellations* comes in:

> Nous suggérons alors que l'idéologie "agit" ou, "fonctionne" de telle sorte qu'elle "recrute" des sujets parmi les individus (elle les recrute tous), ou "transforme" les individus en sujets (elle les transforme tous) par cette opération très précise que nous appelons *l'interpellation,* qu'on peut se représenter sur le type même de la plus banale interpellation policière (ou non) de tous les jours : "hé, vous, là-bas!" (113)

(Althusser here owes a clear debt to Lacan: his *interpellation* is merely a special case of Lacan's "intimation de la parole" [1966, 296] or of his "interlocution" [258].)

Althusser's footnote adds a coercive note and firmly establishes the top-down nature of the transaction: "L'interpellation, pratique quotidienne, soumise à un rituel précis, prend une forme tout à fait 'spéciale' dans la pratique policière de 'l'interpellation', où il s'agit d'interpeller des 'suspects'" (113n18). *L'interpellation policière* brings to bear on the addressee the weight of the law ("Halt in the name of the law!" is what you'll hear if you start running the other way) and sets him up as a suspect, witness, or person of interest. In the context of state intervention (e.g., through the police), *interpeller* becomes performative ("I order you in the name of the law").

BREWSTER'S TRANSLATION

Brewster's translation is not without its merits, not the least of which is the fact that Brewster appears to be quite conversant with *Capital* (I'm referring to the translation done by Samuel Moore and Edward Aveling, as edited by Frederick Engels). Brewster deserves credit for reverting to the canonical terminology of this 1906 English translation rather than using new, possibly more up-to-date equivalents. *Capital* is an iconic text, one whose constructs and terminology have influenced generations of anglophones, Marxist or not: updating the English terminology would destroy this intertextual dimension.

Even so, while I would be the first to admit that subject expertise is more important than purely translational skills, Brewster's translation is in many respects laboured and lumpy, word-bound, betraying a lack of familiarity with idiomatic French or with recent events of utmost interest to the French Left (Althusser's reference to [the demonstrators trapped by the police and crushed to death against the locked gates of the metro] *Charonne* [79] goes unglossed in Brewster's rendering [139]). Brewster seems to be neither comfortable enough with the source idiom and referents nor sure enough of himself as a TL rewriter to cut straight to the content and rearticulate it in idiomatic, instrumental English. "[C]ette reproduction de la qualification de la force de travail tend (il s'agit d'une loi tendancielle) à être assurée non plus 'sur le tas' (apprentissage dans la production même), mais de plus en plus en dehors de la production" (Althusser 1976, 72) becomes "this reproduction of the skills of labour power tends *(this is a tendential law)* decreasingly to be provided for *'on the spot' (apprenticeship within production itself)*, but is achieved more and more outside production" (Brewster 1971, 132; emphasis added). (I would suggest "the reproduction of labour power qualifications tends [generally speaking] to occur no longer on the factory floor [on-the-job training] but increasingly outside the workplace.")

Althusser's sarcastic and slyly colloquial wordplay goes right over the translator's head. "L'immense majorité des (bons) sujets marchent bien 'tout seuls', c'est-à-dire à l'idéologie" (1976, 120), is meant to evoke *ils marchent au quart de tour* but gets Englished rather piously into "the vast majority of (good) subjects work all right 'all by themselves', i.e., by ideology" (Brewster 1971, 181), as opposed to "the vast majority of (worthy) subjects fall into line all by themselves, marching away to the beat of ideology." Brewster's, in short, is an *amateurish* translation. His English is distinctly harder to follow, at times, than Althusser's French—a cardinal sin for the translation of a didactic, instrumental text.

Nowhere is the inadequacy of Brewster's translation more evident than in the passage that launched *interpellation* and its fellow traveller, *hailing*, on such a high-flying career in the North American academy. *Interpellation*—from a strictly semiotic point of view—was a monstrously inept *faux-ami:* where Althusser was visualizing what goes on in the street as a concrete, everyday analogue (and instance) of the concept that he was forging, *interpellation*, in English, is what occurs, sporadically, in the rarefied precincts of European parliaments. Worse still, Brewster's *interpellation* reverses the dynamics of power: where Althusser was thinking top-down (*l'agent de police* stopping you on the sidewalk, perhaps shoving you into a *panier à salade*, and carting you off to the *commissariat*, where you may even be *passé au tabac*—all in the name of the law), the English *interpellation* is bottom-up: a member of the opposition challenging a minister on a point of government policy (*Oxford English Dictionary (OED)*).

Brewster, conscious no doubt of how opaque *interpellation* would be for the anglophone reader, tried to remedy things by dragging in a backup. Unfortunately, *hailing* only made things worse. Its auspicious etymology was at loggerheads with Althusser's intent: *hail* is a variant of the noun *hale*, which (like the German *heil* and its predecessors) signifies health, prosperity, good luck (*OED*, Wahrig, *Deutsches Wörterbuch*).[2] *Hailing* is not even tangential to the wide-ranging semantic potential of *interpeller*, whose *effets de sens* extend from the banal-benign (*interpeller, ou aborder, un passant*: to stop, or accost, or call out to a passerby, e.g. to ask for directions) to the judicial (*se faire interpeller par la justice*: to be arrested, or served a summons, or brought to court). The cops do not "hail" you in English (pas plus que les flics, dans l'exercice de leurs fonctions, ne vous "saluent"). They stop you, flag you down, demand to see your ID, pull you over, or wave you over (particularly if you happen to be speeding); they detain you for questioning (whether as a witness, suspect, or person of interest); they arrest you, execute a warrant for your arrest. You may be summoned by a public prosecutor, dragged into court, hauled before the courts (*interpellé par la justice*) but not *hailed*. Brewster's *hailing* was the worst possible backup for his already disastrous *interpellation*. Yet it is precisely this bicephalic monstrosity that has caught on in the North American academy.

RETRANSLATING ALTHUSSER

For starters, the translator needn't hesitate to "edit" or "revise" Althusser's "notes" in the interest of transparency, clarity, and fluency: it is not up to the translator to convey the rough-and-ready feel of Althusser's writing—this is, after all, an instrumental text. Insofar as the register of translation is concerned, it is, as Brewster recognized, important to preserve the ideological, historical, and intertextual colouring of the essay by reverting to the historically correct Marxist terminology, as established in the first American translation (*the labour process or the production of use-value, the degree of exploitation of labour-power, reproduction of the conditions of production,* etc.).

Such are the text-level strategies that might shape a retranslation. What interests us here, though, is not Althusser's essay per se (not even its insights, its flashes of humour, its bracing mix of religious nostalgia and militant atheism) but its status as the granddaddy of the *interpellation*s and *hailing*s that have worked their way into academic discourse. In this respect, the key problem for the retranslator, as I see it, is to connect with the concrete situation that Althusser is using, in the central passage, as both an analogue and an instance of the process of "subjectification" that he is formalizing. The retranslator has to make sure that she is working *ad rem*, with an unwavering eye on the referent, that she has a precise grasp, not only of the core concept that Althusser is constructing in this passage, but also (and perhaps more importantly) of the street situation that he is using to illustrate and embody it.

Althusser is thinking of the police (on foot) stopping a suspect by shouting out "Hey! You there!" But the concrete, likely urban, situation that he's using as an analogue could be visualized as a different form of police intervention, without losing the essential feature ("in the name of the law!"). When you get stopped for speeding by the constable manning the radar gun, or the OPP officer whose cruiser has been lurking in a hidden side road, or the state trooper coming after you with his blue lights flashing, the operation involves two phases: you're flagged down, then given your ticket. Whether in the urban setting or on the highway, it's the force of the law (of the state) that is brought into play. There is nothing to stop the translator from envisaging this act of authority in the setting of a speed trap rather than an urban street: the exercise of authority is the same.

Where neither Brewster's *interpellate* nor his *hail* is adequate to either the core meaning or its coercive instantiation, English does have one word at least that can convey both: *to flag* (*someone*, or *someone down*, or *someone as something*):

> What I am getting at is that ideology "works," or "operates," by recruiting individuals (every last one of them) as subjects, transforming every single individual into a subject: this it does by what I propose to call *flagging*—precisely as, in everyday life, people constantly get flagged down (e.g., by the police): "Hey! You there!"

Althusser's footnote becomes "Flagging is an everyday occurrence, one that involves specific, codified gestures; when the police flag you, or flag you down, they set you up as a 'suspect.'"[3]

Rewritten in terms of *flagging*, strings of profspeak such as those cited earlier would no longer sound anomalous; better still, they would have an immediate and clear-cut meaning: "By [flagging] a person or a group as a 'colonial subject,' for example, a colonial power makes . . . the subjectivity of that person or group subject to the colonial power," or "the Indians were [flagged] as mystical, primitive, unreliable, mendacious, etc. by the British colonizers" (Robinson 1997, 119).

Paradoxically, though, while *flagging*, extrapolated from its common uses (*flag a taxi, flag down a speeding motorist, flag someone as a threat to security*), is a semiotically viable solution, it might run into difficulties at the strictly pragmatic level. What it would seem to evoke most readily, in current usage, is the kind of third-party operation—*the RCMP had him flagged as a terrorist*—that sets its object up as a nonparticipant "non-person" (Benveniste 1966), rather than the sort of direct-address, vocative transaction—*the police flagged him down for speeding*—central to Althusser's view that it is as addressees that we are co-opted into becoming subjects of the state.[4] *Interpellation*, on the other hand, precisely because it was almost totally unfamiliar, had the advantage of opacity: since few anglophone readers knew what it normally meant, it could and eventually did take on the specific meaning constructed for it by its translated co-text.

FROM PROFSPEAK TO SCHOLARLY DISCOURSE

As amateurish as it is, Brewster's translation is nonetheless of considerable importance from the standpoint, not only of the transmission of ideas, but also of the formation of a whole register of discourse. It is through this translation—through this snippet—that Louis Althusser has been funnelled into North American academic discourse, iterated, glossed, and reglossed. Althusser's essay, as Englished by Ben Brewster—or the core fragment, which is perhaps all that many academics know of it—has become a topos of critical discourse. Althusser, it would seem (at least as the author of this particular essay), has entered the canon and taken on the status of an *auctoritas* —*ipse dixit*—in the North American academy. (In France, it is altogether possible that the text has long since sunk into the same sort of irrelevance as the notoriously dogmatic French Communist Party. Fancy French imports are not always what they are cracked up to be: as Jean Bricmont puts it, "il est amusant de constater que le mot 'postmodernisme' est beaucoup moins utilisé en France qu'aux États-Unis, où ce courant est perçu comme venant de France" [Debray and Bricmont 2003, 84]).

Which leads us to a reflection on translation pathways, terminological pathways, and discursive ruts.[5] Once heavy-handed renderings such as *interpellation* and *hailing* have worked their way into the academic register, chances are that not even a reasonable and reasoned equivalent such as *flagging* would stand a chance of dislodging them. The fact is that language users show an astonishing capacity to *make* sense, motivating and remotivating even the most obscure items. One way that readers have made sense is by ignoring *hail* and exploiting the very opacity of *interpellate*, whose unfamiliarity leaves it open to the new and highly specialized meaning that it acquires—through a process of *terminologization*—in co-texts where it functions as an exponent of Althusser's view. Tejaswini Niranjana, for example, consistently uses *interpellate* while systematically avoiding its backup: "Influential translations (from Sanskrit and Persian into English in the eighteenth century, for example) interpellated colonial subjects," she writes, "legitimizing or authorizing certain versions of the Oriental, versions that then came to acquire the status of 'truths' even in the countries in which the 'original' works were produced" (1992, 33). Homi K. Bhabha, similarly, uses the well-formed and transparent "subjectification," avoids *hailing* altogether, refers only once (with a tip of the hat to Althusser) to "the leaden voice of 'ideological interpellation'" (1994, 46).

Genuine scholars—those who have the intellectual skills and intuition to connive with what the text is "trying to do"—will make silk purses out of even the least auspicious translations. Kaja Silverman goes so far as to read into Brewster's doublet a distinction that is utterly lacking in Althusser's essay. "Althusser refers to the address as 'hailing', and its successful outcome as 'interpellation,'" she writes (1983, 48–49), thereby semiotizing what in itself is no more than an accident of inept translation. This, too, is how language lives, transmuting ineptness into invention.

Still, it is richly ironic that Brewster's translation should have survived most tenaciously precisely where it broke down.

NOTES

1   In *Positions*, the 1976 republication, Althusser footnotes his title ". . . Cet article est composé de *fragments* d'une étude à l'origine plus étendue." Brewster—who must have been translating from the first (1970) publication—appends the following footnote (Althusser's, undoubtedly) to the first subtitle: "This text is made up of two extracts from an ongoing study. The sub-title 'Notes towards an Investigation' is the author's own. The ideas expounded should not be regarded as more than the introduction to a discussion."
2   Etymology plays a decisive (and generally overlooked) role in the formation and persistence of collocational constraints. Ideologically driven attempts to defeat its subterranean workings are generally doomed to failure (see my remarks on feminist attempts to "rehabilitate" words (e.g., *hag* and *crone*) "degraded in patriarchal usage" [Folkart 2006, Chapter 6]).
3   Brewster: "Hailing as an everyday practice subject to a precise ritual takes a quite 'special' form in the policeman's practice of 'hailing' which concerns the hailing of 'suspects'" (1971, 174).
4   Both flagging and flagging-as are of course integral to the workings of subjectification: before a society can flag its members into conforming with the ideal that it seeks to impose, it must implicitly construct that ideal, flagging the abstract-ideal citizen *as* whatever best suits its purposes.

5 See my remarks on what I refer to as "the hired-man effect" (the unstoppable momentum of entrenched translation equivalents, however inept) in Chapter 8 of my *Second Finding*.

REFERENCES

Althusser, Louis. 1976 [1970]. "Idéologie et appareils idéologiques d'état: Notes pour une recherche." In *Positions (1964–1975)*, 67–126. Paris: Éditions sociales.

Benveniste, Émile. 1966. *Problèmes de linguistique générale*. Vol. 1. Paris: Gallimard.

Bhabha, Homi K. 1994. "Interrogating Identity: Frantz Fanon and the Postcolonial Prerogative." In *The Location of Culture*, 40–65. London: Routledge.

Brewster, Ben, trans. 1971. "Ideology and State Ideological Apparatuses (Notes towards an Investigation)." In *Lenin and Philosophy and Other Essays: Translated from the French by Ben Brewster*, 127–86. New York: Monthly Review Press.

Debray, Régis, and Jean Bricmont. 2003. *À l'ombre des lumières*. Paris: Odile Jacob.

Folkart, Barbara. 2006. *Second Finding: A Poetics of Translation*. Ottawa: University of Ottawa Press.

Lacan, Jacques. 1966. "Fonction et champ de la parole et du langage en psychanalyse." In *Écrits*, 237–322. Paris: Seuil.

Marx, Karl. 1906. *Capital: A Critique of Political Economy. Translated from the Third German Edition by Samuel Moore and Edward Aveling. Edited by Frederick Engels. Revised and Amplified According to the Fourth German Edition by Ernest Untermann*. New York: Modern Library.

Niranjana, Tejaswini. 1992. *Siting Translation: History, Post-Structuralism, and the Colonial Context*. Berkeley–Los Angeles: University of California Press.

Robinson, Douglas. 1997. *Translation and Empire: Postcolonial Theories Explained*. Manchester: St. Jerome Publishing.

Silverman, Kaja. 1983. *The Subject of Semiotics*. New York: Oxford University Press.

CHAPTER 9

CONSEQUENCES OF TRANSLATION FOR LEGAL TERMINOLOGY DURING THE MIDDLE AGES AND RENAISSANCE

CLAIRE-HÉLÈNE LAVIGNE

INTRODUCTION

In the sixth century, Justinian I, Emperor of the East, instructed a commission of jurists to compile and correct the classical Roman laws. The commission produced what became known in the West as the *Corpus Iuris Civilis*. This compilation of Roman laws consists of five separate texts: the *Codex constitutionum*,[1] the *Digest*, the *Codex repetitae praelectionnis*, the *Novellae*, and the *Institutes*. It was "rediscovered" (Kuttner 1982) in the West at the end of the eleventh century, and from that time on it was extensively studied by the Glossator School. By the thirteenth century, the Justinian compilation had become, "together with canon law and theology, part of a common learned Christian culture shared by those who occupied positions of authority, both lay and ecclesiastical" (Stein 1999, 66).

In this article, I will examine the evolution of various strategies for translating some of the legal terminology in Book 1, Title 15, of the *Institutes*. Four translations will be considered: two from the Middle Ages and two from the Renaissance. In particular, I will analyze the techniques used to translate the Roman legal terms *adgnatorum (agnatio, onis, f)* and *adgnati (agnatus, i)*, and then determine whether the translators succeeded in transferring the concepts conveyed by those legal terms. After a short "review" of the four translations, I will explain the law covered in 1.15 and give succinct definitions of *adgnatorum* and *adgnati*. Finally, I will analyze the evolution of the translation process for those terms and its consequences for legal terminology.

TRANSLATIONS

The *Institutes,* a "legal textbook for students," was translated twice in thirteenth-century France and then again in 1543. This last translation was "reused" in 1580 by an editor (Chez Jean Poupy) who appears to have reproduced Nicolle de Lescut's translation of the *Institutes* but not the gloss accompanying the 1543 translation. The editor does not specify that he borrowed the translation by de Lescut; he simply mentions that he has used the gloss written in Latin by Jacques Buchereau and translated into Middle French by Guy de La Roche.[2]

ANONYMOUS TRANSLATION (1220–30)

The first translation may have been done between 1220 and 1230. The author is unknown, the text is in prose, and there is no prologue or epilogue. This text probably represents the earliest translation of a text from the *Corpus Iuris Civilis* into Old French. It was apparently quite popular—twenty-seven manuscripts are known to exist.

Félix Olivier-Martin edited the text in 1935. In his introduction, he writes about the possible identity of the translator, the date of the translation, and the origins of the various manuscripts. He does not, however, analyze the translational approaches or methods used.[3]

TRANSLATION ATTRIBUTED TO RICHARD D'ANNEBAUT (1280)

The second translation of the *Institutes* is a verse translation attributed to Richard d'Annebaut. There is only one manuscript of this translation, Harley 4477.2, and one incunabulum printed in Paris in 1485 by Antoine Cayllaut. The translation was completed in 1280, according to its epilogue, but has never been edited. It is approximately 24,000 lines long, including an eighty-four-line prologue and a forty-line epilogue presumably written by the translator.

TRANSLATION BY NICOLLE DE LESCUT (1543)

The third translation was published in Paris in 1543 by V. Gaultherot. It is known as *Les institutions impérialles [de Justinien], avecques certaines gloses et arbre civil, ou sont insérées les formules de demandes ou libelles judiciaulx sur chascune action, le tout mis de latin en françoys par maistre Nicolle de Lescut, secretaire du Duc de Lorraine.* It was re-edited in Paris in 1549 by G. Le Bret.[4] This translation has a table of contents in addition to a prologue containing a dedication to the Duc de Lorraine and a short epilogue, both presumably written by the translator, Nicolle de Lescut. The text is extensively glossed, and de Lescut appears to have translated the original text of the *Institutes* as well as the gloss on the text. The translated text of the *Institutes* is reproduced under the heading "Texte," followed by the gloss under the heading "Glosse."

NEW VERSION BY GUY DE LA ROCHE
The fourth and last "translation" was printed in Paris in 1580 by Chez Jean Poupy. Its complete title is *Les institutes impériales de Justinian, joinctes avec la jurisprudence françoise mise à la marge d'icelles. Esquelles tout le droict ancien romain est descrit et esclarey: Et veu à l'œil, en quoy il est conforme aux loix, ordonnances et statuts de noz roys tres-chrestiens, ensemble aux meurs, us, coustumes, pratiques et observations usitees au Royaume de France. Œuvre tres utile pour tous particiens. Nagueres faict en latin par M. Jaques Buchereau, Conseiller et Referandaire en la Chancelerie de France, et maintenant mises en françois par Guy de La Roche Advocat.* This translation contains a prologue, apparently written by the editor and entitled "Le libraire au lecteur." It also has a table of contents and an alphabetical index but no epilogue. The translation is extensively glossed—so much so that the gloss surrounds the text and appears to have as much importance as, if not more importance than, the *Institutes* themselves. This translation is 894 pages long.

INSTITUTES 1.15: "DE LEGITIMA ADGNATORUM TUTELA"

Title 15 concerns statutory guardianship by agnatic relatives.[5] It consists of an introductory paragraph and three sections. The introductory paragraph states, "Quibus autem testamento tutor datus non sit, his ex lege duodecim tabularum adgnati sunt tutores, qui vocantur legitimi" ("Under the Twelve Tables, agnates are made guardians when there is no appointment by will. We call them statutory guardians"). Section 1 gives a short definition of *adgnati*, provides some examples of who can be *adgnati,* and gives a short explanation of the difference between *adgnati* and *cognati*. Section 2 states that agnatic relatives become guardians not only if the person who died did not have a will but also if the deceased did not appoint someone in his will or if the appointee predeceased the testator. The last section explains how the agnatic tie can be broken by loss of status, while the cognatic tie can never be broken.

DEFINITIONS AND ETYMOLOGIES

In modern law, the Latin term *adgnatus* refers to Roman law and can be defined as "the relatives in the male line from common male ancestor. . . . People from either sex can be agnates, as those who are adopted into a family" (Birks and McLeod 1987, 149 s.v.). To understand the notion conveyed by the term *adgnatus*, a definition of *cognatus* must be given, since the two terms are often used together. The term *cognatus* means "normally a blood relation, including one adopted out of the family or emancipated. So a cognate, unlike an agnate, can be related to another through the female line" (Birks and McLeod 1987, 150 s.v.). According to the *Dictionnaire général de la langue française du commencement du XVIIe siècle jusqu'à nos jours, précédé d'un traité de la formation de la langue* (Hatzfeld and Darmesteter 1890, s.v.), the term *agnation* was first used in French in 1539, *agnat* in 1697, *cognation* in 1243, and *cognat* sometime in the thirteenth century. In 1552, Robert Estienne gave the following definitions of *agnatio* and *cognatio* in his *Dictionarium latinogallicum*: *agnatio* is "parentage du coste du père [relatives on the father's side]," while *cognatio* is "parenté [relatives]."

TRANSLATION OF LEGAL VOCABULARY

In this last section, I will analyze the evolution of the techniques used to translate *adgnatorum (agnatio, onis, f)* and *adgnati (agnatus, i)*. In both cases, I will start by examining the anonymous translation, followed by the translation by Richard d'Annebaut, and I will finish with the translation by Nicolle de Lescut. Unless otherwise specified, I have not reproduced the translation allegedly done by Guy de la Roche since it simply reproduces the text found in the translation by Nicolle de Lescut.

ADGNATORUM (AGNATIO, ONIS, F)

The anonymous translator translates Title 15, "De legitima adgnatorum tutela" ("Statutory guardianship by agnatic relatives")[6] by "Cist titres est des desfendeurs qui sunt donné par loi" ("This title is about tutors that are given by law"). Richard d'Annebaut translates it by "Cest tiltres est quant les orphelins / Sont en la garde a leurs cousins" ("This title is when orphans / Are in the care of their cousins"). Both medieval translators do not try to translate the legal term *adgnatorum* by using an equivalent, a calque, a synonymic binomial, or a circumlocution.

The anonymous translator simply drops any reference to the legal expression *adgnatorum,* while d'Annebaut uses the term *cousins,* which is not a legal term. According to Sainte-Palaye (1875–82), *cousins,* in Old French, can be defined as a family relation. It refers to all relatives, regardless of the degree of kinship and no matter if the relationship is through the male line or the female line. Furthermore, d'Annebaut does not translate *legitima,* creating a shift in meaning by not specifying that the guardianship is statutory.

In 1540, Nicolle de Lescut translates Title 15 by "De la tutelle legitime des parens, prochains, & germains" ("Of Statutory Guardianship by Close and Full-Blood Relatives").[7] The Latin term *agnatorum* is translated as "parens, prochains, & germains." According to Greimas (1997), *parens* is a Middle French word for *père* ("father") or *ancêtre* ("ancestor"), and *prochains* is "état de ce qui est proche (voisinage, parenté)" ("state of someone or something close [neighbouring, relatives]"). In his *Dictionnaire de la langue française du seizième siècle,* Huguet gives the same definitions of both terms. He specifies, however, that *prochain parent* means *proche parent* ("close relative"). Finally, according to Greimas, the French term *germains* means "né des mêmes père et mère" ("born of the same father and mother"). Huguet gives the following definition of this term: "germain (adj.): (frère germain; sœur germaine) frère, sœur de père et de mère" ("[full-blooded brother; full-blooded sister] brother, sister [of the same] father and mother"). It would appear that *germain,* in Middle French, does not refer specifically to the male line. Accordingly, the circumlocution "parens, prochains, & germains" means, in Modern English, "close relatives born of the same father and mother." Nicolle de Lescut's translation of the legal term *agnatorum* does not transfer the legal concept or maintain the semantic field covered in the Latin (i.e., that the relatives must be from the male line). None of the four translators specifies that *agnatorum,* as used in the title, refers exclusively to male relatives.

ADGNATI (AGNATUS, I)

I will now examine whether the translators correct their mistake when translating the legal term *adgnati (agnatus, i)* as used in the introductory paragraph and Section 1 and whether they succeed in transferring the legal concept represented in this expression. This will also enable me to determine whether the translators adapt their translations to the context in which the word *adgnati* is used.

Introductory Paragraph

In the introductory paragraph, the anonymous translator translates *adgnati sunt tutores* by "parant sunt lor desfendeur" without specifying that the *parant* is supposed to be in the male line and share a common male ancestor with the person.[8] *Parant* is defined as "father, family member" (Godefroy 1969; Greimas 1997) or "father and mother, relatives, relations by blood" (Sainte-Palaye 1875–82). The anonymous translator uses a general vocabulary term that does not have a specific, specialized legal meaning. This translation technique allows the translator to follow the Latin text closely; however, it causes a translation error by dropping any reference to the male line.

Richard d'Annebaut's translation is not any more felicitous. D'Annebaut translates the Latin by "La garde en vient a leurs cousins / Qui sont en aage et resnables" ("Their guardianship goes to their relatives / that are of legal age and reasonable").[9] D'Annebaut uses the term *cousins* to translate *adgnati*. As I have already noted, *cousins*, in Old French, can be defined as a family relation from the male or the female line. Furthermore, d'Annebaut adds to the text when he writes that the relatives must be of age and reasonable. This addition by the translator results from the versification process and is one of the characteristics of d'Annebaut's translation. However, it adds to the text a detail that is not in the Latin original.

Nicolle de Lescut translates *adgnati sunt tutores* by "leurs parens prochains germains de ligne masculine seront tuteurs." As we can see, the translator specifies, for the first time, that the "parens, prochains, & germains" must be from the male line ("ligne masculine"), thus successfully transferring the legal concept from the Latin.

Section 1

In Section 1, the anonymous translator translates "Sunt autem adgnati per virilis sexus cognationem coniuncti quasi a patre cognati" ("Agnates are relatives through the male sex, loosely related through the father") by "Li parant sunt cil qui sunt joint as enfans par lynage par devers le pere" ("The relatives that are joined to the children by the father's line"). Two aspects of this translation need to be noted. First, the translator adds the explanation that it is the *enfans* that are joined to the *parent*. In this particular case, his translation is more specific than the Latin. Second, he fails to translate *virilis sexus cognationem*, thereby removing the idea that agnates are relatives through the male line.

Furthermore, the anonymous translator does not give the Latin term in his translation; he adapts his translation to the target culture and does not try to teach his reader the Latin equivalent of his translation.

Richard d'Annebaut's rendering of the Latin text cannot be called a translation in the true sense of the word. It is more a loose adaptation of the notion found in the original.

> Et qui bien y veult adviser
> L'en doit les cousins diviser
> Les uns sont par agnacion
> Les autres par cognacion
> A quel degre que ilz s'estendent
> Cil qui de par masle descendent
> Et les branches et ly cyon
> Sont cousins par agnacion

D'Annebaut explains that, if one wants to be well advised, then one must divide one's cousins into two categories—agnates and cognates—and that the degree of kinship is of little importance: those who come from the male line, directly or indirectly, are agnates. Several aspects of this very loose translation are worthy of note. First and most interestingly, d'Annebaut creates a neologism by importing and calquing the term *agnacion* in Old French. I have already stated that, according to the *Dictionnaire général de la langue française du commencement du XVIIe siècle jusqu'à nos jours, précédé d'un traité de la formation de la langue* (Hatzfeld and Darmesteter 1890, s.v.), the first written attestation of the use in French of the term *agnation* is dated 1539.[10] This is confirmed by the absence of that word in the Godefroy, the Sainte-Palaye, the Greimas, and the Tobler. Furthermore, when using this calque, d'Annebaut does not specify its origin or the fact that it is a loan translation from the Latin, nor does he feel the need to explain the meaning of *agnacion* by the use of a synonymic binomial.[11] He simply gives a loose translation of the definition found in the Latin text.

Nicolle de Lescut translates the Latin *agnati* by "parens communement appellez agnati, & en langue vulgaire, parens germains, coniointctz & attenans aux cousins non germains, par cognation de genre viril" ("relatives normally called *agnati*, and in French [they are called] full-blooded relatives joined to and related to those who are not full-blooded cousins, by a relationship of the male line"). The first element of interest in this translation is that de Lescut incorporates the Latin term and then introduces, by use of the expression *en langue vulgaire*, a polynomial in order to define the Latin term while adding a detail not in the Latin—namely, that the *parens germains* are joined to and related to cousins who are not full blooded. But perhaps the most interesting element in de Lescut's translation is the evolution of his translations of the terms *adgnati* and *adgnatorum*. The first time that de Lescut translates the term *adgnatorum*, he uses the wording "parens, prochains, & germains." He then specifies, when translating *adgnati*, that the relatives are "de ligne masculine" ("from the male line"). Finally, he gives the Latin term and a rather complex definition of its meaning in Middle French.

CONCLUSION

The three translators do not appear to share a common strategy when translating legal terminology, although Richard d'Annebaut and Nicolle de Lescut use relatively similar techniques. The anonymous translator does not refer at all to the Latin original, while d'Annebaut alternates between an incomplete translation of the concept in the Latin and the use of a neologism. Similarly, de Lescut, when translating *adgnatorum*, does not succeed in transferring the concept found in the Latin. However, his translations of *adgnati* convey the meaning of this legal term. Furthermore, he provides his reader with the Latin while giving a French equivalent in *langue vulgaire*. As we have seen, in the case of *adgnatorum* and *adgnati*, the translation process has serious consequences for the transfer of the concepts of those two legal terms. The transfer from the Roman legal system to the feudal legal system is not an easy feat to accomplish.

On a more general note, it would be interesting to analyze the various techniques used by each translator using a larger corpus of translated Latin Roman legal terms. It would then be possible to compare their strategies, to determine whether the strategies change from one period to another or from one translator to another, to analyze the effect of the translation process on the various concepts, and to gauge whether the terminology used by the translators is imported into or exported from the *droit coutumier*. Such a study would shed new light on the implications that translation had on the transfer of legal terminology from one system to another during the Middle Ages and the Renaissance.

NOTES

1. Only fragments of the first code survived.
2. Those findings are preliminary.
3. In this article, I use the Olivier-Martin edition of the anonymous translation.
4. For this article, I use the 1543 edition of this translation. I have a photocopy of this early edition.
5. "De legitima adgnatorum tutela—Quibus autem testamento tutor datus non sit, his ex lege duodecim tabularum adgnati sunt tutores, qui vocantur legitimi. Sunt autem adgnati per virilis sexus cognationem coniuncti, quasi a patre cognati, veluti frater eodem patre natus, fratris filius neposve ex eo, item patruus et patrui filius neposve ex eo." ("Statutory guardianship by agnatic relatives—Under the Twelve Tables agnates are made guardians when there is no appointment by will. We call them statutory guardians. 1. Agnates are relatives through the male sex, loosely relations through the father, as for instance his brother if born from the same father, that brother's son, and the grandson through that son, also his father's brother, that uncle's son, and the grandson through that son.")

   Anonymous 1220–30: "Cist titres est des desfendeurs qui sunt donné par loi—Se aucun sunt a qui desfenderes n'est pas donéz en testament, lor parant sunt lor desfendeor par la loi des XII tablez et cil desfendeur sunt apelé loial. 1. Li parant sunt cil qui sunt joint as enfans par lynage par devers le pere, si conme lor freres de par le pere, ou li filz au frere, ou li onclez, ou li filz a l'oncle."

   Richard d'Annebaut: "Cest tiltres est quant les orphelins / Sont en la garde a leurs cousins—Quant il advient par aventure / Que le pere n'a pas sa cure / A son testament ordonner / De tuteur a ses filz donner / Qui sont jeunes et orphelins / La garde en vient a leurs cousins / Qui sont en aage et resnables / Et par la loy des XII tables / Garde qui ainsy est allee / Est garde loyal appellee / Et qui bien y veult adviser / L'en doit les cousins diviser / Les uns sont par agnacion / Les autres par cognacion / A quel degre que ilz s'estendent / Cil qui de par masle descendent / Et les branches et ly cyon / Sont cousins par agnacion" (Harley 4477.2, folio 87r).

   Nicolle de Lescut: "De la tutelle legitime des parens, prochains, & germains—Ceulx à qui par testament ne sont donnez tuteurs, par la loy des douze tables, leurs parens prochains germains de ligne masculine seront tuteurs, qui sont dictz legitimes. Et sont ledictz parens communement appellez agnati, & en langue vulgaire, parens germains, coniointctz & attenans aux cousins non germains, par cognation de genre viril, comme frere né d'ung mesme pere, le filz du frere, & le nepveu d'icelluy, l'oncle de par pere, le filz d'icelluy & nepveu."

6   In this article, all English translations of the *Institutes* are taken from Peter Birks and Grant McLeod's translation; the Latin text is from the Paul Krueger edition.
7   The editor of the 1580 translation attributed to Guy Buscherau appears to have reproduced Nicolle de Lescut's translation. To simplify my presentation here, I will give the 1580 translation only when there are major differences between that translation and de Lescut's translation.
8   *Desfendeur* is defined as "avocat, defenseur, protecteur" ("lawyer, defender, protector") in Sainte-Palaye (1875–82).
9   *Garde*, in Middle French, refers to the *tutelle* ("guardianship"). See Sainte-Palaye (1875–82).
10 *Le Nouveau Petit Robert*, 2003 edition, gives the same date.
11 Synonymic binomials, as used by the medieval translators, usually occupy an explanatory function in the translation, and they are used in various ways. According to Claude Buridant (1980, 20), binomials can be used to fill a lacuna in the target language. This technique is seen in the very first translations made into Old French. Binomials can also be used to restrict the sense of a general term by adding a term that has a more specific sense. For example, the Latin term *constituere* can be translated by the synonymic binomials *fere et estaublir* (21). However, the most important role played by synonymic binomials in translation is when the translator wants to adapt a learned term calqued on the Latin. Its function in the translation is then either to explain a learned term that is infrequent or possibly unfamiliar to the reader or to help integrate into the vernacular a neologism calqued on the Latin language. Binomials were already being used in this way by the first French translators and became common in Middle French (23 ff.).

REFERENCES

Buridant, Claude. 1977. "Problèmes méthodologiques dans l'étude des traductions du latin au français au XIIIe siècle: Le domaine lexical. Les couples de synonymes dans l'Histoire de France en français de Charlemagne à Philippe-Auguste." *Actes du Colloque des 29 et 30 avril 1977. Linguistique et Philologie (Application aux textes médiévaux)*, 293–324. Centre d'Études Médiévales de l'Université de Picardie. Paris: Librairie Honoré Champion.

———. 1980. "Les binômes synonymiques: Esquisse d'une histoire des couples de synonymes du Moyen Âge au XVIIe siècle." *Synonymies : Bulletin du Centre d'analyse du discours* 4: 5–79.

Estienne, Robert. 1552. *Dictionarium latinogallicum*. http://colet.uchicago.edu/cgi-bin/Estienne.pg.sh?PID=66.

Les 4 livres d'institutes de Justinien en vers. British Library, Harleian Collection, 4477.2.

Godefroy, Frédéric. 1969. *Dictionnaire de l'ancienne langue française et de tous ses dialectes du IXe au XVe siècle composé d'après le dépouillement de tous les plus importants documents manuscrits ou imprimés qui se trouvent dans les grandes bibliothèques de la France et de l'Europe et dans les principales archives départementales municipales, hospitalières, ou privées.* Paris: Kraus Reprint.

Greimas, A.J. 1997. *Dictionnaire de l'ancien français — Le Moyen Âge.* Paris: Librairie Larousse.

Hatzfeld, Adolphe, and Arsène Darmesteter. 1890. *Dictionnaire général de la langue française, du commencement du XVIIème siècle jusqu'à nos jours, précédé d'un traité de la formation de la langue.* Paris: Delagrave.

Huguet, Edmond. 1925–67. *Dictionnaire de la langue francaise du seizieme siecle.* 7 vols. Paris: E. Champion.

Les institutions impérialles [de Justinien], avecques certaines gloses et arbre civil, ou sont insérées les formules de demandes ou libelles judiciaulx sur chascune action, le tout mis de latin en françoys par maistre Nicolle de Lescut, secretaire du Duc de Lorraine. 1543. Paris: V. Gaultherot. Bibliothèque nationale de France shelf-mark FRBNF30670429. (Re-edited in Paris in 1549 by G. Le Bret, Bibliothèque nationale de France shelfmark FRBNF30670430.)

Les Institutes impériales de Justinian, joinctes avec la jurisprudence françoise mise à la marge d'icelles. Esquelles tout le droict ancien romain est descrit et esclarey: Et veu à l'œil, en quoy il est conforme aux loix, ordonnances et statuts de noz Roys tres-chrestiens, ensemble aux meurs, us, coustumes, pratiques et observations usitees au Royaume de France. Œuvre tres utile pour tous particiens. Nagueres faict en latin par M. Jaques Buchereau, Conseiller et Referandaire en la Chancelerie de France, et maintenant mises en françois par Guy de La Roche Advocat. 1580. Paris: Chez Jean Poupy. (Bibliothèque nationale de France shelf-mark FRBNF30742179.)

Les Institutes de Justinien en français. Traduction anonyme du XIIIe siècle. 1935. Intro. Félix Olivier-Martin. Paris: Société anonyme du recueil Sirey.

Justinian. 1955. *Imperatoris Iustiani Institutionum.* Libri Quatuor, with commentary and excursus by J.B. Moyle. London: Oxford University Press.

Justinian's Institutes. 1987. English text trans. Peter Birks and Grant McLeod, Latin text Paul Krueger. London: Duckworth.

Kuttner, Stephen. 1982. "The Revival of Jurisprudence." In *Renaissance and Renewal in the Twelfth Century,* ed. R. Benson and G. Constable, 299–323. Cambridge, MA: Harvard University Press.

Sainte-Palaye, Jean Baptiste de la Curne de. 1875–82. *Dictionnaire historique de l'ancien langage françois.* Niort: L. Favre.

Stein, Peter. 1999. *Roman Law in European History.* Cambridge, UK: Cambridge University Press.
Tobler, Adolf, and Erhard Lommatzsch. 1886. *Tobler-Lommatzsch Altfranzosisches Worterbuch: Adolf Tobler nachgelassene Materialien bearbeitet und mit Unterstutzung der Preussischen Akademie der Wissenschaften hrsg.* Berlin: Weidmann.

CHAPTER 10

SEBASTIAN BRANT'S *DAS NARRENSCHIFF* IN EARLY MODERN ENGLAND: A TEXTUAL VOYAGE

BRENDA M. HOSINGTON

INTRODUCTION

Sebastian Brant's *Das Narrenschiff,* first published in Basel in 1494, was one of the most popular works of the late fifteenth and early sixteenth centuries. It is a biting satire of human morals and activities comprising a series of chapters displaying various sins and errors as exempla of *Narrheit* or "folly." Although Brant's work presents a telling picture of German society in his time, its significance and relevance go far beyond the confines of Germany and the fifteenth century, as is attested by its many editions, reprintings, and translations into several languages at regular intervals between 1494 and 1650. It is with two of these translations that the present article is concerned.

The first, Jacob Locher's *Stultifera navis* (Basel, 1497, 1498), was also the most influential of all the translations because it made the work accessible to an international audience by being in the lingua franca of the day, Latin, and serving as the text from which most subsequent translations were made, either directly or indirectly, wholly or in part. Locher was a pupil of Brant, and his work was overseen by Brant himself. Locher did, however, make some changes in the organization of the chapters and the verse forms, converting Brant's rhyming couplets into a variety of classical metres. More important, he omitted and added much, while changing the tone from Brant's familiar and at times earthy German into that of a more learned discourse, as one might expect from a Latin version. The second translation, the subject of this study, is Alexander Barclay's verse rendering *The shyp of folys of the worlde . . . translated out of Laten, Frenche, and Doche into Englysshe,* published in London in December 1509 by Richard Pynson. It contained Locher's Latin version, which served as Barclay's base text.[1] The French text to which Barclay alludes is Pierre Rivière's untitled 1497 verse translation of Locher, to which Barclay often turns, although for none of the passages that we will be discussing, but the reference to the "Doche" [German] is misleading, for there is no trace whatsoever of Brant's original text in his translation. Barclay's translation followed hot upon the heels of another English rendering, Henry Watson's *The Shyppe of Fooles*, a translation of Drouyn's 1498 prose version of Rivière, published in July 1509 by Wynkyn de Worde (Hosington 2006). The popularity and esteem that Brant's *Das Narrenschiff* enjoyed on the Continent obviously inspired Pynson and de Worde, the two major printers in England at the time, who must have hoped to repeat the success (Carlson 1995, 290–94).

DOMESTICATING AND "ENGLISHING" STRATEGIES

Barclay's *Shyp of folys* has been discussed, as has Watson's rendering, in Aurelius Pompen's (1925) study of Brant's *Narrenschiff* in English, a useful, detailed, though very dated work, especially in terms of translation studies. Our focus, unlike Pompen's, must of necessity be narrower. It will be on Barclay's "englishing" of the text, in other words on the ways in which Barclay makes his text relevant and significant for his English audience. Englishing was widely used by the translators of the early modern period, but perhaps the best-known example is in John Florio's translation of Montaigne's *Essais*, where French rivers and geographical features become English ones. In far more recent times, this technique has been seen, on the one hand, as a strategy of "dynamic translation" trying to "relate the receptor to modes of behaviour relevant within the context of his own culture" (Nida 1964, 159); on the other, it has been criticized as "ethnocentric translation" that "domesticates" an original and thereby destroys its very essence (Meschonnic 1973; Berman 1985). In Barclay's time, it raised no such concerns. Barclay himself refers to his intention to make his text relevant to his audience in his translation of Locher's prologue and then proceeds to use various "domesticating" strategies throughout the other paratexts (prologues, dedicatory poems, addresses to the reader, etc.) and the text itself.

Of the twelve paratexts accompanying Locher's text, only five are translated by Barclay. Of these five, four are "domesticated." The first technique used is the most obvious one, the translator's naming of himself either by substituting his own name for the original translator's or simply introducing himself as the translator. Thus, Barclay turns Locher's "Excusatio Jacobi locher Philomusi" into "A. Barclay excusynge the rudenes of his translation" (f.i^v), and Locher's plea for his readers' understanding in "Celeusma" into one for "no dysdane / Thoughe Barclay haue presumed of audacitie" (f. v). In the final paratext, Locher's "Argumentum in narragoniam," untitled in the English, Barclay tells us that he did the translation while at the "Colege of Saynt Mary Otery," translating it out of "Laten, Frenche and Doche." He then continues translating Locher's text in the first person as if he were the original translator or author, a common practice in medieval and Renaissance translation and one not necessarily intended to mislead.[2] Barclay tells us in "The Prologue of J. Locher" (Locher's "Prologus") that Locher had first translated Brant's work, then that of a Frenchman whose name he does not know (Rivière); he now wishes to "redres the errours and vyces of this oure Royalme of Englonde" as previous translators did for their countries, however unworthy a language English may be for such a task (a commonplace in early modern paratexts). Barclay hopes for neither reward nor praise, wishing only to "clense the vanyte and madnes of folysshe people of whom ouer gret nombre is in the Royalme of Englonde" (ff. viii-ix). His appears, then, an act of patriotic duty. This sentiment will be echoed again and again in prefaces to translations throughout the sixteenth century.

To carry out this duty and make the work relevant to his readers, Barclay uses another englishing technique. He adds or substitutes English place names for German ones in his translation. In "The Prolog" (Locher's "Hecatostichon"), he says that none is deemed wiser "betwene London and Hull" than a rich, fat man (f. x, l. 49). Locher had simply "Prudentes nimium se tamen esse putant" (l. 30), "for all that they think themselves very wise" (my translation). Hull is also in tandem with Lyn (King's Lynn in Norfolk) in "Barclay the translatour to the foles," Locher's "Celeusma." Barclay asks where the ship should put into port, Hull or London, then adds "no hauen in Englonde be denayd" so full is it of fools (f. v) [l. 3]. In "The Prologue" (Locher's "Hecatostichon"), he claims that London is so full of fools that the ship would be overloaded, exclaiming "from London rockes Almyghty God us saue!" and warning "London galantes" not to try to board (f. x) [l. 13-14].

Barclay states in his "Prologue of J. Locher," as we have seen, that he is translating Brant's work for the good of the English, in order to correct their "errours and vyces." Crucial to that purpose, as he obviously saw it, was the domestication of the text in order to increase its relevance to his audience, both national and local. The strategies that he employed to this end were many. The translation also, however, had another aim: to increase patriotism and to propagandize on behalf of the monarchy. While Jamieson (1966, xviii–xix) calls the *Shyp of folys* "an English ship, formed after the Ship of Fools of the World," claiming that "the national tone and aim of the English 'Ship' are maintained throughout with the greatest emphasis," and that Barclay was "actuated by . . . patriotic motives," he supports his view only by quoting the appropriate passages in Barclay's "Prologue of J. Locher." No mention whatsoever is made of the translation itself. This the present study seeks to rectify by focusing on the various translation strategies used to achieve this englishing, which include changes made to the original as well as additions and omissions.

Barclay uses four strategies to make Brant's satire relevant to England: referring to England in various ways, naming local places and people in the county in which he was living when he wrote the *Shyp of folys*, effecting cultural shifts in his text, and expressing nationalistic and ideological sentiments different from those of Locher.

REFERENCES TO ENGLAND

Barclay introduces England into his text, again by using four distinct strategies. The first concerns additions that he made to his original. Sometimes he simply adds a reference to England or adds England to a list of countries found in Locher. For example, he translates quite closely Locher's tirade against angry women, but his tongue-in-cheek statement that the unfaithful, hypocritical woman acts as if "none were lyke hir in Englonde nor in Fraunce / In all vertues" (f. cxxix) [II, p. 7] is added. In the chapter "Of Folys that Dispyse Wysdome . . . A Lamentacion of Barclay," Barclay deplores the fact that "The newe disguyses hath left Almayne and Fraunce / And come to Englonde" (f. ccli^v) [I. 285]. Elsewhere, he takes the English to task for their "disordered loue and veneryous" that causes them to commit crimes to pay for their lust and adds that, without them, "All the feters and gyues of Englonde shulde rust" (f. xxxvii) [I. 83]. Finally, in a statement that suggests that the English were ever hard drinkers, he says that noisy night revellers are not as bad "in this Royalme" as "beyonde the se," although he has discussed the subject "in englysshe tunge"; "drunken glotany," however, is worse (f. cxxv) [I. 299]. At other times, Barclay adds England to a list of countries given in the Latin. For example, in the chapter on the universal ship of fools, he keeps several of Locher's countries that have their fair share of fools but changes others while adding England, Wales, and Scotland (f. cclxi) [II. 308]. In the discussion of variance in table manners from one country to another, he adds that the Greeks, Latins, and Germans use things contrary to "the vse of Englonde," which he adds to Locher's France and Spain (f. ccxliii) [II. 264]. He also inserts England, Wales, and Ireland into a list of countries whose wonders have drawn visitors (f. lxxii^v) [I. 177].

On other occasions, Barclay uses a different strategy: he substitutes England for another country. Three out of the four examples of this technique not surprisingly concern Germany and the Germans. Locher asks why quarrelsome Germany has adopted clothes made of skin that scarcely cover people's pudenda, thereby losing her reputation ("ne ve tuam perdas famam"); Barclay implores England to mend her ways, or "Thy noble name and fame can nat endure" (f. xxi) [I. 39]. Locher entreats the Germans to be powerful and strong, but Barclay says, "O englysshe states I humbly you requyre / Vnto your kynge of hert and mynde be true," changing not only the country but also the subject of his request, fidelity to the monarchy rather than power (f. ccxviii) [II. 206]. Locher also reminds Germany that had she sought wisdom her ancient fame would not have deserted her; Barclay translates the sentiment exactly but transfers it to "the noble royalme of Englonde" (f. ccxlvii) [II. 277].

Barclay also inserts English place names into his text. They all occur in stanzas that he has added to rather than translated from Locher's text. No need to go over the sea to witness Venus's ribaldry, he exclaims, you can buy it at St. Martin's in Westminster, or Tower Hill, or the Stews, the notorious red-light district on the south bank of the Thames, so that all London will soon be full of it (f. lxxiv) [I. 178]. The reference to Westminster's ribaldry also occurs in the chapter on "disordered love and veneryous" (f. xl^v) [I. 83]. As for simple folly, England is so full of it that, wherever the ship lands, be it in London or Bristol, there would be "mariners" to climb aboard (f. cclxii) [II. 309].

A final strategy always available, although rarely desirable, to the translator is omission. Only once does Barclay resort to this when wishing to english his text. Locher upbraids the stammering Germans ("Theutonicos inter balbos") on whom his Latin verbs would be lost; Barclay omits the Germans, thereby widening his satiric aim to include all who reject learning such as his, although he keeps silent in their company, "Lyst by moche speche my latyn shuld be spent" (f. xiv) [I. 21].

PERSONAL REFERENCES

I have mentioned Barclay's use of England and English place names to make his text more relevant to his readers. Perhaps Barclay also had in mind a potential local audience since he often inserts references to people and places that he knew personally. As I noted, he tells us in his prologue that he wrote the *Shyp of Folys* while he was chaplain "in the Colege of saynt Mary Otery," in Devon. He dedicated it to Thomas Cornish, suffragen bishop of Bath and Wells but also warden at St. Mary's. In Chapter 1, on the uselessness of books, Barclay says bitterly that flattery and the ability to hunt with hawks rather than learning are likely to make one a "Person [parson] of Honyngton or of Clyst" (f. xiv^v) [I. 22], both near Ottery. There is only one example of a local name being substituted for a Latin one. Locher's two-line address praising Ticio (f. ccxlvii) is replaced by four stanzas praising Barclay's old friend John Bisshop, who, the translator tells us, first read the translation and encouraged its publication (f. ccxlviii) [II. 282–83]. The names of other local people are simply added to the text: "my mayster kyrkham," a local knight, high sheriff of Devon, and benefactor of Honiton (Pompen 1925, 189), whom Barclay says he served as chaplain, is praised for his meekness and generosity (f. clxi^v) [II. 81]; in the same chapter, a certain "Mansell of Otery" is criticized for robbing the poor (f. clxi^v) in what Jamieson (1966, xxxvii) calls the only severe personal reference in all of Barclay's writings. In "The unyversall shype," Mansell reappears with one Soper, both called stealing tailors, and in the company of cheating millers and bakers and three other unidentified people, Jack, Charde, and Robyn Hyll, who might of course be fictitious.

CULTURAL SHIFTS

A third way in which a translator can domesticate a text is by changing or adding cultural referents in the target text. Again, Barclay avails himself of this method in a variety of areas, six to be exact. The first provides the most examples. Barclay rigorously translates each of

Locher's references to "vinum" as "wine and ale," thereby making the text more relevant to an ale-drinking country such as England.[3] For example, in the chapter on gluttons and drunkards, a diatribe against immoderate wine drinking, Locher's "vini moderatior vsus / Nil nocet" (f. xliv, ll. 31–32) is translated as "in eche thynge ought to be had measure / Wyne ne ale hurteth no maner creature" (f. xliv^v) [I. 97]. Similar shifts occur no fewer than ten times. On one occasion, Barclay adds an English ale-related proverb to his original: "By the ale stake knowe we the ale house" (f. xviii). Cultural shifts also occur when Locher's money and measurements become English. Criticizing priests who have many benefices, Locher says, "Hunc sed amor nummi," which becomes "So for the loue of the peney and ryches" (f. lxvi) [I. 157]. Barclay also blames priests and clerks who chatter in the choir stalls and whose devotion is therefore superficial, claiming that it is "nummus" that inspires them: "The peny them prycketh vnto deuocyn" (f. clxxxxiii) [II. 156]. In the chapter on new fashions, which Barclay completely revamps, he changes Locher's focus from the indecency of contemporary clothing and fashions to the waste of money that they incur, warning unthrifty fools that they will have "no Peny them to socour at theyr nede" (f. xix) [I. 36]. Castigating cooks and butlers for stealing their masters' food and drink, Locher says that they waste "lagenas Bacchi," flagons of wine, but Barclay englishes this to "galons and potels," the potel being a measurement of two quarts (f. clxv^v) [II. 92].

Other cultural referents that Barclay changes or adds are literary, social, and historical. Three times he refers to the "gest of Robyn Hode," "gest" having the double meaning of a narrative recounting of the exploits of the famous English outlaw or any idle tale. When Locher upbraids people for despising the Bible and prophets and preferring "nugas... aniles," old wives' tales, Barclay says, "No scripture thynke they so true nor so gode / As is a folysshe yest of Robyn hode" (f. xxxiv) [I. 72]. Babbling priests, exclaims Locher, recount "fabulas... et nugas," fables and trifles. Barclay expands this to "And all of fables and Iestis of Robyn hode / Or other tryfles that skantly ar so gode" (f. clxxxxiv) [II. 155]. In the "Addicion of the Syngularyte of Some Newe Folys," Barclay adds a whole stanza to Locher's farewell to fools and is at pains to point out that he has written "no iest ne tale of Robyn Hode"; nor has he desired "For Phylyp the Sparowe the dirge to synge" (f. cclxx) [II. 331]. The "dirge" in question is *The Boke of Phyllyp Sparowe*, a poem written by Skelton, with whom Barclay was not on the friendliest of terms (Pompen 1925, 272–73).

All but one of the cultural shifts of a social nature concern crime and the law. Criticizing foolish people's desire for new fashions and clothes, Locher says that it leads to "crimina vita," a life of criminality; Barclay makes this very specific by mentioning the prison of Newgate in London where criminals' garments are offered for sale (f. xvi) [I. 37]. According to Brant and Locher, bad judges are to be shown no grace in the ship of fools. Barclay adds an envoy in which he warns the young "Studentes of the Chauncery," the Court of the Lord Chancellor of England and a court of equity, to liberate justice from the fetters in which their fathers had imprisoned it (f. xvii) [I. 27]. He also sarcastically suggests in the chapter on old dishonest fools that, if a father teaches his son correctly how to be an extortioner, he could "be made Juge of the comon place"—that is, a judge in the Court of Common Pleas in London, where one citizen could bring a civil case against another (f. xxiii) [I. 43]. The one cultural addition that has nothing to do with the law is in a series of four stanzas original to Barclay, inserted into the chapter on the uselessness of books. Here he effects a shift in focus from those who collect books but do not read them to those who succeed in life despite their ignorance. Lords, clerks, and lawyers are the particular object of his ire, but so are "gentlemen": "that thoughe one knowe but the yresshe game / Yet wolde he haue a gentyllmannys name" (f. xiv) [I. 21]. For Barclay, "the yresshe game," a type of backgammon, supersedes books as a means of getting ahead in the land of fools.

The final examples of cultural shift concern three places and one figure of historical significance to an English reader, all added to Locher's text. In the chapter on old dishonest fools who teach their sons bad ways, we saw the satire levelled at judges. Several stanzas later it is customs officers who are similarly targeted. Barclay adds that he hopes they will have posts in Lynn, Calais, or Dieppe. King's Lynn was a port dealing with the cities of the Hanseatic League, whose monopoly over the wool trade the English broke by 1500; Calais, the one English possession in northern France after 1371 and so assimilated that it seemed almost part of England, replaced Bruges as the wool staple in 1493 at the behest of Henry VII; Dieppe, an English possession until 1346, was one of France's busiest ports, receiving English ships and goods. In 1509, when Barclay was translating his *Shyp of folys*, the fierce trade and customs tariff disputes with the French, Northern Europeans, and Venetians in the late 1490s, and in which the English had fared quite well, were a fairly recent memory, hence Barclay's allusions to Lynn, Calais, and Dieppe.

The memory of the historical figure, however, was stronger still. Barclay, after translating Locher's passage on evil men quite closely, retaining his examples and adding only King David to the list, creates a whole stanza on "Richarde, lately kynge of price / In Englonde," guilty of ambition, "gyleful Couetyse," and murder. Fortune smiled upon him for two or three years, Barclay says, but then "god sende hym punysshment / By his true seruant the red Rose redolent" (f. xlii) [I. 87]. The allusion of course is to Richard III, who after multiple murders reigned for the last two years of the Wars of the Roses (1483–85) before being vanquished by Henry Tudor, the "red rose redolent" [fragrant] of the Lancastrians. The reputation of Richard as the personification of evil was well established by the time that Barclay was writing, while Henry VII, founder of the Tudor dynasty, had died but eight months before the publication of *The Shyp of folys*. As an englishing technique to make the translation more relevant to Barclay's audience, then, the evocation of Richard and Henry would have been very successful. As a technique to further Tudor propaganda, it also played a role.

PATRIOTISM

The Tudor dynasty, and Henry VIII in particular, are bound up with the patriotism, nationalism, and ideology that inspire some of the other changes that Barclay made in his translation. Many writers have spoken about the connection between translation and patriotism in the sixteenth century.[4] Barclay does indeed betray glimpses of his national pride, despite the faults he finds in England and satirizes through the changes that I have mentioned. One such glimpse is in the chapter on pride and boasting. Locher demonstrates his patriotism by criticizing those who spurn Germany's fine places of learning and boast of having studied abroad. Barclay does likewise but substitutes England for Germany, telling boasters that, if they want "to study cunnynge [knowledge or wisdom] and ydelnes despyse / The royalme of Englonde myght for them suffyse." He then adds a whole stanza praising the "noble men endued with scyence" in England who can teach wisdom and eloquence and who make travelling to the ends of the Earth nothing to brag about (f. clxxxxvi) [II. 160]. Barclay also stirs up the patriotism of his readers by evoking their patron saint, Saint George, whom he asks to help him launch his ship full of fools who refuse to learn (f. ccxii)

[I. 206]. While Locher says in a long chapter deploring the decay of the Catholic Church simply that "Regi caelica turba favet," "the heavenly host helps the king" (my translation), Barclay adds the line "For God and his saynts shall helpe hym for to fyght / Saynt George our patrone shall eke augment his myght" (f. ccxvi) [II. 206].

This chapter on the ruin and decay of the Catholic Church and the upsurge of the Turkish threat, a reality by the time *Das Narrenschiff* and its translations were written given the Turks' successful incursions into the Holy Roman Empire and their uneasy peace treaty of 1503 with Venice and Hungary, sees Barclay making the most radical changes to Locher's text in terms of nationalism and ideology. In this, Barclay was but proceeding in the same way as Rivière and Drouyn, who also domesticated the chapter for their French readers, and Watson, who patriotically englished this chapter more than any other. Brant, Locher, and all the translators that I have mentioned agreed that the Catholic Church had to unite against the Turks; however, whereas the two Germans appealed to the Holy Roman Emperor Maximilian to lead the crusade, the others appeal to their respective monarchs. Similarly, whereas Brant and Locher praise their fellow Germans and appeal to them to take up arms—with Locher adding an even more specific reference to his countrymen the Swabians—Rivière and Drouyn direct their compliments and encouragement to the French, Watson turns the chapter into a eulogy of the English and their kings, while, as Pompen says (1925, 155), Barclay uses the occasion to vent his patriotic or royalist feelings. Again, the ways in which he does this, first in Chapter 46 on the "Great Myght and Power of Folys" and then in Chapter 99 on the ruin of the Catholic faith, are varied.

Barclay's stanzas in Chapter 46 on the young King Henry VIII, who acceded to the throne on April 22, 1509, have no source in Locher's text. Since the colophon of *The Shyp of folys* tells us that the translation was made in 1508, Barclay must have added them, in the form of an envoy, to his text some time between April and December when the translation went to print.

In them, Barclay reminds princes that their offences are worse than those of simple folk and that they must rise above "lowe people," not only in rank but also in virtue. They must "lerne to lyue by the rede Rose redolent." The metaphor, previously used to refer to Henry VII, as I noted, reappears in the refrain of all five stanzas but is now applied to his son, Henry VIII, "Harry clene of concience," who has ended wars and is administering justice and disbursing alms. The paean ends with an appeal to England to show him obedience (f. cxxxv) [II. 16–17]. It reflects the optimism and promise felt after Henry VIII's accession to the throne and prepares us for the further eulogy of the monarch and appeal to English patriotism developed in Chapter 99.

After enumerating the successes of the heretics and the conquests of the Turks, and appealing to the countries of Europe to unite against such threats, all of which Barclay translates quite closely, Locher launches into an elaborated version of Brant's eulogy of Emperor Maximilian. At this point, Barclay alerts his reader in the margin that he has changed Maximilian for Henry VIII and he reworks the thirteen stanzas that follow accordingly.[5] He keeps Locher's analogy between Maximilian and certain heroes of classical antiquity but transfers it to Henry. He also changes Maximilian's standard of the eagle, emblem of the Holy Roman Empire and enough to destroy the Turks, to Henry's royal coat of arms bearing lions rampant: "There shall ne Turke be abyll to indure / His rampynge Lyons rorynge in theyr rage" (f. ccvii) [II. 206]. This is followed by the invocation of Saint George, as I mentioned earlier, and an appeal to the "englysshe states" to rally around their king and save Christendom, corresponding to Locher's appeal to the German people and their leaders. Some lines later, Locher returns to eulogizing Maximilian, who is at hand, he says, and has all the qualities requisite for victory. In Barclay's translation, Maximilian is once again metamorphosed into "the noble Henry of Englonde," who of course shares all the emperor's virtues.

Barclay then leaves Henry aside to praise another monarch who could head the crusade, James IV of Scotland, and to appeal to England and Scotland to unite against their common foe, the Turks. Jamieson (1874, xxx) and Pompen (1925, 153–54) say that this is unheard of on the part of an Englishman in 1509 and certainly denotes Barclay's Scottish birth, which is probable although never proven. Neither notes the fact that James had in fact concluded a "treaty of perpetual peace" with Henry in 1502 and married his sister in 1503. Nor do they mention James's ambition to lead a European crusade against the Turks, or the fact that James represented, in the eyes of his contemporaries, the ideal monarch—brave, warlike, handsome, generous in dispensing justice, and cultured. In short, he conformed to the portrait that Barclay paints of him. Despite the treaty and marriage union, however, relations were starting to become fraught again between England and Scotland by

1509, and Barclay's plea for the "Englysshe Lyon" with his "wysdome and ryches" and the "Scottis vnicorne" with his "myght and hardynes" to join forces must have seemed most timely. Whatever Barclay's motive in adding these stanzas, they contribute to domesticating the chapter, which heightens the patriotic and monarchal sentiments expressed elsewhere in the work.

CONCLUDING REMARKS

Opinions have differed over the years as to the extent and success of Barclay's domesticating in the *Shyp of folys*. Jamieson, writing in 1874, said that Barclay had "painted for posterity perhaps the most graphic and comprehensive picture now preserved of the folly, injustice and iniquity which demoralised England at the beginning of the sixteenth century" and went on, as I mentioned earlier, to praise the translator's Englishness (xviii–xix). Charles Herford, writing but a dozen years later (1886, 348), contends on the contrary that Barclay could never have given us a "genuinely English voyage," as does the anonymous author of *Cock Lorell's Bote* (c. 1510), largely inspired by Barclay's *Shyp of folys*. Contradicting this point of view is Edwin Zeydel, who in 1944 and again in 1967 states that Barclay's is a "new ship, which carries the fools of sixteenth-century England," rather than a translation of Brant or even Locher (1944, 96; 1967, 29). Albert Baugh, too, claims that Barclay is "intent on localizing the fools in England, which he does so effectively that few would have believed his book of foreign origin, had he not so candidly confessed it" (1967, 351). With this last comment we come extremely close to the transparent, or invisible, type of translation that does not appear a translation, which Lawrence Venuti contends has been the preferred one in England since Dryden (1995, 309). It was certainly the one preferred by Barclay some 200 years earlier. I am not suggesting that Barclay chose to translate within a proscribed theoretical framework, given his silence on the matter and the absence of any coherent body of translation theory in the beginning of the early modern period. He was, however, like all translators to varying degrees, rewriting his source text according to the cultural values of his audience. Furthermore, he was avowedly rewriting it in order to correct the vices and follies of his compatriots. Like Brant's and Locher's, his was a moral vision that encompassed all humankind, but a special place was reserved for his own countrymen. By employing a series of translating strategies, not discussed in detail by any of the commentators whom I have mentioned, I hope to have demonstrated how Barclay achieved the englishing that is a hallmark of his *Shyp of Folys*.

NOTES

1 All quotations from both Locher and Barclay are taken from Barclay (1509), in which the Latin provided is that of the Lyons 1498 reprint. Page references are to this text. However, page references are also given in brackets to a later edition of 1570 having only the English translation and re-edited in two volumes by T.H. Jamieson in 1874.
2 Barclay translates Locher's claim that he is translating "verbum nos verbo minus reddere (vt Flaccus ait)" as "it is nat translated worde by worde accordynge to ye verses of my actour," omitting the reference to Flaccus [Horace], but then adding "some tyme addynge, sometyme detractinge and taking away such thinges as semeth me necessary and superflue" (f. xii). This indeed he has amply done. He similarly translates Locher's appeal for his readers' understanding on account of his youth, "et teneros lanuginsi annos considerauerint," a topos in medieval and Renaissance paratexts, as "ye shall holde me excused if ye consider . . . my vnexpert youthe." The remainder of Barclay's passage is taken not from Locher but from Rivière's 1497 *La nef des folz du monde*.
3 It is ironic that Barclay makes this cultural shift from wine to wine and ale since Locher had made a similar shift but in reverse, so to speak: in *Das Narrenschiff*, Brant criticizes the excessive *beer* drinking prevalent in Germany.
4 See, in particular, Amos (1920, 88–89); Matthiesson (1931, 2), who says that "the translator's work was an act of patriotism"; and Sweeting (1940, 44–46).
5 The marginal note reads "Mutator laus Maximiliani Romanorum regis in laudem Henrici octavi Anglorum regis" ("The praise of King Maximilian of the Romans is changed into praise for King Henry VIII of the English") (my translation). It is noteworthy that of the four English and French translators, only Barclay alerts the reader to the change of monarch. Rivière silently changes Maximilian to Charles VIII and Drouyn to Louis XII, while Watson includes Maximilian but silently adds Henry VIII.

REFERENCES

Amos, Flora Ross. 1920 [1973]. *Early Theories of Translation*. New York: Columbia University Press. Reprint, New York: Octagon Press.

Barclay, Alexander. 1509. *The shyp of folys of the worlde.* London: Richard Pynson.

Baugh, Albert C., ed. 1967. *A Literary History of England.* 2nd ed. New York: Appleton Century Crofts.

Berman, Antoine. 1985. "La traduction et la lettre, ou l'auberge du lointain." In *Les Tours de Babel: Essais sur la traduction.* Mauvezin: Trans-Europe Express.

Brant, Sebastian. *Das Narrenschiff.* 1494. In *Sebastian Brant's* Narrenschiff, ed. Friedrich Zarncke, 1–115. Leipzig: Georg Olms.

Carlson, David. 1995. "Alexander Barclay and Richard Pynson: A Tudor Printer and His Writer." *Anglia: Zeitschrift für Englische Philologie* 113: 283–302.

Drouyn, Jehan. 1498. *La grant nef des folz du monde auec plusieurs satyres: Aditions nouuellement adiousteez par le translateur.* Lyon: Balsarin.

Herford, Charles H. 1886. *Studies in the Literary Relations of England and Germany in the Sixteenth Century.* Cambridge, UK: Cambridge University Press.

Hosington, Brenda M. 2006. "Henry Watson, 'Apprentyce of London' and 'Translatoure' of Romance and Satire." In Olivier Bertrand and Jacqueline Jenkins, ed. *The Medieval Translator 9.* Turnhout, Belgium: Brepols.

Jamieson, T.H., ed. 1874 [1966]. *The Ship of Fools Translated by Alexander Barclay.* 2 vols. Edinburgh: William Paterson. Reprint, New York: AMS Press.

Locher, Jacob. 1497, 1498. *Stultifera navis.* Basel: Johann Bergmann.

Matthiesson, F.O. 1931. *Translation: An Elizabethan Art.* Cambridge, MA: Harvard University Press.

Meschonnic, Henri. 1973. "Propositions pour une poétique de la traduction." In *Pour la poétique II,* 305–66. Paris: Gallimard.

Nida, Eugene. 1964. *Toward a Science of Translating: With Special Reference to Principles and Procedures Involved in Bible Translating.* Leiden: E.J. Brill.

Pompen, Aurelius. 1925 [1967]. *The English Versions of "The Ship of Fools": A Contribution to the History of the Early French Renaissance in England.* London: Longman, Green. Reprint, New York: Octagon Books.

Rivière, Pierre. 1497. *La nef des folz du monde.* Paris: Jean Philippe Mansteuer and Geoffrey de Marnef.

Sweeting, Elizabeth J. 1940. *Early Tudor Criticism, Linguistic and Literary.* Oxford: Basil Blackwell and Mott.

Venuti, Lawrence. 1995. *The Translator's Invisibility: A History of Translation.* London: Routledge.

Watson, Henry. 1509. *The Shyppe of Fooles, Translated out of Frenche.* London: Wynkyn de Worde.

Zeydel, Edwin H. 1944. *The Ship of Fools by Sebastian Brant: Translated into Rhyming Couplets with Introduction and Commentary.* New York: Dover Publications.

———. 1967. *Sebastian Brant.* New York: Twayne Publishers.

CHAPTER 11

CRITICIZING TRANSLATIONS:
THE NOTION OF DISPARITY

JEAN DELISLE

Disparity is endemic to the translator's art.
—Georges Mounin, *Les belles infidèles* (1955)[1]

Never definitive, a translation, even the best, is a dissonance unresolved!
—Marion Graf, *L'écrivain et son traducteur en Suisse et en Europe* (1998)

INTRODUCTION

Criticizing a literary translation is not about making subjective value judgments, nor about conveying a feeling, an impression, a pleasure in the reading. On the contrary, it is about performing a close analysis of the work, understanding its deeper meaning and how this meaning is rendered in the target language. As Antoine Berman (1995) demonstrates in reference to a poem by John Donne, the undertaking is more demanding than it may appear. The critic must be able to discern the translator's project, for every translator worthy of the name is guided in his or her rewriting by a purpose, a plan, be it explicit or implicit. This only makes sense, since translating a literary work is rather like pursuing the same writerly task that produced the original.

This global intention determines most of the many decisions that the translator makes throughout the re-creation. Style, rhythm, tone, register, syntactic structures, and vocabulary are only some of the elements weighed. And if the translation in question is historical, then the critic must have equal knowledge of two sets of circumstances: those surrounding the translation itself and those surrounding the source text's creation—the author and his or her era, the prevailing literary and linguistic conventions, the expectations of the target readership. All aspects of historical context are relevant, be they sociopolitical, literary, linguistic, religious, even economical. Once this general context—the work's original horizon of expectation—has been determined, the critic can analyze the text itself.

Although a translation exists as an autonomous work—one should be able to read it independently—it is still an echo of its source, and that is why comparison has an important, if not exclusive, role in criticism. Comparative analysis is not about ensuring that each and every element of the original has been transposed. This petty inventorial approach, this checking to see if every word has been rendered in good and due form—this has nothing to do with real criticism. Such a method is founded, rather, on the false assumption that a translated work must be identical word for word to its original, a perfect mirror image. More than one critic has denounced this specular conception, this literal utopia. Translation should not be a "lie trying to pass itself off as something it can never be" (Renken 2002, 96). In essence, to translate is to tell again but to tell *differently*. A translation is not a photographic reproduction but a *representation*. The distinction is vital, and its consequences for the criticism of translations are far reaching.

History tells us that, on the whole, excessively literal translations have not been well received or considered successful,[2] unless of course literalism is the norm for a certain type of text—the Bible, for example—or the norm in a given period or social context. The critic, understanding his task as he should, tries rather to determine whether the translated work offers the same literary properties as the first, the same semantic cohesion, the same aesthetic qualities, the same underlying unity. In a word, the same *signifiance*. The work's "signifiance" is its deepest, most integrated level of meaning. For translators, as most criticism seems to suggest (Delisle 2001), it is an ideal rarely attained. For the most part, translations actually disconcert, jar, upset the reader, give her what Maurice Gravier has called "translation sickness,"[3] a condition resulting from the inevitable "disparity"—sometimes great, sometimes little—that target texts demonstrate with respect to their source texts.

We might better understand the notion of disparity, central to translation theory and translation criticism specifically, by first addressing the term's definition in commonly consulted dictionaries. This initial lexical exploration will afford insight into the notion's more important implications.[4]

Appearing in seventeenth-century French, *disparate* came from the Latin *disparatus:* "different, dissimilar, unequal." At first, the word was used in rhetoric and designated a "contradictory statement." I will note in passing that the word, from the beginning, is rooted in discourse. It came to French through the Spanish *disparate*, which referred to "an extravagant act, an extravagance, a prank," and took on henceforth its pejorative connotation of "shocking contrast." In French, *disparate* is both an adjective and a noun. From the adjective, two acceptations: "A. [*of two or more objects, persons*] in discord, out of harmony with its surroundings; standing out in shocking, disagreeable, bizarre contrast," and "B. [*of a group, an ensemble*] made up of diverse, dissimilar, unmatching elements" (*Trésor de la langue française informatisée* 2002). Marked in modern French dictionaries with the labels *vx* and *litter* ("archaic" and "literary"), the noun *disparate* expresses a discord, a lack of harmony, a contrast, a shocking dissimilarity between two or more things or persons. Now feminine, the word was masculine in Balzac's day.

The French synonyms and quasi-synonyms of *disparate* reinforce the word's pejorative sense: *bigarré, boiteux, composite, décousu, discordant, dissonant, divergent, faux, hétéroclite, hétérogène, incongru, inconsistant, inharmonieux, mélangé,*[5] synonyms to which we might add *asymétrique, mal assorti, patchwork,* and even *salmigondis.* The word thus refers to something that clashes with its environment, breaks unity, sounds out of tune, disrupts, and upsets. Among its antonyms: *assorti, harmonieux, homogène.*[6]

The English dictionaries record only the adjective *disparate,* which has the same sense as its French homograph. A few rare works, such as *The American Heritage Dictionary of the English Language* (4th edition, 2000), include the noun *disparateness,* as describing the character of something "1. fundamentally distinct or different in kind; entirely dissimilar" or "2. containing or composed of dissimilar or opposing elements."

In French as in English, incongruity is one of the notion's defining properties:[7] "Containing or made up of fundamentally different and often incongruous elements" (*Merriam-Webster Online Dictionary*). The English *disparate* translates the French adjective, but it is *disparity* that translates the French noun. Rather than "*This translation contains many disparates," one would say "This translation contains many disparities." Just what is *disparity* in translation?

In translation studies, *disparity* describes stylistic incoherencies and discordances affecting the translated work. When compared to the original, the translation demonstrates a lack of linguistic, stylistic, and tonal unity, among others. The lack manifests in a juxtaposition of incompatible registers, in semantic distortion (*impropriétés*), anachronisms, archaisms, lexical inconsistencies, breaks from literary convention, an unwarranted conversational tone or dialect. In French, the word has been used indifferently in its singular and plural forms. The translator Paul-Louis Courier (1772–1825), for example, writes, "You find that I have completed Amyot's version [Longus's *Pastoral*] *with such skill* that one does not notice too much disparity between what is his and what I have added."[8] Marie Delcourt (1891–1979), translator of Euripides' complete dramatic works into French, sets the term against the notion of *homogeneity*: "Seventeenth century French classicism, mindful of homogeneity in all things, rejected disparity in any form" (1925, 13). As for the translator Edmond Cary, he wrote while keeping in mind the historians and critics who would eventually judge the translations of today: "It is not inconceivable that modern translators, who now seem so direct and authentic, will ring doubly false in the near future when the disparities they produce today are compounded with those arising when the acoustics inevitably change" (1963, 36). Although absent in specialized dictionaries, the term is nevertheless currency, we can see, among translators, critics, and translation historians.

The notion of *disparity* is one of the universals of translation, appearing in the discourse as frequently as Greimas's semantic isotopies, to name one example. All forms of translation are susceptible to disparity, be they source or target oriented, historic or contemporary. Spotting them is a matter of addressing larger units of signification, of examining their particularities systematically. A phrase removed from context is less likely to contain disparities. Here is a rather banal example. Let us say that an editor writes the acronym for the United Nations Education Science and Culture Organization in two, even three, different forms: UNESCO, U.N.E.S.C.O., Unesco. This kind of inconsistency is the result of editorial oversight. Disparities, as we will see later on, occur rather on the broader, stylistic level.

Moreover, disparity should not be confused with false sense, even nonsense, in translated works. No fewer than 100 gaffes of this sort have been counted in the French version of J.D. Salinger's *Catcher in the Rye* or *L'attrape-cœurs*. The translator confused *horserace* with *racehorse*, rendered one for the other. It seems that she also confused *terrific* and *figure* with their French cognates *terrible* (*fearsome, awesome*) and *figure* (*face*). "She had a terrific figure" thus became "*Elle avait un visage terrible" ("She had a fearsome face") (Brodin 1970, 336–37). Then there is the Russian poet, novelist, and translator Kornei Chukovsky (1882–1969), who spotted in many Russian translations of English and French works innumerable semantic errors similar to the ones inflicted on the French *Catcher in the Rye*. The Russian rendering of *une adresse de singe* left readers imagining a monkey's place of residence rather than its agility, the intended sense of *adresse* in this case. Another example is the *pont* (*deck*) of a ship, which became the Russian equivalent for *bridge*, not to mention the *plongeur à l'hôtel* (dishwasher) that became a *bather in a hotel* (Chukovsky 1984, 95).

It goes without saying that this sort of gaffe diminishes a translation's overall quality. But this does not necessarily imply disparity. False senses are, rather, the result of the translator's lapsed attention or insufficient knowledge. They point to a lack of training (an amateur or improviser) or experience (a novice), to an insufficient knowledge of the languages in question (a pseudo-bilingual), or to a failure to infer properly, to make appropriate contextual assumptions (an error in methodology or a false conception of translation). Precisely speaking, this is not a stylistic error, although in many pseudo-translations authors have been known to fabricate disparities to trick their readers into believing that they are reading a translation (Toury 1995, 212–15). In these cases, disparity is literary artifice, a rhetorical device.

Disparities are errors of an altogether different nature. In the ensemble of significations that make up the translated text, a disparity is both "out of place" (belonging to another *style* or *genre* of writing) and "out of nature" (an element differing in its very nature from those surrounding it). Chukovsky says it well: "The translator's art consists to a significant degree in being guided by a vital sense of style. . . . He who is insensitive to style has no right to undertake a translation: it would be like trying to reproduce an opera he has seen but not heard" (1984, 97). Grammar teaches us how to form and connect words, but there is no teaching the artist's creative agency of words, the very definition of style. Literary talent cannot be taught, even in creative writing programs. Style for the writer, just like colour for the painter, is a matter of perspective, vision. "It is an absolute way of looking at things," Flaubert said. Writing with style means understanding the "mechanics" of language and mastering its resources. Style links form with expression. To break form is to break style; to break style is to denature a piece of writing. Even Helen Tracy Lowe-Porter (1876–1963), translator of Thomas Mann, affirms that "The translation of a book which is a triumph of style in its own language, is always a piece of effrontery" (1973, xxv). Disparities are breaks in style. How and where such breaks occur is relative: one translation's disparity is not necessarily another's.

Perhaps the easiest type of disparity to spot in translated texts is the anachronism or archaism. In the second stanza of Hugh Hazelton's (2004) poem "Serra do Roncador," for example, the word *path* has been turned into *sente*, an archaism in French. Nothing in the original seems to justify this.

I am coming to you
  down from the mountains
  mist rising in myriad
  pillars from the jungle
	Je viens à toi
	  du fin haut des monts
	  dans la brume qui lève
	  entre les mille fûts de la jungle

I am coming to you
  on a path through tall, cooling palms
  and giant ferns
  smelling fresh with rain
	Je viens à toi
	  par fraîche sente sous hautes palmes
	  et fougères géantes
	  à l'odeur ravivée par la pluie

—translated by Laurent Lachance (ATTLC 2004)

The word *sente*, dating from the seventeenth century, is rather surprising here. So is the syntax of the verse, which has a medieval ring—"Nécessité fait gens méprendre / Et faim saillir le loup du bois" (Villon). The following versions, still by no means flawless, fare better by maintaining the simple vocabulary of the original and maintaining a unity of language and tone:[9]

Je m'avance vers toi
  du pied de la montagne
  la brume se lève myriades
  de piliers sortant de la jungle
Je m'avance vers toi
  par un sentier ombragé de grands
    palmiers
  et de fougères géantes
  sentant bon la pluie
	Je viens à toi
	  en dévalant la montagne
	  dans la brume qui, de la jungle
	  s'élève en myriades de piliers
	Je viens à toi
	  sur un chemin traversant les frais
	    palmiers
	  et les fougères géantes
	  à la senteur fraîche de pluie

—translated by André Debbané (ATTLC 2004)	—translated by Jean-Paul Daoust (ATTLC 2004)

Certain contemporary translators, trying to re-create a style or to apply their own style to a historical text, will try to paint with the colours of faraway times and places, those of the Homeric age, for example. Motivated by artistic intentions, they will juxtapose (often without knowing, I should say in their defence) a variety of incompatible elements: contemporary conversational registers, the language of medieval epic poetry, the noble tones of classical tragedy, a vocabulary dating to feudal times. All of this in an effort, quite commendable in itself, to ring archaic, rustic, to create the *illusion* of historical language and sensibilities. These are the snares awaiting the authors of so-called learned translations, like many of those published in nineteenth-century France—the period of historical translation—by translators such as Paul-Louis Courier, Émile Littré (1801–81),[10] and Charles-Marie Leconte de Lisle (1818–94).

Rare are those who avoid these pitfalls by translating through "coloured glasses" (Mounin 1994, 91). Unlike the *"cibliste"* group, who translate through clear glasses, tailoring their texts to the target language and culture, these *"sourcier"* translators strive to conserve the source text's foreignness, traces of its language, period, and culture. Through translucent yet coloured glasses, the text "reads like a translation," but this is a small price to pay for drawing the reader out of his familiar surroundings, sending him back to a more exotic time and place. It is easy to see how such translators risk filling their texts with all manner of disparities. Making assumptions about the mores and sensibilities of a remote civilization, and then transposing these assumptions coherently into a target text, comprise an artistic enterprise fraught with peril. It is difficult to avoid drawing on many and diverse periods of a language's history in the effort to generate a sense of exoticism. This is why so few translators achieve the tour de force of re-creating a work free of disparity, a work poetically coherent, relating to its source synchronically as well as diachronically.

Most of the deforming tendencies that Antoine Berman attributes to literary translation in *La traduction et la lettre ou l'auberge du lointain* describe disparities. These tendencies, we recall, include "rationalization, clarification, extension, refinement and vulgarization, qualitative and quantitative depreciation, homogenization, the destruction of rhythms, the destruction of underlying or supporting signifying systems, the destruction of internal text systems, the destruction of vernacular language, the destruction of idioms and idiotisms, the erasure of polyphony or language layering" (Berman 1999, 53).[11] Moreover, *cibliste* or "ethnocentric" translations are no less subject to disparity.

Friedrich Schleiermacher (1768–1834) also intuited the notion of disparity. On the subject of lexical systems circulating in a literary work like blood in a living organism, he warned translators against what he called a "colorful variety." The translator is to be praised if

> he succeeds in maintaining similarity with respect to the more important objects in specific writings (or even in individual parts of them only), so that no single word gets a multiplicity of quite different replacements, or so that a colorful variety does not prevail in the translation where in the original a clear relationship of expressions is presented without discontinuities.... (Schleiermacher 1992, 46)

Schleiermacher argued in favour of respecting the author's own lexical choices.

This is why Milan Kundera frequently tears into his translators. Put off by his repetitive style, they reflexively resort to synonymy. Repetition is viewed as "inelegant," something to be avoided at all costs, so they run to their thesauruses.[12] This reflex may be a way for the translator to show creativity. But its systematic application undermines the lexical systems underpinning the many themes crossing each other in the work. Every disruptive synonym is a disparity. This is why the author of *The Betrayed Testaments* asks the translator to respect "the author's personal style," "his supreme authority" in the matter, instead of bowing to "conventional style" (Kundera 1993, 132–34). This is because the literary work transgresses the conventional writing style found in pragmatic texts. For Kundera, there is only one rule: "a word is repeated because it is important, because it is meant to resound acoustically and symbolically through the paragraph, the page" (138). Consequently, it should be repeated in the translation. Style is the author's signature. Disparity is the mark of a bad forgery.

The risk of dissonance is just as great in translations produced collectively. Could several collaborators possibly possess the same understanding of a text, turn its style uniformly, coherently? "Having many translators on the same work results inevitably in dissonance" (Mayoux 1959, 80). Such an endeavour is hopeless if we define translation as the transmission of the original's message while conserving its singular style and force. This is the ideal. It is also translation's ontological paradox. The ambition most often fails, because "each text has a sound, a color, a movement, an atmosphere of its own" (Larbaud 1946, 69). To avoid disparity, the translator must adapt to the "particular" style of each author.

The idea may be a truism, but its practical consequences are still enormous, for "translating does not turn one language into another so much as it turns one style into another, one linguistic singularity into another linguistic singularity" (Rolin 2002, 54). One cannot dress every stranger in the same outfit. Neither can one go around mixing sartorial styles. Just how would someone look in a top hat, a ruff, a toga, and patent-leather shoes? Disparities often lend such a comical appearance to translations. And this is why it is difficult to correct translations and maintain their coherence. The Orientalist Jean-Louis Burnouf (1775–1844) was convinced: "I have never believed that a good translation could come of correcting a bad one. At the very least, one will never achieve by this means the same tonal unity and integral harmony essential to any creative work" (1933, xix).

As we have just seen, disrespecting the source text's lexical patterning can result in disparity. However, the latter can take other forms as well. We know, for example, that every metaphor in a work does not necessarily contribute to an overall aesthetic and that certain commonplace metaphors are better rendered by metaphors equally commonplace in the target language, so that readers of the latter will not afford them any special significance. Conversely, translating literally a metaphor of no aesthetic value often results in disparity. How many translators have succumbed to fascination and invested casual metaphors with undue stylistic importance? Under the spell of strange-seeming yet perfectly commonplace rhetoric, they see exotic wonders and take pains to transpose them in the target text, often violating the target language. Maurice Blanchot (1972, 173) is not the only one to have seen that "the language we translate appears richer in imagery and more concrete than the language into which we translate."

Here are a few examples. The French translator of George Szanto's novel *La condesa María Victoria* turns "For less than a blink, fear took Pitando's eyes" into "*Pendant moins d'un clignement d'œil, la peur s'empara des yeux de Pitando," a disconcertingly literal formulation, to say the least. Why not the much simpler "La peur se lit aussitôt dans les yeux de Pitando"? The same translator is behind *Le libraire a du flair*, the French version of Richard King's novel. He turns the bookseller's words "People think books walk into the store and float up onto the shelves" quite literally into "Ils [les livres] n'entrent pas tout seuls dans le magasin pour flotter dans les airs jusqu'aux rayons. . . ." Here as well the translator's abusive and awkward literalism creates disparity. Would the passage not have been better served by "Ils n'entrent pas tout seuls dans la librairie et ne se placent pas d'eux-mêmes, comme par magie, sur les rayons"? In the same detective novel, the author marks character dialogue with the usual "she said," "I responded," "I asked," "I told her." These verbs do not betray any attempt at stylistic effect. But, for whatever reason, the translator alternates between the common inverted tag "a-t-elle dit," "ai-je répondu," "ajouta-t-il," and the non-inverted tag "j'ai demandé," "j'ai répondu," "j'ai grimacé," as we see in the following passage: "'It's Sam, Sam Wiseman,' I told her, shaking her offered hand. 'Maybe you know me from the bookstore, Dickens & Company. I work there,' I added modestly" (King 2002, 234); translation: "Je m'appelle Sam, Sam Wiseman, *j'ai dit* en serrant la main tendue. Vous m'avez peut-être vu à la librairie Dickens & Company. C'est là que je travaille, *j'ai ajouté* modestement" (King 2003, 285; emphasis added). Why not "ai-je dit," "ai-je ajouté"? Over the long haul, the repetition of this type of disparity becomes irritating. And I could go on multiplying examples, showing how disparities occur in all lexical and discursive categories.

CONCLUSION

All things said, disparity, excepting its motivated use in pseudo-translations, affects the aesthetic and literary value of a work judged in the light of contemporary norms. The unity of the text is disrupted, and in the worst cases the result can be an aesthetically displeasing "piecemeal" or "patchwork." At the prosodic, rhythmic, acoustic, or "musical" levels (primarily of poetic texts), a disparity is dissonance, harmonic discord, the false note in the score. A lack of unity that disconcerts the reader, conflicts with his or her linguistic and aesthetic sensibility. Having closely examined translations from different historical periods, Georges Mounin (1910–93) was one of the first, if not the first, to reveal the problem's enormous scale. In his *Belles infidèles*, he asks translators to be conscious of disparity's depreciative effect on the quality of their work and to exercise utmost vigilance. For him, disparity is truly "endemic," a defect in the translator himself: *"This near total lack of receptiveness to disparity,"* Mounin (1994, 99) writes, "must be widely denounced, for it can be found everywhere among learned translators who, fascinated by isolated language problems, lose sight of the whole." However, learned translators are not the only ones who seem to be insensitive to disparity. Examination of all sorts of contemporary translated texts suggests that all translators are affected, to some extent, by this endemic defect.

When well executed, criticism uncovers "great translations," helps us to appreciate the subtleties involved in the translator's art, gives us an idea of the exceptional talent of those able to re-create, following the conventions of the art, the aesthetic and the poetic of a literary work. Sometimes the miracle does indeed happen. However, we must keep in mind that the standards of acceptability vary from period to period and from genre to genre. Yesterday's successful translation can be today's tissue of disparities (remember the anachronisms of seventeenth- and eighteenth-century French translations). This is translation's paradox. To the translations of yesterday, not only the standards of today should be applied.

NOTES

1   Unless otherwise specified, all quotations referencing works in a language other than English have been translated by Ryan Fraser, a professor at the School of Translation and Interpretation at the University of Ottawa.
2   Throughout history, theorists and practitioners have attested to this. I reference many of them in "Le sens à travers l'histoire de les traduction [...]" (Delisle 2005). Here is what two literary translators and contemporaries of George Sand (1804–76) have to say: "A literal translation is more satisfying to academics, but it is a dead translation" (Cary 1963, 32); "Literal translation is like to love for Marguerite Duras and a few others: necessary but impossible" (Barilier 1990, 17). "Some masterpieces are still buried under the icy shroud of literal translation" (Sand 1860, 106).
3   "The multiplication of these little bumps and jars [linguistic imprecision, the attribution of false meanings] creates a vague malaise, hard to define, that reminds one of the first symptoms of sea sickness. One might call it 'translation sickness'" (Gravier 1973, 42). Two years earlier, Jacques Olivier Grandjouan expressed a similar opinion in his *Linguicides:* "The accumulation of impropriety upon impropriety has the strangest effects" (1971, 207–08).
4   The word is absent in dictionaries specializing in literary terms (Dupriez 1984; Cuddon 1998; Gorp et al. 2001), in dictionaries of linguistics (Dubois

et al. 1994; Crystal 2003), and in dictionaries specializing in translation studies (Shuttleworth and Cowie 1997; Baker 1998; Delisle, Lee-Jahnke, and Cormier 1999).

5   *motley, ill assorted, patchwork, disjointed, discordant, dissonant, divergent, false, heterogeneous, sundry, incongruous.*
6   *assorted, harmonious, homogeneous.*
7   Which is not the case with the word *eclectic.*
8   Translation by Ryan Fraser; the original reads, "Vous trouvez que j'ai complété la version d'Amyot [La *Pastorale* de Longus] *si habilement,* dites-vous, qu'on *n'aperçoit point trop de disparate* entre ce qui est de lui et ce que j'y ai ajouté..." (Courier 1926, 80–81).
9   Twenty-four translators have tried their hand at this poem. For the word *path,* eleven chose *sentier,* six *chemin,* one *cheminer,* one *piste,* and two *sente.* The others didn't translate the word at all (ATTLC 2004).
10 On the subject of the historical reconstructionist Émile Littré, who translated Dante's *Inferno* into fourteenth-century *langue d'oïl* as if it were translated by a fourteenth-century translator (Littré 1847), Alain Rey (1970, 288) writes that "Romance scholars were quick to discover prosodic anomalies and linguistic oddities" (my translation). The philologist's examination of this sort of translation unearthed a viper's nest of disparities.
11 Translation by Ryan Fraser; the original reads "la rationalisation, la clarification, l'allongement, l'ennoblissement et la vulgarisation, l'appauvrissement qualitatif, l'appauvrissement quantitatif, l'homogénéisation, la destruction des rythmes, la destruction des réseaux signifiants sous-jacents, la destruction des systématismes textuels, la destruction (ou l'exotisation) des réseaux langagiers vernaculaires, la destruction des locutions et idiotismes, l'effacement des superpositions de langues."
12 Translators' views on the subject of repetition, Nitsa Ben-Ari (1998, 77) demonstrates, seem to be ambivalent and obey contradictory norms:

There is a tendency not to transfer original repetitions—not out of carelessness nor out of linguistic constraints, but out of normative stylistic considerations, on the assumption that repetitions are not 'elegant' and reflect a poor vocabulary; on the other hand, a seemingly contradictory phenomenon occurs, in which new repetitions are introduced by the translators.... New repetitions are added as a result of other normative considerations, like the wish to embellish or amplify the text.

It is therefore important to address the question of repetition while keeping in mind the target culture's standards of acceptability and the status (canonical or otherwise) of the work at hand.

REFERENCES

The American Heritage Dictionary of the English Language. 4th ed. http://www.bartleby.com/61/ (consulted June 6, 2004).
ATTLC. 2004. "Mots en mouvement." Association des traducteurs et traductrices littéraires du Canada, http://www.attlc-ltac.org/move.htm (June 21, 2004, version; consulted July 21, 2004).
Baker, Mona, ed. 1998. *The Routledge Encyclopedia of Translation Studies.* London: Routledge.
Barilier, Étienne. 1990. *Les belles fidèles: Petit essai sur la traduction.* Collection "CTL" 9. Lausanne: Centre de traduction littéraire, Université de Lausanne.
Ben-Ari, Nitsa. 1998. "The Ambivalent Case of Repetitions in Literary Translation: Avoiding Repetitions: A 'Universal' of Translation." *Meta* 43 (1): 68–78.
Berman, Antoine. 1995. *Pour une critique des traductions: John Donne.* Bibliothèque des idées. Paris: Gallimard.
———. 1999. *La traduction et la lettre ou l'auberge du lointain.* 1985. Paris: Seuil.
Blanchot, Maurice. 1972 [1949]. "Traduit de. . . ." *La part du feu.* Paris: Gallimard.
Brodin, Pierre. 1970. "Traduit de l'Américain." In *The World of Translation*, 335–41. New York: PEN American Center.
Burnouf, Jean-Louis. 1933. Introduction. *Histoires,* by Tacitus, trans. Henri Bornecque. Paris: Garnier.
Cary, Edmond. 1963. *Les grands traducteurs français.* Geneva: Librairie de l'Université Georg.
Chukovsky, K [Chukovskii, Kornei]. *Vysokoe iskusstvo [A High Art].* English translation: *The Art of Translation.* Trans. and ed. Lauren G. Leighton. Knoxville: University of Tennesee Press, 1984.
Courier, Paul-Louis. 1926. *Daphnis et Chloe ou les pastorales de Longus suivies des pamphlets.* Paris: Larousse.
Cuddon, John A. 1998. *A Dictionary of Literary Terms and Literary Theory.* 4th ed. Oxford: Blackwell.
Crystal, David. 2003. *A Dictionary of Linguistics and Phonetics.* Oxford: Blackwell.
Delcourt, Marie. 1925. *Étude sur les traductions des tragiques grecs et latins en France depuis la Renaissance.* Brussels: Lamertin.
Delisle, Jean. 2001. "L'évaluation des traductions par l'historien." *Meta* 46 (2): 209–26.
———. 2005. "Le sens à travers l'histoire de la traduction: de l'antiquité à la fin du xixe siècle." In *La théorie interprétative de la traduction: Regards croisés (vol. II),* ed. F. Israël and M. Lederer, 211–228. Paris: Paris: Minard.]

Delisle, Jean, Hannelore Lee-Jahnke, and Monique Cormier, eds. 1999. *Terminologie de la traduction / Translation Terminology / Terminología de la traducción / Terminologie der Übersetzung.* FIT Monograph Collection (1). Amsterdam: John Benjamins.

Dubois, Jean, et al. 1994. *Dictionnaire de linguistique et des sciences du langage.* Paris: Librairie Larousse.

Dupriez, Bernard. 1984. *GRADUS: Les procédés littéraires.* c. 1977. Collection "10/18" 1370. Paris: Union Générale d'Éditions.

Gorp, Hendrik van, et al., eds. 2001. *Dictionnaire des termes littéraires.* Paris: Honoré Champion.

Graf, Marion, ed. 1998. *L'écrivain et son traducteur en Suisse et en Europe.* Geneva: Zoé.

Grandjouan, Jacques Olivier. 1971. *Les linguicides.* Paris: Didier.

Gravier, Maurice. 1973. "La traduction des textes dramatiques." In *Exégèse et traduction*, ed. D. Seleskovitch. Spec. issue of *Études de linguistique appliquée* (12): 39–49.

Hazelton, Hugh. 2004. "Serra do Roncador." *Ellipse* 71: 32.

King, Richard. 2002. *That Sleep of Death.* Toronto: Dundurn Group.

———. 2003. *Le libraire a du flair.* Trans. François Barcelo. Montréal: Libre Expression.

Kundera, Milan. 1993. *Les testaments trahis.* Paris: Gallimard.

Larbaud, Valery. 1946. *Sous l'invocation de saint Jérôme.* Paris: Gallimard.

Littré, Émile. 1847. "La poésie homérique et l'ancienne poésie française." *Revue des deux mondes,* t. XIX, year 17 (July 1): 109–61.

Lowe-Porter, Helen Tracy. 1973. "Translator's Note." In *Buddenbrooks*, by Thomas Mann, trans. Helen Tracy Lowe-Porter, and *Lübeck As a Way of Life and Thought,* trans. Richard Winston and Clara Winston, xxv. New York: Alfred A. Knopf.

Mayoux, Jean-Jacques. 1959. "Enquête de la FIT sur la qualité des traductions." *Babel* 5 (2): 80.

Merriam-Webster Online Dictionary. http://www.m-w.com/cgi-bin/dictionary (2004 version; consulted June 30, 2004).

Mounin, Georges. 1994 [c. 1955]. *Les belles infidèles.* Collection "Étude de la traduction." Lille: Presses Universitaires de Lille.

Renken, Arno. 2002. *La représentation de l'étranger: Une réflexion herméneutique sur la notion de traduction.* Collection "CTL" 42. Lausanne: Centre de traduction littéraire.

Rey, Alain. 1970. *Littré, l'humaniste et les mots.* Collection "Les essais" 150. Paris: Gallimard.

Rolin, Olivier. 2002. "Écriture et traduction." In *Du pareil au meme: L'auteur face à son traducteur,* ed. Henri Awaiss et al., 53–54. Collection "Sources et Cibles." Beyrouth: ETIB, Université Saint-Joseph.

Salinger, J.D. 1951a. *The Catcher in the Rye.* Boston: Little, Brown.
———. 1951b. *L'attrape-coeurs.* Trans. Annie Saumont. Paris: Robert Laffont.
Sand, George. 1860 [*c.* 1856]. "À Monsieur Régnier." In *Théâtre de George Sand,* t. 3: 97–109. Paris: Michel Lévy; Leipzig: Alphonse Durr.
Schleiermacher, Friedrich. 1992. "On the Different Methods of Translating." In *Theories of Translation,* trans. Waltraud Bartscht, ed. Rainer Schulte, 36–54. Chicago: University of Chicago Press.
Shuttleworth, Mark, and Moira Cowie. 1997. *Dictionary of Translation Studies.* Manchester: St. Jerome Publishing.
Szanto, George. 2001. *The Condesa of M.* Toronto: Cormorant Books.
———. 2003. *La condesa María Victoria.* Trans. François Barcelo. Montréal: XYZ éditeur.
Toury, Gideon. 1995. *Descriptive Translation Studies and Beyond.* Translation Library 4. Amsterdam: John Benjamins.
Trésor de la langue française informatisé. http://atilf.atilf.fr/tlf.htm (October 12, 2002, version; consulted June 6, 2004).

CHAPTER 12

TRANSLATION MEMORY AND "TEXT"

LYNNE BOWKER

INTRODUCTION

Translation technology has been increasing in popularity over the past decade. As the volume of text to be translated increases, so does the pressure on translators to be able to work quickly and efficiently. Many translators are turning to technology in the hope that it can help them to increase their productivity. Whenever a new way of working is introduced, there will inevitably be effects on both the process and the product. This article will focus on the effects that one particular type of translation technology—a tool known as a translation memory (TM)—can have on text. In recent years, a number of observations have been made with regard to the impact that TM tools can have on the quality of target texts. A few of these observations have been made by researchers, but many have been pointed out by practising translators or localization specialists who have employed these tools in their work.[1] In this article, I will summarize these observations and add some of my own to present an overview of how text can be affected by TM tools. The article begins with a brief description of what is understood by the notion of "text"; it then goes on to consider why text is relevant to translation. Next the TM tool is introduced, and the basic way in which it works is explained. This is followed by a discussion of some of the ways in which the use of TMs has had an impact on text and translation. The paper closes with a discussion about new developments in the field of translation technology that have been inspired by experiences with TM systems.

WHAT IS "TEXT"?

Lexical items and syntactic structures are the building blocks of language. According to Mona Baker (1992, 111), they have "meaning potential," but this potential is realized only in text. Similarly, M.A.K. Halliday and Ruqaiya Hasan (1976, 25) describe text as "the basic unit of meaning in language." Text has features of organization; it is not a random collection of sentences and paragraphs. Rather, the sentences and paragraphs depend on one another—they have connections within and among them. There are various kinds of connections, including both cohesion and coherence.

Cohesion refers to the network of surface relations that link words or expressions to one another (i.e., lexical or grammatical dependencies). Meanwhile, coherence is the network of conceptual relations that underlies the surface text (i.e., semantic or meaning dependencies). Cohesion is a property of text, whereas coherence is a facet of the reader's evaluation of a text. The mere presence of cohesive markers (e.g., pronouns, deictics, lexical repetition, synonymy, substitution, ellipsis, conjunction, punctuation) cannot create a coherent text. For a text to be coherent, the cohesive markers must reflect semantic relations that make sense. Nevertheless, cohesive markers are valuable because they can facilitate the interpretation of the underlying semantic relations.

WHAT IS THE RELEVANCE OF "TEXT" FOR TRANSLATION?

The aim of a translator, in most cases, is to achieve equivalence at text level. Translators typically want their translations to be accepted as texts in their own right, and they may not even want these texts to be recognized as translations. To achieve text-level equivalence, translators clearly have to work with lexis and syntax, but it is also essential for them to view the text as a whole. In the words of Albrecht Neubert (1999, 123), "The way a word has to be rendered is a function of its role in the text. . . . Translating them [words] involves translators taking both the lexical and the textual system requirements into account." To understand the message contained in the source text (ST), translators must read the entire text through at least once before beginning to translate. When it comes to producing a target text (TT), translators must keep in mind that features of text organization may be language and culture specific. For instance, languages may have different strategies for achieving cohesion, and the overall level of cohesion that is desired may even differ between languages. As part of the translation process, translators need to adjust the organizational features of the ST to create a TT that meets expectations of the way in which texts are organized in the target language. According to Baker (1992, 112), when these organizational features are not adjusted, readers are often able to identify the text as a translation, even though it appears to be lexically and grammatically "normal."

WHAT IS A TRANSLATION MEMORY TOOL?

A TM is essentially a type of linguistic database used to store STs alongside their translations. The translations in question have been produced by human translators, and the TM makes it possible to retrieve sections of previously translated texts in order to "recycle" these translations into a new TT. Detailed descriptions of how TMs work can be found in a number of different places in the literature (e.g., Bowker 2002; Somers 2003), so I will provide here only a brief summary of the most salient points.

The data in a conventional TM are organized in a specific way. STs and TTs are first divided up into segments, which typically correspond to sentences or sentence-like units (e.g., headings, tables in a cell, items in a list). Corresponding segments from STs and TTs are aligned or linked together and stored in the TM database as translation units, as illustrated in Figure 1.

When a translator receives a new ST to translate, the TM system begins by dividing this new text up into segments. Then the TM

Figure 1: Sample translation units stored in a TM database

Translation unit 1	EN	**Strikes and lockouts**
	FR	**Grèves et lock-outs**
Translation unit 2	EN	For the duration of this agreement, the employer and the association agree as follows.
	FR	Pendant la durée de la présente convention, l'employeur et l'association conviennent de ce qui suit.

automatically compares each segment from the new ST against the source language segments stored in the TM database. If it finds a matching segment, the TM system retrieves the relevant translation unit and presents it to the translator, who can accept, modify, or reject the proposed translation.

There are a number of different types of matching segments that can be retrieved by a TM system. Two of the most common include exact matches and fuzzy matches. An exact match is one that is perfectly identical (with regard to the appearance of the character string) to the segment from the new ST that is to be translated. A fuzzy match is a partial match. In other words, the new segment and the segment retrieved from the database have some part(s) in common, as shown in Figure 2. The general idea is that, with a bit of editing, it may be possible to reuse at least some of the previously translated text in the new translation. The user can set the threshold for a fuzzy match anywhere between one percent and ninety-nine percent. Most users tend to work with a threshold in the area of sixty-five percent to seventy percent because, if the threshold is set too high, potentially useful matches may not be retrieved, and if the threshold is set too low the matches that are retrieved may not be very helpful.

Figure 2: Example of a fuzzy match retrieved from a TM database with differences underlined

New ST segment to be translated	EN	The employer shall not <u>order</u> a lockout, and members of the <u>organization</u> shall not take any strike action, <u>work slowdown, or work stoppage</u>.
Fuzzy match retrieved from TM database	EN	The employer shall not <u>call</u> a lockout, and <u>the</u> members of the <u>as</u>sociation shall not take any <u>form of</u> strike action, <u>work stoppage, or work slowdown</u>.
	FR	L'employeur ne déclarera aucun lock-out, et les membres de l'association ne déclencheront aucune forme de grève, d'arrêt de travail, ou de ralentissement de travail.

HOW HAS "TEXT" BEEN AFFECTED BY TRANSLATION MEMORY TOOLS?

Now that we have a basic understanding of how a TM tool operates, let us consider the impact that such tools can have on text. The first thing to emphasize is that TMs are not intelligent tools. They operate on the basis of character string matching. Therefore, when a match from the TM database is presented as being 100 percent identical to the new ST segment, this means that the character string in question is identical, but semantics and context are not taken into account. Problems could arise, for example, in the case of polysemy. A segment such as "Empty the pipe" would have a different meaning, and therefore a different translation, in a text about plumbing (pipe = *tuyau*) than it would in a text about smoking (pipe = *pipe*). The correct concept would likely have been made clear in a previous part of the text, but since the sentence from the TM database is presented out of context there is no way for the translator to refer back to it.

Another important point to remember is that texts as such are not stored in the TM database. As described in the previous section, the STs and TTs are divided up into segments, and the corresponding source and target language pairs are stored together as a translation unit. Each unit is stored in isolation—once it has been removed from the text, there is no way for the translator to find out which text it originated in or what its former position was in that text (e.g., whether it was sentence three or sentence seventeen). In the words of Catherine Arrouart and Claude Bédard (2001, 30), a TM is actually a memory of sentences out of context. This can be problematic because, as previously noted, sentences in a text generally depend on each other in various ways. For instance, when we read or write the third sentence in a text, we can refer back to information already presented in the first two sentences, which means that it is possible to use pronouns, deictics, and other references. However, if we take the third sentence in isolation, then the antecedents of such references may not be clear.

Furthermore, because languages do not have a one-for-one correspondence or the same stylistic requirements, individual sentences in a TT may not depend on each other in precisely the same way in which individual sentences in the ST do. As described by Neubert (1999, 127), "the translation is a new text buzzing with words that relate to those of the original not only as individual items but also as pointers to a complex and total textual experience." Similarly, Geneviève Roux-Faucard (2005, 205)[2] points out that translators who are trying to convey the overall message of a text might ideally choose to map information to the TT sentences in a way that differs from how that information was originally organized in the ST sentences. In this way, two texts that can be considered to be equivalent when taken as a whole may not consist of individual pairs of equivalent sentences. To translate the overall message of the text, translators often need to work outside the artificial boundaries of sentences, so the sentence-by-sentence approach imposed by TMs may not be conducive to effective translation of the text's message as a whole.

Because TM tools process a series of sentences, rather than a text, translators sometimes react by using what Mogensen (2000, 28) refers to as "Orwellian linguistics" to maximize recyclability; the reference is to George Orwell's book *1984*, in which the language "Newspeak" is "cutting the language down to the bone." Mogensen suggests that TMs are not only changing the way in which translators work but also impacting the resulting translations. For instance, translators may choose to structure the sentences in the TT in a way that follows the structure of the ST. This might include translating one ST sentence by one TT sentence, rather than taking a long ST sentence and splitting it into several shorter TT sentences (or combining several short ST sentences into one long sentence in the TT). It could also include following the syntax of an ST segment, such as using the passive voice in the TT if it was used in the ST. Other tactics include the avoidance of synonyms and of pronouns or other referents, which creates what Mattias Heyn (1998, 135) refers to as "peep-hole translations." Instead, lexical items are repeated. While lexical repetition can be used as a cohesive device (Halliday and Hasan 1976, 278), it is not normally used to the exclusion of all others. Even within a given language, different text types vary in style and in the nature and density of their cohesive ties. The general result of Orwellian linguistics is a text that is inherently less cohesive or coherent, less readable, and of a lesser overall quality. It may be grammatically correct, but it risks containing oversimplified syntax, monotonous rhythm, and a lack of diversity.

Consistency is often promoted as a benefit of using TMs. However, Magnus Merkel (1998) conducted a survey of technical translators using TMs to see if they felt that such consistency was always desirable. The translators who were surveyed warned that a proposed match must always be evaluated within the new context as it may not always be automatically acceptable. In particular, they advised using caution before applying "consistent" translations in different structural contexts (e.g., in a sentence versus in a heading versus in a table cell).

In fact, TMs may even hinder consistency in some cases. A TM may contain texts that were written by different authors for different clients and subsequently translated by different translators. The terminology preferred by one client may not be the same as—or indeed appropriate for—the documents of another. In addition, the terminology in some fields evolves quickly, so that, even if a text contained appropriate terminology when it was initially stored in a TM, this terminology may have changed by the time a translator consults the TM for help with a new translation. The translator therefore risks incorporating outdated terminology into a new TT. If a translator consults a TM and merges terminology from a variety of different documents into the new TT, then the translator risks creating what is sometimes referred to as a terminology "train wreck" (Topping 2000).

A similar observation is made by Bédard (2000), who notes that not only individual terms but also entire sentences can be misused to create a new TT. Each text and each translator will have a different style, and when sentences from a variety of texts are brought together, the resulting text could be a stylistic hodgepodge that Bédard refers to as a "sentence salad." This is similar to the notion of *disparity* described by Jean Delisle (p. 162 in this volume). According to Delisle, disparities are breaks in style: "*disparity* describes stylistic incoherencies and discordances affecting the translated work. When compared to the original, the translation demonstrates a lack of linguistic, stylistic, and tonal unity, among others."[3] Using a fashion analogy, Delisle (p. 167) compares a disparate translation to someone wearing a mixture of sartorial styles—"a top hat, a ruff, a toga, and patent-leather shoes." He goes on to note that translations produced collectively are particularly susceptible to disparity. In the case of a translation produced with the help of a TM, it may be technically true to say that one translator was ultimately responsible for producing the target text; however, if that translator recycled material that was stored in the TM by other translators, then the resulting text will reflect the different styles of these previous translators. It is highly unlikely that the original source text has been created by simply cutting and pasting together individual sentences taken from a range of other documents, so it is questionable whether this approach should be used to produce a TT, which is also a text in and of itself.

Another problem that may arise when working with a TM is that the translator may be influenced by the segment presented by the system.

In other words, after seeing a suggestion presented by the TM, it may be difficult for the translator to think of a different way of expressing that notion. The translator may therefore use the suggested translation even if it does not fit very well into the text as a whole. This may be exacerbated in cases where translators are working under extreme time pressures, when it is tempting to incorporate a suggestion that is "good enough" rather than composing one that is "good." A text containing one or two "good enough" sentences might still be acceptable on the whole; however, a text composed primarily of "good enough" sentences might fall considerably short of the mark.

Lack of experience may also be a factor that causes some novice translators to be unduly influenced by the suggestions presented by the TM. A novice may not have the confidence to question the suitability of a proposal, particularly if the use of the TM has been mandated by the client or company. An experiment conducted by Lynne Bowker (2005) revealed that both time pressures and lack of translation experience can be factors that lead translators to incorporate inappropriate TM suggestions into the TT. Proper training is therefore essential.

Lack of training or understanding of how TM systems work can lead to other problems as well. Lanctôt (2001, 30) recounts the following scenario where multiple translators are sharing a single TM over a network. It may be that translator A, for example, works by ploughing through a text to complete a full rough draft, and he then goes back over the text a second and third time to clean up any outstanding problems (e.g., terminological, stylistic). In contrast, translator B's approach is to go more slowly, doing terminological research and addressing stylistic concerns as he goes along. In Lanctôt's scenario, translator B is frustrated by the suggestions proposed by the TM—many of which were produced as part of translator A's first rough draft and should not have been stored in the TM in the first place.

A number of the issues raised above lead to the question of TM database development and maintenance. To increase the chance of getting a match, the TM databases should be as large as possible. However, to improve the quality of a match, it makes sense to create a database of texts that are as similar as possible with regard to subject matter, terminology, style, and text type. These two requirements are often at odds with one another. To build a large database, texts would be gathered from different authors/translators, different text types, et cetera. This approach can lead to problems of terminological "train

Translation Memory and "Text"

wrecks" and "sentence salads," among others. In contrast, if one were to restrict the contents of a TM to texts produced by a single author/translator and texts of a specific type, then the TM database might contain only a handful of texts and produce very few matches. Balance and good judgment seem to be the keys here.

With regard to maintenance, it is important to keep in mind that information stored in a TM has been produced by humans, and it is not necessarily error free. Lanctôt (2001, 30) provides the following account of a translator who carefully stores all his translations in a TM but who does not update the contents to reflect corrections made by the client to the final document. When the client sends a document that closely resembles a version of a document previously translated the year before, the translator uses the TM and blithely reproduces the same errors in the new translation. The client is irritated because the same passages that were corrected last year need to be corrected again. This is not the kind of added value that the client was looking for. In addition, as noted above, there could be cases where a translation was indeed correct when it was initially entered into the database, but it may become outdated over time (e.g., if the terminology changes).

In cases where the commissioner of an ST knows that the text is intended for translation, and that this translation will be done with the help of a TM, the commissioner may request that the ST author write this text using a "controlled language," which means a language that uses a reduced vocabulary and syntax. Controlled languages have been used for some time with machine translation systems (e.g., Lockwood 2000); however, it is clear that they can also be used with TM systems in order to increase the number of matches found. In this way, TMs are affecting not only the way in which TTs are produced but also the way in which STs are written.

CONCLUDING REMARKS

The above discussion of TMs and their impact on translation may lead readers to believe that such tools have no place in translation, which is, after all, concerned primarily with the production of texts. However, this may be too drastic an assumption. Clearly, such tools are not appropriate for the production of all types of text; however, there are some translation jobs for which they could prove to be useful. For instance, TMs have already proven to be valuable in helping to translate updated versions of technical documents, such as computer manuals, where only a small percentage of the document changes from one version to the next. Identifying the precise characteristics of texts that are amenable to translation with the help of TMs is an area currently under investigation (e.g., Circé 2005), but more research is needed.

Another point that can be considered is whether or not all translations need to be of the highest quality. Bédard (2000) proposes that translation jobs could be classified into one of three categories: prestige quality, certified quality, and industrial quality. The last of these, he argues, could be done with the help of tools such as TMs. This proposal is in line with findings reported by a number of researchers working with machine translation systems who observed that, for certain types of texts, clients are very willing to accept a lower quality in return for a lower price or faster turnaround time (e.g., Hutchins 2001; O'Hagan and Ashworth 2002, 154). In fact, as pointed out by John Hutchins (2001), it is typically the translators themselves, not the clients, who are resistant to the idea of poorer-quality translations. Clearly, professional pride is important; however, in the current climate, where the demand for translation far exceeds the number of available translators (ABI 2002, 2–8), it may be necessary to be more selective about which types of texts are deserving of high-quality human translation and which can be reasonably handled with the help of tools such as TMs.

Additional research on issues such as the ideal unit of segmentation could also mitigate the negative impact that such tools can have on text. Bert Esselink (2000, 363), for example, suggests that the paragraph, rather than the sentence, might make a better unit of segmentation. If paragraph-based segments were employed, then translators could feel free to use references or to split or join sentences within a paragraph. It is probable that fewer matches would be retrieved from the TM for paragraph-based segments; however, if a match were retrieved, then it would likely require less editing than a sentence-based match, and because a greater amount of context is preserved the resulting translation would likely be more coherent and readable.

We should also keep in mind that these TM systems are the first generation of tools of this type. Their development represents a breakthrough in translation technology, but the research will not stop here. Now that translators have been using these tools for a few years, observations such as those summarized in this paper can hopefully be used to bring about improvements in the next generation of TMs.

For instance, Elliott Macklovitch and Graham Russell (2000, 145) have already suggested that it would be useful to build a feature into TMs that would allow the original text to be reassembled from its constituent sentences. In this way, the translator would be able to refer to a larger context when evaluating the appropriateness of a translation unit for inclusion in a new TT.

The value of having a complete text, rather than a series of independently stored sentences, has also inspired the creation of another type of translation technology, sometimes called a corpus-based or bitext tool.[4] While it does not fall under the narrow definition of TM that applies to the conventional tools (i.e., a tool that maintains a database of SL and TL sentence pairs), it does fall under a broader definition proposed by Macklovitch and Russell (2000, 137), who regard a TM simply as "an archive of past translations structured in such a way as to promote translation reuse."

In a corpus-based tool, the overall "text" is preserved. Corresponding segments of STs and TTs may still be aligned at the sentence level, but it is the complete text that is stored in the database rather than a series of sentence pairs. Because the texts have not been divided into segments, these tools typically operate by searching for matching character strings of any length (e.g., from a single word to an entire text). When a match is found between a character string in the new ST and one in the bitext database, the matching portion of the previous translation is highlighted for the translator's reference, but it remains within its full-text context.

In closing, it is worth noting that even translators who do not use TMs may fall victim to disparity. In fact, Delisle (p. 169 in this volume) suggests that disparity is an endemic problem that affects all translations to some extent. However, unless a translator is vigilant, the use of a TM could exacerbate this problem. I should therefore emphasize that TM tools are designed to help, not to replace, translators. Translators who want to make intelligent use of such tools need proper training and must use their judgment about whether and how to apply such tools to the translation of a given text.

NOTES

1   Observations made by practitioners have been reported in a number of magazines aimed primarily at language professionals, such as *Circuit*

(e.g., Lanctôt 2001), the magazine produced by the Ordre des traducteurs, terminologues et interprètes agréés du Québec (OTTIAQ); *Traduire* (e.g., Bédard 2000), produced by the Société française des traducteurs (SFT); or magazines such as *Language International* (e.g., Mogensen 2000) or *Multilingual Computing and Technology* (e.g., Topping 2000).

2   The original French text by Roux-Faucard is as follows: "les traductions ne reproduisent pas un découpage du sens déjà effectué par la succession des phrases du texte original, mais restructurent fortement et diversement son organisation : pour une même unité de sens, la formulation équivalente peut donc figurer à des places très différentes à l'intérieur du segment traduit, voire dans le segment précédent ou le segment suivant."

3   Although Delisle is discussing literary translation in particular, I believe that this concept could be applied to translation in general.

4   Examples of some corpus-based tools, which have varying degrees of automation, include MultiTrans (www.MultiCorpora.ca), LogiTerm/ LogiTrans (www.Terminotix.com), and Find (www.Beetext.com).

REFERENCES

Allied Business Intelligence (ABI). 2002. *Language Translation, Localization, and Globalization: World Market Forecasts, Industry Drivers, and eSolutions.* Oyster Bay, NJ: ABI.

Arrouart, Catherine, and Claude Bédard. 2001. "Éloge du bitexte." *Circuit* 73: 30.

Baker, Mona. 1992. *In Other Words: A Coursebook on Translation.* London: Routledge.

Bédard, Claude. 2000. "Mémoire de traduction cherche traducteur de phrases. . . ." *Traduire* 186: 41–49.

Bowker, Lynne. 2002. *Computer-Aided Translation Technology: A Practical Introduction.* Ottawa: University of Ottawa Press.

———. 2005. "Productivity vs Quality? A Pilot Study on the Impact of Translation Memory Systems." *Localisation Focus* 4 (1): 13–20.

Circé, Karine. 2005. "Traduction automatique, mémoire de traduction, ou traduction humaine? Proposition d'une approche pour déterminer la meilleure méthode à adopter, selon le texte." MA thesis, University of Ottawa.

Esselink, Bert. 2000. *A Practical Guide to Localization.* Amsterdam: John Benjamins.

Halliday, M.A.K., and Ruqaiya Hasan. 1976. *Cohesion in English.* London: Longman.

Heyn, Mattias. 1998. "Translation Memories: Insights and Prospects." In *Unity in Diversity? Current Trends in Translation Studies*, ed. L. Bowker, M. Cronin, D. Kenny, and J. Pearson, 123–36. Manchester: St. Jerome Publishing.

Hutchins, John. 2001. "Machine Translation and Human Translation: In Competition or in Complementation?" *International Journal of Translation* 13 (1–2): 5–20.

Lanctôt, François. 2001. "Splendeurs et petites misères . . . des mémoires de traduction." *Circuit* 72: 30.

Lockwood, Rose. 2000. "Machine Translation and Controlled Authoring at Caterpillar." In *Translating into Success: Cutting-Edge Strategies for Going Multilingual in a Global Age,* ed. Robert C. Sprung, 187–202. Amsterdam: John Benjamins.

Macklovitch, Elliott, and Graham Russell. 2000. "What's Been Forgotten in Translation Memory." In *Envisioning Machine Translation in the Information Future,* ed. J.S. White, 137–46. Berlin: Springer.

Merkel, Magnus. 1998. "Consistency and Variation in Technical Translation: A Study of Translators' Attitudes." In *Unity in Diversity? Current Trends in Translation Studies,* ed. L. Bowker, M. Cronin, D. Kenny, and J. Pearson, 137–49. Manchester: St. Jerome Publishing.

Mogensen, Else. 2000. "Orwellian Linguistics." *Language International* 12 (5): 28–31.

Neubert, Albrecht. 1999. "Words and Texts—Which Are Translated? A Study in Dialectics." In *Word, Text, Translation,* ed. Gunilla Anderman and Margaret Rogers, 119–28. Clevedon: Multilingual Matters.

O'Hagan, Minako, and David Ashworth. 2002. *Translation-Mediated Communication in a Digital World.* Clevedon: Multilingual Matters.

Roux-Faucard, Geneviève. 2005. "Une didactique de la traduction à partir des langues périphériques: Le 'régime spécial' à l'ÉSIT. " *Meta* 50 (1): 194–209.

Somers, Harold. 2003. "Translation Memories." In *Computers and Translation: A Translator's Guide,* ed. Harold Somers, 31–46. Amsterdam: John Benjamins.

Topping, Suzanne. 2000. "Sharing Translation Database Information: Considerations for Developing an Ethical and Viable Exchange of Data." *Multilingual Computing and Technology* 11 (5): 59–61.

CHAPTER 13

AN EVALUATION METHODOLOGY FOR COMPARING TWO APPROACHES TO SEARCH AND RETRIEVAL IN TRANSLATION MEMORY DATABASES

FRANCIE GOW

INTRODUCTION

Translation memory (TM) tools help human translators to recycle portions of their previous work by storing previously translated material. This material is aligned, which means that segments of the source texts are linked with their equivalents in the corresponding target texts. When a translator uses a TM tool to translate a new text, the tool identifies similarities between segments of the new text and the source texts that are stored. The translator may then choose to insert or adapt the previous translation of that segment. Therefore, search and retrieval functions are an essential component of all TM tools. However, not all TM tools approach these tasks in the same way.

In conventional TM tools, the aligned texts are divided into sentence-level source and target translation units for storage in the database. Each sentence of a new source text is compared with the units stored in the database, and the system proposes matches that are exact or similar. This is referred to as a sentence-based approach to search and retrieval. A different and more recently developed approach involves storing full source- and target-text pairs (known as bitexts) in the database and identifying identical character strings of any length. This is referred to as a character-string-within-a-bitext (CSB)-based approach to search and retrieval.

Because the second approach is more recent, traditional techniques for evaluating TM tools do not take into account this fundamental difference (e.g., Benis 1999, 2000; Höge 2002; Zerfaß 2002). This paper presents a new evaluation methodology that can be used to compare the two approaches to search and retrieval fairly and systematically, first by defining "usefulness" as a measurable attribute, then by measuring the usefulness of the output of each approach in an identical translation context.[1] For the practical experimentation, TRADOS[2] will be used as a representative example of a TM that uses the sentence-based approach, while tools using the CSB-based approach will be represented by MultiTrans.[3]

DESIGNING A COMPARATIVE EVALUATION METHODOLOGY

According to the Expert Advisory Group on Language Engineering Standards (EAGLES 1995), a good evaluation methodology should have the following characteristics:

- validity: end users should be able to infer from the measurement values obtained what effect the tool will have on their productivity;
- reliability: an evaluation should produce similar or identical results when repeated in the same context by different evaluators;
- efficient applicability: the evaluation should be performable with the least effort possible, especially by the end users.

These characteristics were prioritized in that order for this project. Although TRADOS and MultiTrans were chosen as representative tools for each approach, the methodology had to be applicable to other tools as well. Finally, usefulness had to be defined as a measurable attribute.

In this methodology, usefulness is defined as a function of validity, time saved, and time spent. Usefulness and time savings are overlapping concepts. If a match is invalid in a given context, then it is useless to the user and automatically wastes time. This is serious, since TM technology is supposed to accelerate the translation process. However, the inverse is not necessarily true. A valid match is useful if and only if it saves time in terms of research, typing, or revision. Even a valid match is useless if it takes more time to find and retrieve it than to translate the segment from scratch.

In designing a methodology to compare the usefulness of output from sentence-based searches versus CSB-based searches, it is important to account for the relationship between validity and time. For any given unit of text to be translated, each tool will produce one of five results:

(1) no proposal;
(2) an invalid proposal (which necessarily wastes time);
(3) a valid proposal that wastes time;
(4) a valid proposal that has no effect on time; and
(5) a valid proposal that saves time.

Category 5 is the only desirable result. Category 1 cannot be measured, Category 4 can be ignored, and Categories 2 and 3 must be penalized. The tool will require a certain amount of effort by the user to generate results even in Category 5, and this effort must also be considered (in terms of time).

PREVIOUS WORK IN TM EVALUATION: OBJECTIVE AND SUBJECTIVE APPROACHES

Some researchers have used the concept of edit distance to evaluate the usefulness of matches proposed by a TM tool (e.g., Simard and Langlais 2001). The US-based National Institute of Standards and Technology defines edit distance as the "smallest number of insertions, deletions, and substitutions required to change one string . . . into another" ("Levenshtein Distance" 1999). A small edit distance between two strings implies similarity.

Edit distance could be used to approximate the usefulness of proposed translations by measuring them against a model translation. The advantages of this approach are reliability and efficient applicability (after the initial cost and effort of programming an algorithm). The disadvantage is its questionable validity, since there is no one agreed formula to measure edit distance, and it is unrealistic to assume that only one model translation is possible.

The subjective approach involves human translators manually applying a rating system to each match proposed by a given system (e.g., Somers 1999).[4] The advantage of this approach is its validity, since humans are better than computers at identifying useful matches.

Although there may be slight variations between the results, a group of evaluators will likely agree on the majority of cases.

Disadvantages include the time required to perform the evaluation and the fact that the rating can only be applied *after* the evaluator has seen the proposals made by the tool. One of the factors that evaluators must consider in deciding the usefulness of a proposal is whether they already knew the information or whether they would have had to spend time looking for it. Once a proposal is in their heads, it is impossible to mentally "erase" it, making it difficult in many cases to judge whether they would have considered that suggestion before it was proposed.

SOLUTION: A MODIFIED SUBJECTIVE APPROACH

Because validity was a high priority, I favoured a modified version of the subjective approach. The biggest problem that needed to be solved was the difficulty for evaluators in determining the usefulness of a proposal after being influenced by that proposal. The solution involved shifting the determination of usefulness to an earlier stage of the evaluation process, before the application of the TM tools.

A mark-up procedure was developed in which the evaluator reviews the input text independently of the TM tool and marks items (terms, titles, phrases, sentences, paragraphs, etc.) that would require research in a real translation situation (see Figure 1). This step provides an unbiased snapshot of which proposals one particular translator would consider useful, against which the output of the tools can be measured. This snapshot would vary depending on the translator creating it, but for comparative purposes it is enough that the same snapshot be applied

Figure 1: An extract from marked-up text; underlined sections correspond to "questions" to which the translator is hoping to find "answers" in the TM

Descriptions de tâches
Directeur régional, services administratifs et installations (AS-07)
Résultats axés sur le service à la clientèle :
Assurer la gestion et la direction des programmes et services suivants au sein du Ministère : immobilier, télécommunications, acquisitions des biens et services (installations), services administratifs (bureautique, courrier, gestion de l'information, formulaires, politiques environnementales).

An Evaluation Methodology

to each tool being tested. It essentially provides a checklist of questions to be answered. Scores can be generated depending on whether tool X answers each question completely, partially, or not at all, and these scores can be compared formally with a similar set of scores generated for tool Y.

PRETRANSLATION PROCESS

In the next step, new texts are "pretranslated" in each tool. The evaluator proceeds through the text, allowing the TM tool to propose matches. The evaluator inserts the most suitable option, if any, into the text. This involves human judgment, but most translators would get similar results. The evaluator does not edit the output or perform any manual translation.

The resulting output in both systems is partially translated text. In TRADOS, some sentences will be in the source language, while others will be in the target language. The MultiTrans output will still be in the source language, with target-language text strings dispersed throughout. The challenge here is comparing these two different forms of output fairly.

In TRADOS, it is always worthwhile to check for possible matches, since an entire sentence replaced in the text saves time, even when the translator already knows the translation. In MultiTrans, it is not necessarily worthwhile for a user to check the database for matches for a short string that the user already knows how to translate. The evaluator therefore cannot indiscriminately check the database for every single chunk for which a match exists, since this does not reflect the real use of the tool.

This is where the marked-up text described in the previous section is useful. When the tool indicates that a string in the input text is in the database, the evaluator can consult the marked-up text to see whether that particular part is marked. If so, then the database should be checked. If not, then it can be assumed that the translator can translate that section manually in less time than it takes to check the database and insert a match. In that case, the string should be ignored.

SCORING SYSTEM

Most evaluation methods are biased toward the sentence-based approach. If a sentence is evaluated in MultiTrans, and three separate "chunks" of that sentence are replaced, does that constitute a single unit or three? To solve this problem, the scoring system was divided into two parts: a time gain score and a time loss penalty. They are combined to create a composite score. The time gain score (score 1) was given twice the weight of the time loss penalty (score 2) in calculating the composite score (score 3). The tool that generates the highest composite score for a particular set of texts will extract the most useful information for similar jobs.

The time gain score is applied to each sentence (or heading) of the input text that contains target text, whether the entire sentence appears in the target language or just parts of it. In this case, the same scoring table can be applied to the output of both tools, as illustrated in Table 1.

Table 1: Score 1— Time gain score in TRADOS and MultiTrans

Information provided by TRADOS or MultiTrans	Score
Multiple-word unit inserted, no changes (n = # of words in source language unit)	$2 + n/2$
Multiple-word unit inserted, minor changes required (punctuation or capitalization)	$1 + n/2$
Multiple words inserted, major changes required (word order, additions or deletions)	1
Single word (translator always has to verify whether suggestion is suitable in new context, even for 100% matches, so usefulness is negligible)	0
Answers implied questions identified in mark-up phase, regardless of changes required (q = # of questions answered within a given unit)	$2q$
Bonus added to score if one tool finds information that the other tool misses	1

In contrast, the time loss penalty is applied to each unit as defined by the system in question. In TRADOS, the units are sentences (see Table 2), and in MultiTrans the units are the character strings that have been replaced with target-language text (see Table 3). Any action that the evaluator must perform (e.g., clicking open a unit to check for matches in TRADOS, deciding whether to "fetch" matches in MultiTrans, or assessing which, if any, of the proposed matches is suitable for insertion in either tool) implies a loss of time, which must be penalized.

Table 2: Score 2—Time loss penalty in TRADOS

Proposals generated	Penalty
Unit opened, no match	-0.5
100% match	-0.5
One fuzzy match	-1.5
2 to 4 fuzzy matches	$-1.5-(n-1)/4$
5 or more fuzzy matches	-2.5

Table 3: Score 2—Time loss penalty in MultiTrans

Amount of input unit highlighted	Proposals generated	Penalty
No highlight	N/A	0
Full unit highlighted	Fetch yields one match	-1.5
	Fetch yields 2 to 4 matches	$-1.5-(n-1)/4$
	Fetch yields 5 or more matches	-2.5
Portion of unit highlighted	No fetch performed	-0.5
	Fetch yields one match	-2
	Fetch yields 2 to 4 matches	$-2-(n-1)/4$
	Fetch yields 5 or more matches	-3

The composite score for each system was derived using the following formula: composite score = 2(score 1) + score 2.

APPLICATION OF SCORING SYSTEM

The texts chosen for the experiment were statements of qualifications for employment. At an average length of 228 words (1.5 pages), they were ideal for testing purposes. They were written mostly in sentence fragments (e.g., "Driver's licence required"), and although they contained little internal repetition they had a high degree of external repetition, which made them good candidates for use with TM tools (Bowker 2002, 113).

The mark-up procedure was applied to ten new statements of qualifications, and TRADOS and MultiTrans databases were created, each of which contained the same set of 100 previously translated statements of qualifications. A time gain score and a time loss penalty were applied to each of the ten input texts, as shown in the sample worksheet in Figure 2.

Figure 2: Sample worksheet showing the results obtained from each system and the application of the scores

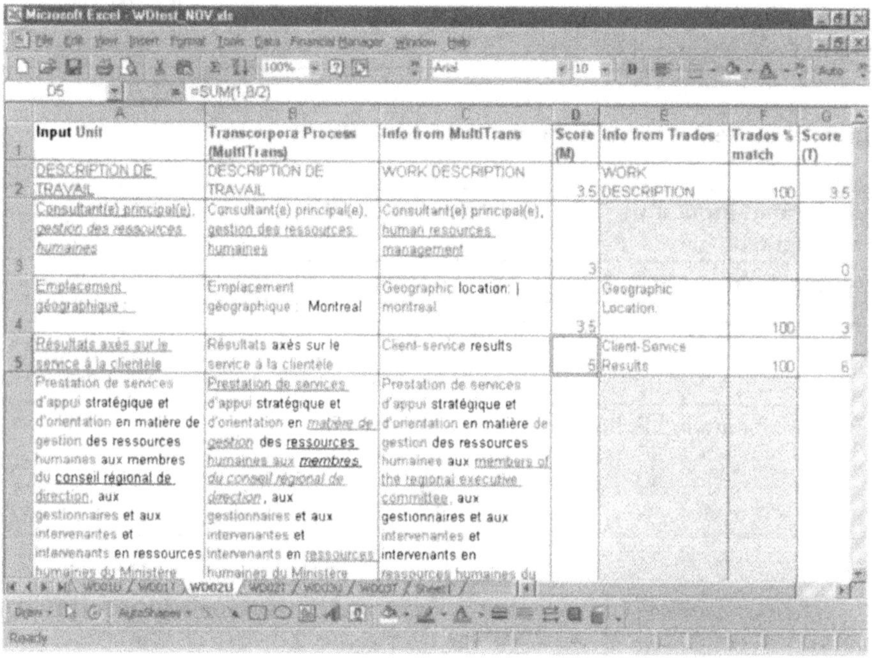

	A	B	C	D	E	F	G
1	Input Unit	Transcorpora Process (MultiTrans)	Info from MultiTrans	Score (M)	Info from Trados	Trados % match	Score (T)
2	DESCRIPTION DE TRAVAIL	DESCRIPTION DE TRAVAIL	WORK DESCRIPTION	3.5	WORK DESCRIPTION	100	3.5
3	Consultant(e) principal(e), gestion des ressources humaines	Consultant(e) principal(e), gestion des ressources humaines	Consultant(e) principal(e), human resources management	3			0
4	Emplacement géographique :	Emplacement géographique : Montreal	Geographic location: | montreal	3.5	Geographic Location	100	3
5	Résultats axés sur le service à la clientèle	Résultats axés sur le service à la clientèle	Client-service results	5	Client-Service Results	100	6
	Prestation de services d'appui stratégique et d'orientation en matière de gestion des ressources humaines aux membres du conseil régional de direction, aux gestionnaires et aux intervenantes et intervenants en ressources humaines du Ministère	Prestation de services d'appui stratégique et d'orientation en matière de gestion des ressources humaines aux membres du conseil régional de direction, aux gestionnaires et aux intervenantes et intervenants en ressources humaines du Ministère	Prestation de services d'appui stratégique et d'orientation en matière de gestion des ressources humaines aux members of the regional executive committee, aux gestionnaires et aux intervenantes et intervenants en ressources humaines du				

The results were concatenated to generate the scores shown in Table 4.

Table 4: Test result

Sum of scores for 10 input texts	Time gain score		Time loss penalty		Composite score	
	MultiTrans	TRADOS	MultiTrans	TRADOS	MultiTrans	TRADOS
	490.5	502	-360.25	-175.25	620.75	828.75

The time gain scores were very similar, indicating that for this text type TRADOS and MultiTrans identified roughly the same amount of useful information. However, MultiTrans generated a greater time loss penalty, indicating that the evaluator had to spend more time accessing, assessing, and inserting the useful information.

This is not necessarily a general trend. TRADOS is more suitable for the statements of qualifications tested, but there are other text types for which MultiTrans may be better suited. Potential users should remember that there is no "best tool," only a most appropriate tool for a given job. Also, this test applies only to automatic search and retrieval functions; it does not take into account the other features of the tools.

A breakdown of the results revealed general differences between the performance of the automatic search and retrieval functions in TRADOS and MultiTrans. TRADOS offered a small number of high-quality matches (long and requiring little or no editing), thereby saving time. However, TRADOS missed useful information below the sentence level that MultiTrans found. MultiTrans generated far more proposals. The increased choice in translation options could lead to a better translation but requires more time. The units replaced by MultiTrans were generally much shorter than those replaced by TRADOS. More editing time was required to fit the matches into the sentence, but more terminological information was provided to the user.

CONCLUSIONS

The methodology provides a valid and reliable comparison of the two approaches to searching for and retrieving information from a database. It is not as efficiently applicable as an edit distance algorithm, but this trade-off seems to be necessary to ensure validity. The process can be customized to different translation situations, ensuring a result that reflects each user's particular needs.

The sentence-based approach is better suited to text types with sentence-level repetition, and the CSB-based approach is better suited when the repetition occurs below the sentence level. An additional interpretation of the results described above is that the sentence-based approach is better for seasoned translators who are familiar with the terminology and concepts in their fields of specialization, and who are mainly interested in saving time, while the CSB-based approach may be of greater use to translators at an earlier point in their careers, when the translation database is more valuable for the information that it contains than for its time-saving potential.

A final point is that fuzzy matching, a technique associated with the sentence-based approach, and the strict character-by-character matching associated with the CSB-based approach need not be mutually exclusive. Since this research was performed, various developers of computer-aided translation tools have begun advertising their efforts to combine the two approaches in a single tool. These functional hybrids will hopefully combine the best features of each approach, resulting in a real step forward for translators.

NOTES

1. This paper is based on my MA thesis (Gow 2003). Professor Ingrid Meyer was a member of the jury who examined this thesis, and she recommended that the results be published.
2. See http://www.sdl.com.
3. See http://www.multicorpora.ca. Note that the MultiTrans tool is not advertised as a TM per se, perhaps to differentiate it from tools using the sentence-based approach; however, it still fits the broad definition of TM provided by Elliott Macklovitch and Graham Russell (2000, 137), who describe a TM as "an archive of past translations structured in such a way as to promote translation reuse."
4. Note that the article by Harold Somers actually discusses subjective approaches to evaluating example-based machine translation (EBMT), a technology that is closely related to TM.

REFERENCES

Benis, Michael. 1999. "Translation Memory from O to R." http://www.transref.org/u-articles/Benis3.asp (consulted May 5, 2005).

———. 2000. "How the Memory Measured Up." http://www.transref.org/u-articles/Benis4.asp (consulted May 5, 2005).

Bowker, Lynne. 2002. *Computer-Aided Translation Technology*. Ottawa: University of Ottawa Press.

Expert Advisory Group on Language Engineering Standards (EAGLES). 1995. *Evaluation of Natural Language Processing Systems: Final Report*. http://issco-www.unige.ch/projects/ewg96/ (consulted May 5, 2005).

Gow, Francie. 2003. "Metrics for Evaluating Translation Memory Systems." MA thesis, University of Ottawa.

Höge, Monika. 2002. "Towards a Framework for the Evaluation of Translators' Aids Systems." PhD diss., Helsinki University.

"Levenshtein Distance." 1999. In *Dictionary of Algorithms and Data Structures*, ed. Paul E. Black. National Institute of Standards and Technology, http://www.nist.gov/dads/HTML/editDistance.html (consulted May 5, 2005).

Macklovitch, Elliott, and Graham Russell. 2000. "What's Been Forgotten in Translation Memory." In *Envisioning Machine Translation in the Information Future*, ed. John S. White, 137–46. Berlin: Springer Verlag.

Simard, Michel, and Philippe Langlais. 2001. "Sub-sentential Exploitation of Translation Memories." In *Proceedings of MT Summit VIII: Machine Translation in the Information Age* [CD-ROM], ed. B. Maegaard. Santiago de Compostela, Spain, September 18–22, 2001.

Somers, Harold. 1999. "Example-Based Machine Translation." *Machine Translation* 14 (2): 113–57.

Zerfaß, Angelika. 2002. "Comparing Basic Features of TM Tools." *Language Technology Supplement, Multilingual Computing, and Technology* 13 (7): 11–14.

CHAPTER 14

CORPORA AND TRANSLATION

RODA P. ROBERTS
AND JACQUELINE BOSSÉ-ANDRIEU

INTRODUCTION

Human translation has become increasingly computerized over the past thirty to thirty-five years. Beginning with the word processors and the term banks of the 1970s, translators have turned to computers for assistance with at least three different tasks: documentary and terminological research, translating itself, and physical production of the translation. As of the 1990s, electronic corpora have played a major role in the first of these tasks: translation-related research.

What exactly constitutes a corpus? The term *corpus* can in fact be interpreted in a narrow or broad sense. According to Antoinette Renouf (1987, 1), it is "a collection of texts of the written or spoken word, which is stored and processed on computer for purposes of linguistic research." In other words, she limits the term to machine-readable texts that are selected and compiled for a specific purpose. However, Geoffrey Leech and Steven Fligelstone (1992, 115) broaden the definition of *corpus* when they state that it consists of "bodies of natural language material (whole texts, samples from texts, or sometimes just unconnected sentences), which are stored in machine-readable form." This definition is wide enough to cover all computerized material, including what is found on the Internet. In this paper, we will consider corpora in both senses, distinguishing between the two by designating corpus in the narrow sense of "linguistic corpus" or LC and corpus in the broad sense of "general corpus" or GC.

We will begin by discussing certain types of corpora that are particularly useful for translation. We will then focus on the use of corpora in translation research. We will first categorize translation problems and then use a sample text to identify translation problems, and finally we will show how corpora can be used to find possible solutions.

TYPES OF CORPORA

Since not all types of corpora are equally useful for translation, it is important to begin by identifying those that are particularly so. However, just as there is no complete agreement on the definition of *corpus*, so too there is some disagreement on the different types of corpora that can constitute LC or be found in GC. Consensus is lacking not only on the designations of the corpus types but also on their definitions and their number.[1] Indeed, rather different classifications of corpora have been suggested by John Sinclair (1982), Douglas Biber (1994), Mona Baker (1995), Graeme Kennedy (1998), and others. Our intention here is not to try to resolve inconsistencies in the different classifications and definitions provided. Rather, we will identify three generic types of corpora that translators may find particularly interesting, using a suitable (but not necessarily generally accepted) term, and define them. These three generic types are determined on the basis of two criteria: the number of languages contained in a corpus, on the one hand, and the degree and type of "similarity" between sets of texts contained in a corpus, on the other. They are presented below.

Unilingual corpora contain texts in one language only. Thus, the British National Corpus contains a number of texts in English.

Bilingual/multilingual translation corpora[2] contain texts in two languages ("bilingual") or more than two languages ("multilingual"), with original texts in one language and translations of those originals in the other language or languages. The pairs or sets thus created contain texts that are equivalent in content and style although different in language. An example of a bilingual translation corpus is the *Hansard*, which contains translated English/French texts from the journal of debates in the Canadian House of Commons: the speeches have been translated by very seasoned translators, mainly from English into French but also some from French into English.

Bilingual/multilingual comparable corpora[3] contain original texts in two or more languages that are similar in content, style, and function and can therefore be "compared," but they are not source texts and translations as is the case with translation corpora. An example of a bilingual comparable corpus is Textum (set up specifically for the needs of the Canadian Bilingual Dictionary Project): it contains, for instance, journalistic texts in English and French, published in newspapers of similar standing, written during the same period, and covering more or less the same events. Each set of language texts can also be used as a unilingual corpus.

All three types of corpora can be "stand-alone"—that is, set up to meet the particular needs of a group of users—or found on the Web. In other words, they can be LC or GC. One advantage of LC over GC is that LC is more focused than GC since it is established to meet specific needs. Another advantage is that LC can be exploited using concordancers, such as PAT, WordSmith, and MicroConcord, specially chosen by users to respond to their needs, while text collections on the Internet have to be exploited using either the concordancer attached to a given collection (which is often more limited in functions than commercially available concordancers) or a regular Web browser, which does not provide a concordance. Thus, the bilingual translation corpus *Hansard*, mentioned above, is now available on the Internet, but the concordance program on the Internet is much more simplistic than the one available with the stand-alone version. However, given that the majority of translators cannot afford to set up their own corpora, the Internet, which contains both specifically created corpora and millions of other texts and which can be considered loosely as a vast undefined corpus, is an essential working tool for translators.

TRANSLATION PROBLEMS

Before demonstrating how both LC and GC can be used by translators to resolve many of the translation problems that they face, we should categorize these problems. First, translation problems can be classified as source text-related or target text-related. In other words, are the problems related to comprehension of the source text or to transfer into the target language? Second, translation problems must be subdivided into three main categories on the basis of the nature of the problem, which can be encyclopedic, linguistic, or textual. We define *encyclopedic problems* as general subject-related problems as well as more specific problems dealing with proper nouns—that is, a lack of familiarity with the topic of the text or with specific places and people mentioned in the text. We define *linguistic problems* as those attached to specific words and phrases—that is, problems related to the comprehension or translation of a given word or phrase. And third, we consider textual problems as those concerned with text types and the internal organization of specific types of texts—that is, problems related to the identification or reproduction of a given text type. While encyclopedic problems are encountered primarily in the source text and textual problems mainly in the target text, linguistic problems can arise equally in the source text or in the target text.

SAMPLE TEXT
These general categories of translation problems will be illustrated using the following text.

MISSILE DEFENCE PROGRAM

Mr. Irwin Cotler (Mount Royal, Lib.): Mr. Speaker, the second petition, again signed by many residents of my constituency, seeks to draw the attention of the House to the following: that the Government of Canada may be asked to support the U.S. national missile defence, NMD, program to be operated by the North American aerospace defence command; that NMD is a unilateral initiative of the United States which plans, as it states in this petition, to dominate space by integrating space forces into war fighting capability; that NMD would be a step toward the deployment of weapons in space and lead to a new arms race; and that it would violate the 1972 anti-ballistic missile treaty and run counter to Canada's commitment as a signatory to the non-proliferation treaty to promote complete nuclear disarmament. These treaties are the cornerstones of the international non-proliferation arms control and disarmament regimes long supported by Canada. Therefore the petitioners call upon Parliament to declare that Canada objects to the national missile defence program of the United States and ask that Canada play a leadership role in banning nuclear weapons and missile flight tests.

This English text is from the *Hansard*. The translators who translate the debates are generalists since the debates cover a wide range of topics and text types. So we are going to show how a generalist freelance translator can take advantage of corpora to render this text into French.

Given the space limitations here, we will focus primarily on the English source text and various source text-related problems. However, we will show, although more briefly, how certain problems of translation into French can also be resolved using corpora.

SOURCE TEXT-RELATED PROBLEMS

During the first stage of translation, the comprehension stage, translators try to ensure that they have fully grasped the meaning of the text. To do so, they need to fill in gaps in both their encyclopedic knowledge and their linguistic knowledge.

Source Text-Related Encyclopedic Knowledge

Situating the Source Text

Before a translator begins working on a text, she needs to know something about its "situationality," which has been defined by Albrecht Neubert and Gregory Shreve (1992, 84) as "the location of a text in a discrete sociocultural context in a real time and place." The freelance translator would undoubtedly be aware that the text she has been assigned is an extract from the Canadian *Hansard*. And, if she is a Canadian, she will no doubt know that the *Hansard* is the journal of debates in the House of Commons. But since the *Hansard* does not constitute regular reading material for most Canadians, she will probably want to have a quick look at one or two issues of *Hansard* to be able to better situate her text. They can be obtained via the Internet at http://www.parl.gc.ca/37/1/parlbus/chambus/house/debates/006_2001-02-05/HAN006-E.htm. For instance, she can see the table of contents for House proceedings on February 5, 2001, and can then click on any section to see what it contains. Thus, by clicking on the section "Petitions," she can find texts similar to the one that she has to translate and can thus situate the latter in terms of the overall contents of the *Hansard*.

Researching the Topic of the Text

To be able to translate the English text presented above with confidence, the translator needs to know something about the missile defence program, the topic of the text. This information is again best obtained via the Internet (i.e., GC), since LC are often less up to date and are set up to provide concordance lines rather than full texts.

Using the search engine Google and the search term *missile defence program*, we obtained 26,600 hits in 0.79 seconds! Obviously, the large number of results obtained can be daunting, but we found what we were looking for in Results 1–10. Clicking onto the Web address http://www.acq.osd.mil/bmdo/bmdolink/html/nmd.html, we found the following text, which was short but served our purpose very well.

> National Missile Defense Program
> The National Missile Defense (NMD) system is being developed to protect the United States against a limited attack by long range ballistic missiles. The current National Missile Defense effort has the goal of establishing a defense of all 50 states against a limited missile attack by a "state of concern." It is not a follow-on to the Strategic Defense Initiative, though we do leverage some of the technologies developed in the 1980s. A Joint Program Office, headed by the NMD Program Executive Officer, manages the NMD Program and has the responsibility to achieve multi-service interoperability. The key NMD components include ground based interceptors (GBI), an X-band radar (XBR), Upgraded Early Warning Radars, Battle Management/Command, Control and Communications (BM/C3) and space sensor technology. The Ballistic Missile Defense Organization (BMDO) is responsible for managing, directing, and executing the Ballistic Missile Defense (BMD) Program. The program focuses on: Theater Missile Defense (TMD), National Missile Defense (NMD), and advanced ballistic missile defense technologies.

This text tells us what the goal of the National Missile Defense Program is, what its key components are, and how it fits into the overall Ballistic Missile Defense Program. This information is certainly sufficient for a translator's needs. If, however, the translator wishes to learn more about the Missile Defense Program, there is a list of related areas at the end of this Internet text that she can click on for further information.

Researching Information to Understand Specific Statements
Encyclopedic information is also required to understand the following sentence in the text: "it [National Missile Defense Program] would violate the 1972 anti-ballistic missile treaty and run counter to Canada's commitment as a signatory to the non-proliferation treaty to promote complete nuclear disarmament." For someone not very

familiar with the many treaties in the area of nuclear disarmament, it would not be clear if the speaker was referring in this context to one treaty (the 1972 one), which Canada signed, or to two distinct treaties (the 1972 anti-ballistic missile treaty and a nuclear non-proliferation treaty), the second of which it signed. Again, the Internet provides clear answers. Using search terms suggested by the source text ("1972 anti-ballistic missile treaty" and "nuclear non-proliferation treaty") at www.google.com, we managed on the first try to locate two texts (http://www.clw.org/ef/bmdbook/abmtreat.html and http://www.fas.org/nuke/control/npt/ respectively), which indicate the following: (1) the 1972 anti-ballistic missile treaty, officially known as the "Treaty on the Limitation of Anti-Ballistic Missile Systems," has two signatories, the United States and the Soviet Union, agreeing to severely limit strategic (or so-called national) anti-ballistic missile defences in order to forestall a predictable interaction between opposing defensive and offensive strategic forces; and (2) the nuclear non-proliferation treaty, officially known as the "Treaty on the Non-Proliferation of Nuclear Weapons" (NPT), which opened for signature on July 1, 1968, and entered into force with the deposit of US ratification on March 5, 1970, which obligates the five acknowledged nuclear weapon states (the United States, Russian Federation, United Kingdom, France, and China) not to transfer nuclear weapons, other nuclear explosive devices, or their technology to any non-nuclear weapon state and makes non-nuclear weapon states undertake not to acquire or produce nuclear weapons or nuclear explosive devices. It is thus clear that the speaker was referring to two separate treaties, both dealing with nuclear weapons, but only one of which Canada signed.

Researching Abbreviations and Acronyms

The only other encylopedic information that the translator would need to thoroughly understand this text is the full name that the abbreviation NMD stands for, but that is provided in the source text itself: "the U.S. national missile defence, NMD, program." However, if the source text had not provided the full name, the Internet texts used above would have readily filled that knowledge gap.

Source Text-Related Linguistic Knowledge

The other main types of source text problems faced by translators consist of problems related to the meanings of linguistic elements contained in the text. Of course, the translator can always have recourse to dictionaries for such problems, but print dictionaries, which are limited by space restrictions, do not always present a given meaning of a word, especially if it is highly specialized or rare, or do not account for all the nuances of meaning that a word may have, and many dictionaries available either in CD-ROM format or online are merely computerized versions of print dictionaries and therefore have the same deficiencies. The combined use of dictionaries (print or computerized) and corpora is therefore the translator's best chance of fully grasping the meaning of linguistic elements. We will illustrate this using two elements from the English text presented above: *missile flight test*, which is specialized vocabulary and a multiword lexical item, and *cornerstone*, which is an element of general language used figuratively in the context.

Specialized Vocabulary: *Missile Flight Test*

The problems with *missile flight test* begin with the fact that such a multiword lexical item can be interpreted differently depending on how it is segmented: "a test flight for missiles" or "a flight test for missiles" (versus other types of tests). In the English text, there is nothing to indicate which of these interpretations pertains. So we turned to an LC, Textum, to see how the words *missile, flight,* and *test* were used in combination in other texts. In a journalistic subcorpus extracted from the *Wall Street Journal*, both *missile flight test* and *missile test flight* were found, both used along with the word *ban* as in the text under consideration. However, the concordance lines (sample presented below) permitted no discrimination between the two multiword units.

> \>\> "missile flight tests"
> 216197752, . . . vors a ban on missile flight tests, an idea that is a cousin of . . .
>
> \>\> "missile test flights"
> 129755358, . . . proposes a ban on missile test flights, he backed nuclear-freeze pro . . .

Even longer contexts, such as the following, were of little help.

> 165913776, Governor Dukakis bought into their peacenik theology of a nuclear freeze, a ban on missile flight tests, and the "fantasy" of strategic defense.

Turning next to the Internet using the search engine Google, we learned, via a number of industry and government texts, that the NMD program missile testing was termed *missile flight test*.

> First Brimstone Missile Flight Test Successful
> http://www.boeing.com/news/releases/1999/photorelease/photo_release_990823n.htm
>
> Missile Defense Flight Test Scheduled for Summer 2001
> http://www.usinfo.state.gov/topical/pol/arms/stories/01032707.htm
>
> Joint Air-to-Surface Standoff Missile Flight Test
> http://www.af.mil/photos/Sep1999/991599a.html

A search for *missile test flights* also yielded a number of pertinent results, including the following.

> Will Facility Monitor US Missile Test Flights? Observers Say Tarawa Tracking Station Expands Chinese Eavesdropping . . .
> http://www.fas.org/irp/news/1998/05/980513-tarawa.htm

But since the term *missile flight test* was used in official US government documents (which was not the case with *missile test flights*), we decided that the speaker of the source language text was using *missile flight test* appropriately in the sense of "flight test for missiles" versus other types of tests.

General Vocabulary: *Cornerstone*
The word *cornerstone* is used figuratively in the English source text: "These treaties are the cornerstones of the international non-proliferation arms control and disarmament regimes long supported by Canada." But what exactly is the sense of *cornerstone* here? Can treaties be the *cornerstones* of regimes? We began our search for an answer using a lexical database for English, WordNet, found on the Web at http://www.cogsci.princeton.edu/~wn/. The noun *cornerstone* has three senses in WordNet, of which the first was the only appropriate one.

> 1. basis, base, foundation, fundament, groundwork, cornerstone — (the fundamental assumptions underlying an explanation; "the whole argument rested on a basis of conjecture")

But to find out whether we can speak of "cornerstone *of*... regimes," we have to turn to corpora per se. We used the LC Textum since the search was purely linguistic. Here we found one occurrence (repeated), in the subcorpus English Canadian Press, of *cornerstone* near *regimes:*

> 418725865, . . . federal public service, medicare, the Canada Pension Plan, a new labor code, the Canadian Assistance Plan (the cornerstone of the welfare system), new regulatory regimes for transportation . . .

While the context does not read "cornerstone *of* . . . regimes," it does fortuitously provide an example of "cornerstone *of* the . . . system," which can be considered quasi-synonymous. While the research in this linguistic corpus revealed that, although the phrase *cornerstone of regimes* does not seem to be commonly used, the concept that it presents is legitimate.

TARGET TEXT-RELATED PROBLEMS

During the second stage of translation, which involves transfer into the target language, the problems faced by translators are primarily linguistic but may also be textual. Linguistic problems are related to the search for equivalents, while textual problems are concerned with how a similar text is organized in the target language.

Target Text-Related Linguistic Problems

The search for equivalents in the target language can be undertaken using bilingual translation corpora (if they are available) or unilingual target-language corpora. The use of both will be illustrated with some of the words and terms discussed above.

Equivalent for Proper Name: *Non-Proliferation Treaty*

We first searched for the official French equivalent of *non-proliferation treaty* using the bilingual translation corpus *Hansard*. By inserting the expression *non-proliferation treaty*, we obtained a total of fifty-six matches, presented alongside the parallel French text, of which we present two below.

1. Le traité sur la non-prolifération des armes nucléaires
Nuclear Non-Proliferation Treaty

2. Comme partisan du traité de non-prolifération, le Canada appuie le droit des pays en développement de se doter d'une technologie nucléaire à des fins pacifiques seulement.
As a supporter of the non-proliferation treaty, Canada supports the right of developing countries to develop nuclear technology for peaceful means only.
http://www-rali.iro.umontreal.ca/TransSearch/TS-complex-uen.cgi

Two main equivalents are found in this corpus: *traité sur la non-prolifération* (= treaty on non-proliferation) and *traité de non-prolifération* (= treaty of non-proliferation). To confirm which of the proposed equivalents is the most appropriate, the translator can turn to unilingual corpora (either LC or GC). Thus, a search in one Canadian subcorpus of Textum, Presse canadienne française, revealed seventy-seven occurrences of *traité de non-prolifération* as opposed to five of *traité sur la non-prolifération*. Since this corpus is a journalistic one, we felt it necessary to consult the Internet to find the official designation of the treaty: Google provided forty-six matches for the former term (including at least one official text), versus twenty-four matches for the latter term (including at least one official text). At this point, the translator should realize that both terms are in use and appropriate but may well base her final choice between the two equivalents on the frequency of use of *traité de non-prolifération*.

Equivalent for General Vocabulary: *Cornerstone*

In principle, the Internet is more useful in the case of specialized vocabulary than general vocabulary, especially when the latter is used in figurative senses. However, this is not the case with *pierre angulaire*, the normal equivalent for *cornerstone* in both its literal and its figurative senses. Although all bilingual dictionaries provide *pierre angulaire* as the equivalent for *cornerstone* in both types of senses, none of them provides an example of usage. We therefore turned to the Internet to see whether *pierre angulaire* could be used in the same type of construction as *cornerstone of . . . regimes*. Of the fifty Google matches checked, over forty showed *pierre angulaire* used in the figurative sense, but not a single one was followed by a plural noun. So, to further check the use of the construction "pierre angulaire *des* + abstract noun," we turned to the LC Textum. In the first subcorpus consulted (Presse canadienne française), eleven occurrences of *pierre angulaire des X* were found, seven of which included an abstract noun, one of them being *programmes*.

206132308, . . . e nationale. Pierre angulaire des programmes de la droite franç . . .

377849953, . . . taque à cette pierre angulaire des programmes sociaux canadiens . . .

Thus, we confirmed the usage that we were seeking.

Target Text-Related Textual Problems

Textual problems related to the target text can vary greatly. They can involve generic characteristics (e.g., what are the normal complimentary closes in formal letters in the target language?) or cohesive devices (e.g., are linking devices such as *therefore* used more in target language texts than in source language texts of the same type?) or simply style. In the case of the translation of the English text presented above, there are no particular textual problems. However, the translator might like to see how petitions by members are presented in French in the *Hansard*. To do this, she can turn again to *Hansard* online (at http://www.parl.gc.ca/37/1/parlbus/chambus/house/debates/006_2001-02-05/han006-f.htm) and use the French version to see how petitions are presented in French.

CONCLUSION

The analysis of problems of translation related to the source text chosen and the search for answers in LC and GC as presented above raise some issues. First and foremost, research in corpora is more time consuming than dictionary research because dictionaries provide answers based on prior research—generally in corpora these days—whereas corpora provide raw data that the translator must analyze. However, corpora often provide more material than do dictionaries, which gives the translator greater freedom of choice.

Second, since most translators today have access to the Internet and therefore to what we have termed GC, this is the type of corpus that is most used. However, given the large number and variety of texts available on the Web, their quality is uneven, from the points of view of both content and (especially) language. It is often difficult to tell whether a given text is really an original text or a translation. And, given the fact that many Web-based texts are "anonymous," the author's reputation cannot be used as a factor in evaluating the quality of the documentation. Translators, therefore, need to use discretion in their choice of Web-based texts.

There is no doubt that specially designed linguistic corpora contain texts of better quality. Moreover, they are often more useful than GC to translators looking for solutions to linguistic problems. However, most translators do not have the time or energy or know-how to set up a personal LC. But if translators are called upon to translate a long and specialized text, it may nevertheless be worth their while to use what Krista Varantola (2003) has called a "disposable corpus": that is, one designed quickly to meet a specific need. And if they regularly translate texts in a given specialized area, establishing an LC containing texts from that area would be a wise move. Finally, with translators increasingly receiving source texts in electronic format and generally producing translations in the same format, it would be relatively easy for them to set up a bilingual translation corpus comprised of their own work. However, in their newfound enthusiasm for corpora, translators must not forget traditional translation tools such as dictionaries, for it is only by using the two in combination that they will be able to do the best job in a timely fashion.

NOTES

1. Jennifer Pearson (1998, 43–44) outlines some of the problems in this regard:
   > As corpus linguistics is a relatively new field of enquiry, many new terms have been coined. In addition to corpus we read of subcorpora, components of corpora, special corpora and specialized corpora, monitor corpora and reference corpora, archives and general corpora, full text corpora, sample corpora, parallel corpora and comparable corpora. Some of these terms have been assigned more than one meaning, others are not yet fully defined.

2. These are often termed simply *translation corpora*. However, this term could be misleading since a corpus can be made up entirely of texts in one language that are translations from other languages.

3. Our definition of *comparable corpus* is very different from that proposed by Mona Baker (1995, 234), according to whom such a corpus consists of two sets of texts in the same language: original texts in a given language and translations into the same language. What we call *comparable corpus* contains what R.R.K. Hartmann (1980) has termed *paired texts*.

REFERENCES

Baker, M. 1995. "Corpora in Translation Studies: An Overview and Some Suggestions for Future Research." *Target* 7 (2): 223–43.

Biber, D. 1994. "Using Register-Diversified Corpora for General Language Studies." In *Using Large Corpora*, ed. S. Armstrong, 179–202. Cambridge, MA: MIT Press.

Hartmann, R.R.K. 1980. *Contrastive Textology: Comparative Discourse Analysis in Applied Linguistics*. Heidelberg: Julius Groos Verlag.

Kennedy, G. 1998. *An Introduction to Corpus Linguistics*. London: Longman.

Leech, G., and S. Fligelstone. 1992. "Computers and Corpus Analysis." In *Computers and the Written Text*, ed. C.S. Butler, 115–39. Oxford: Blackwell.

Neubert, A., and G. Shreve. 1992. *Translation as Text*. Kent, OH: Kent State University Press.

Pearson, J. 1998. *Terms in Context*. Amsterdam: John Benjamins.

Renouf, A. 1987. "Corpus Development." In *Looking Up: An Account of the COBUILD Project in Lexical Computing*, ed. J. Sinclair, 1–40. London: HarperCollins.

Sinclair, J. 1982. "Reflections on Computer Corpora in English Language Research." In *Computer Corpora in English Language Research*, ed. S. Johansson, 1–6. Bergen: Norwegian Computing Centre for the Humanities.

Varantola, K. 2003. "Translators and Disposable Corpora." In *Corpora in Translator Education*, ed. F. Zanettin, S. Bernardini, and D. Stewart, 55–70. Manchester: St. Jerome Publishing.

CHAPTER 15

THE CONTEXTUAL TURN
IN LEARNING TO TRANSLATE[1]

KRISTA VARANTOLA

FROM TURN TO TURN

Over the past decades, it has been possible to discern a number of "turns" in translation studies. These turns have manifested changes in focus areas of translation research. The turns have usually been defined as ten-year periods that have conveniently coincided with the actual decades in the Christian calendar. So far, we have seen the heydays of linguistic, cultural, and historical turns, and we have talked about translators' visibility as a potential turn. The emphasis is now shifting to issues of social relevance and quality in translation. Maybe we can even claim that we are now about to enter yet another turn in translation studies.

The important thing to keep in mind is that these different turns are by no means discrete or exclusive shifts of emphasis. The main impacts of all of them are still felt and remain relevant. It is even likely that some turns will be revitalized in the future when we feel the need to focus on them again. In fact, all these research areas show how multifaceted the translation process is in reality and how the various aspects of multilingual communication can be highlighted in the study of translation.

In that framework, it is actually surprising how little attention the translating aspect of translation has received in translation studies. Naturally, there are a number of very useful language-specific "how to"-style instruction books and other practical guides for students of translation, but not a great deal has been written with translating in focus. Studies on the use of corpora in translation are notable exceptions (e.g., Laviosa 1998; Bernardini and Zanettin 2000; Bowker and Pearson 2002; Zanettin, Bernardini, and Stewart 2003; Olohan 2004). In my opinion, however, the time is now ripe for yet another emphasis, which I would like to call a "contextual turn in translating."

Why would we want to focus on such a practical aspect of translation? My main argument is that the recent major developments in the tools of translation, such as dictionaries and corpora, merit this emphasis on the practical aspects of translation. Their effect on the actual translating process is fundamental and deserves a much more systematic treatment than is the case today. In this way, the benefits of the new technologies also become familiar in the training and practice of translation. This new interest area became visible at a recent CULT symposium (Corpus Use and Learning to Translate, Barcelona, 2004) where a number of talks concentrated on the benefits of extractable corpus information for translation. Good examples of such research foci are the Internet as a corpus, comparable corpora, as well as information on contextual equivalence and semantic prosody in corpus data. What seems to have been largely overlooked in the context of translating, however, is the potential of modern dictionaries.

THE HAPPY THREESOME

In this article, my starting point is the competent human translator and his or her information needs. The question is how modern linguistic tools, such as dictionaries and corpora, can help the translator during translation. By competent, I mean somebody who knows how to make decisions about translation strategies, how to translate, and which aspects to take into account and balance in the process. In the actual performance, however, our competent translator needs help in the decision-making process: consultations with other human experts, help from dictionaries and glossaries, information from parallel and comparable texts, et cetera. The need for this external help is particularly marked if the translation task is tricky, a special domain text, a translation into the translator's second language (L2), a very special text genre, or any other challenging task.

My claim is that, owing to developments in language technology and electronic processing of linguistic data, the translators' problem-solving techniques have changed dramatically over the past decade or so. Electronic dictionaries, general and specialized corpora, corpora and corpus analysis tools, and the Internet have all contributed to making the translators' lives easier: these tools have lessened translators' anxiety levels, made translators less frustrated and more confident about their decisions. To summarize, the new tools and resources have made it easier for translators to match competence with equally high-level performance (Varantola 2003, 59).

A MEETING PLACE

I will concentrate on the major changes that have taken place in dictionary making and corpus compilation and discuss how these developments and the electronic medium have changed the work of the human translator.

Thanks to the electronic medium and text analysis tools, information available in dictionaries and corpora is slowly converging. One sense of *converge* is "to come from other places to meet in a particular place." We can think of translators as the third party coming to this meeting place. Translators collaborate with dictionary and corpus information and interact with it while performing a text production task. In essence, dictionaries and corpora are, however, very different tools.

Dictionaries are systematized analyses about words, while corpora are non-systematic collections of text. Yet modern dictionaries are based on large corpora, and the developments in dictionary compilation are the basic raison d'être behind the collection of large corpora, such as the British National Corpus (BNC) and the HarperCollins Bank of English. Nevertheless, we need to keep in mind that lexicographers' corpus needs are very different from translators' corpus needs, and I will return to this aspect later.

Corpora, on the other hand, are by definition context bound. Lexical items do not appear in isolation in them. Instead, corpora display the use of lexical items in "real" language, but today modern dictionaries manage to systematize this real language to an unprecedented extent. Corpora and corpus tools help dictionary makers to manipulate the data and dissect corpus information with anatomical precision.

DICTIONARIES

Traditionally, dictionaries aimed at giving a context-free presentation of the meaning of a lexical item. This is no longer true, however. The electronic format has brought with it a number of freedoms that are now being exploited and experimented with in dictionary making. Similar developments are also taking place in terminology work. Context-free definitions of concepts within a particular domain were for a long time the theoretical ideal in terminological theory, but they are now often replaced by less rigid, contextually relevant definitions, which are much more transparent to non-specialist users.

This development is to a great extent a result of the availability of large special-domain corpora that help the terminologists to realize that even expert terminology is subject to individual interpretations. It is also very difficult to control once it has been let out of the glossary into the real world to be used by human users in different contexts and settings.

Modern dictionaries also tend to contain much more encyclopedic information than was traditionally considered acceptable in lexicography. The usage examples are selected from representative samples, and the ordering of word senses is more often than not based on their "real" frequencies in the outside world. Furthermore, collocational information is more adequate and helpful. Some electronic dictionaries, such as the *Collins Cobuild English Dictionary* (2001), even provide access to more examples in the form of concordances from the corpus data that lie behind the dictionary. Thanks to corpora, lexicographers have become aware of new regularities and systematic behaviours in language use, such as chunking and semantic prosody. They have also been able to incorporate this new information even in print-format dictionaries such as the *New Oxford Dictionary of English* (1998) and the *Macmillan English Dictionary for Advanced Learners* (2002).

It has also become clear to dictionary makers that word sense is a much more fluid category than previously thought. On the whole, I think that we are coming round to the view that language use is much more probabilistic than we expected and far less rule governed than we would like it to be.

MEANING

Prominent corpus lexicographers have frequently expressed their doubts about the validity of "word sense" as a distinct and clear-cut category. Sue Atkins has been quoted as claiming, "I don't believe in word senses" (Rundell 2002, 146). Michael Rundell himself has stated that "word meaning can be regarded as (at best) yet another form of prototype" (147). Patrick Hanks's conclusion is that "words do not have separate meanings but meaning potentials which may be activated in particular contexts" (2000, 7). Annie Zaenen discusses word meaning in the context of the generative lexicon and states that, "Instead of listing subsenses, the generative lexicon aims at making them result from the combination of the general meanings of the various words in a sentence" (2002, 232). A final nail in the coffin of isolatable meaning distinctions is Hanks's comment that "Word meaning (if such a thing exists at all) is extremely vague and unstable. A word can have about as many senses as a lexicographer cares to perceive" (2002, 159). Furthermore, in bilingual dictionaries, a translation equivalent, the gloss or glosses on the right-hand side should be regarded as an approximation or key to the meaning of the entry word (Varantola 2002, 36).

What, then, is word meaning? Should we scrap the category altogether? I do not think that we need to take such a drastic measure; rather, we need to accept the fact that word meaning is a fluid and probabilistic category. We thus need to accept the inherent uncertainty of the category and instead record tendencies and preferences and resort to the concept of core meaning and prototype theory when we describe the meaning potential of a lexical item (see *New Oxford Dictionary of English* 1998). We also need to pay much more attention to phraseology and the combinatory tendencies of words, to the prefabricated units of language (see Cowie 1998). Likewise, we need information on variation and on the metaphorical nature of language use. A good example of the latter is *conversation*. Rundell (2002, 145) states, "conversation is a journey." Corpus evidence shows that it drifts, revolves around, veers, wanders, and moves.

An example of how corpus findings can be incorporated into dictionary entries is found in *The New Oxford Dictionary of English* and the *Macmillan English Dictionary*, which also include information on semantic prosody. In the latter dictionary, for example, the entry for the verb *cause* states

> **cause** verb [transitive]
> to make something happen, usually something bad:
> *a politician who causes controversy wherever he goes*
> *The fire was caused by an electrical fault.*

Semantic prosody is something that native speakers intuitively know about but cannot pinpoint. Corpus information, therefore, is essential in providing the quantitative evidence for it. Ingrid Meyer, Kristen Mackintosh, and Krista Varantola (1997) discussed this phenomenon when they studied the uses and senses of *virtual* in present-day English. Corpus information clearly shows how the traditional use of *virtual* in the sense of "almost the same as" usually has a negative semantic prosody and mainly occurs with headwords that describe something undesirable.

Linguistic categories in general also tend to be more fluid and prototypical than is generally acknowledged. Word-class definitions are particularly notorious. Defining *forgiving* as an adjective or a verb is far from clear-cut in English. Likewise, it is not always easy to differentiate between an adjective and an adverb in actual use. The adverb class is often used as a suitable drawer for items that are difficult to categorize (see, e.g., Rundell 2002, 146). Whatever the drawbacks, it would be difficult to deny the usefulness of linguistic categorization. It is certainly clarifying and helpful in the description of language but at the same time should not be treated as the ultimate and unchanging truth. We should actually be very happy about the inherent uncertainty that we have to live with when dealing with language. Fluid categories are a richness, a precondition, and a catalyst for language and meaning change.

Future dictionaries also need to focus more on lexicographic relevance. Rare words and senses tend to get equal prominence in dictionaries. This is probably adequate for native speaker dictionaries but certainly misleading in learner dictionaries. Pragmatic information is one aspect that does not yet receive enough attention in dictionary entries. As Hanks points out, the conversational use of *right* is much more common in spoken corpus data than *right* in the sense of "true" or "correct" (2002, 157).

However hard we try, we must nevertheless accept the fact that dictionaries will never fully reflect language use in real time. Dictionaries aim at establishing and capturing and systematizing the more permanent and established features of language and its lexis. Corpora, particularly dynamic corpora such as the Internet, can live in real time and include expressions that have not yet made it into the dictionary or should never make it into the dictionary.

CORPORA

Like dictionaries, corpora come in many forms and formats. Lexicographers use corpora to compile dictionaries and translators to help them with translation problems. While lexicographers specifically benefit from large balanced and permanent tagged corpora of the BNC type, with a hundred million words or more, translators seek help in much smaller targeted repositories of running text that can be disposable, self-made raw corpora, parallel translation corpora, or comparable corpora in two or more languages. But whatever the corpus format, the information is by definition context bound; at the same time, the context is the only source of information about the use and meaning of the target item. This naturally means that corpora are also much more cumbersome to use than dictionaries, in which the information has been preprocessed in order to help the user make the right choice. With corpora, we need corpus analysis tools, simple or sophisticated, and technical analysis skills before we can get anywhere with the information available in the corpora.

The Internet, of course, provides the user with a huge, versatile, and forever-changing dynamic corpus, but it is not the final solution. It is too large to be processed with conventional corpus tools such as concordancers or word frequency analyzers. The information is not validated in any way, and all responsibility falls on the user and the user's linguistic skills and intuition.

WHAT ARE CORPORA GOOD FOR?

Corpora are not word-oriented in the conventional sense. In the context of corpus processing, a word is typically understood to be a meaningful string of letters separated by blanks from its fellow items. Nor is a searchable unit size in a corpus determined in the same way as it is in dictionaries. This helps the user to find out about the use of chunks and longer passages in the text without the burden or need of further categorization. Corpora can be easily manipulated and dissected to cater to particular user-defined needs.

In up-to-date corpora, users can observe synchronic language change in progress (see Meyer, Mackintosh, and Varantola 1997; Meyer 2000). Meyer, Mackintosh, and Varantola report on the extensions in meaning of the word *virtual* in its information technology sense and on its novel syntactic behaviour ("virtually yours," "they met virtually"). This new behaviour became apparent in the uses of *virtual* in the Oxford Reader Corpus. This corpus is based on information about new words and novel uses of English vocabulary sent to the editors of the *OED* by readers all over the world. James Murray, the chief editor of the first edition of the *OED*, had already pointed out that individuals notice out-of-the-ordinary uses of words, whereas ordinary uses often remain unnoticed. Today corpora can fix this problem by providing evidence of the frequency of occurrence of different uses.

In a way, time-bound newspaper corpora also illustrate how closely tied language use is to what is happening in the outside world, how new meanings develop in the manner of a linguistic chaos theory, in a way that cannot be predicted. We all know how words ending in *–gate* have become prolific in English since the incident at the Watergate building complex in Washington. Although the original context may now mean nothing to the user, *-gate* is still a usable ending that is easy to decode to mean "scandalous" in English and has even been heard in spoken Finnish with the same connotation.

Corpora can reassure the user. A hesitant translator can confirm his or her intuition by checking the uses of any particular stretch of text in a suitable corpus and finding out whether the expression is really used in the particular context that the translator has in mind. Corpora also enable fuzzy searches and serendipitous finds. It is possible to find information that the user did not think of asking for but nevertheless needs and applies. This normally happens when the user's query is expressed in a fuzzy and nonspecific manner. Corpora can also solve genre- or text-type-related stylistic issues, such as issues related to the choice of appropriate terminology for different user groups.

"WORDNESS"

"Wordness" in corpora and wordness in dictionaries are two very different concepts. All corpus words do not fulfill the stringent criteria of dictionary words. Those words cannot be defined as "a meaningful string of letters separated by a blank" but need to be established units and have permanent-like, encapsulated meanings that native speakers of the language are able to identify. Sporadic creative uses and nonce words do not have a place in the dictionary, but neither do all possible compounds, word combinations, or derivatives deserve a slot in the dictionary.

Translators, however, need information about both dictionary and corpus words. They may want to know whether a multiword item that they themselves have constructed is really used in practice and, if used, whether the context is relevant. I could not find *iron-bar lever* in any of the dictionaries that I had at my disposal, but I could verify by a Google search that the expression existed and that it existed in the context in which I wanted it to exist.

DICTIONARIES AND CORPORA AS INTELLIGENT TOOLS

Before describing my wish list, I need to define what I mean by *intelligence* in this context. In my opinion, intelligent dictionaries and corpora would interactively help users to find the answers that they are looking for. Interactivity would thus be a means of getting closer to the users' real needs first by helping them to specify their queries and then by providing them with the answers. I also believe that it makes sense to discern between *shallow* and *deep intelligence* in the user interfaces of dictionaries and corpora.

Intelligent Dictionaries

Shallow intelligence could be used to describe what spell-checking systems and cross-referencing links in dictionary entries do. These systems help in determining the correct spelling and in finding synonyms, near synonyms, antonyms, and more "mechanical" information in general. Deeper intelligence, on the other hand, would entail access to user-definable user profiles, user-specified filters and display modes, such as browser modes and look-up modes, full and reduced displays of data categories, user alerts, et cetera. The dictionary entry would thus consist of a larger selection of data categories than is now customary.

These data categories would give detailed information on collocational patterns, offer information on semantic prosody, semantic valency, and sense differentiation, and provide access to compatible corpus data. In addition, the dictionary entries could provide further information, such as links to alternative sources of information (e.g., encyclopedias, domain-specific information, and multimedia displays where appropriate). The system should also be a learning system that learns from user search pattern logs and remembers the information that it has acquired in this way.

Intelligence in Corpora

Raw, non-tagged, or POS-tagged corpora could be described as tools of shallow intelligence, because the user is left to handle the manipulation, dissection, and interpretation of the results. Similarly, stand-alone analysis tools are useful but "raw" tools—general and non-customized tools—that require user intervention at every stage.

Corpora that are syntactically and semantically tagged would offer a much greater potential for displaying corpus data according to a variety of parameters. Such corpora could be linked to dictionary entries, and bidirectional access between dictionaries and corpora would become possible. Sophisticated corpus compilation tools, automatic taggers, and parsers would help in compiling both monolingual corpora and multilingual parallel and comparable corpora.

In other words, my wish list incorporates

- compilation and corpus capturing tools for putting together balanced corpora according to user-defined criteria;
- potential for word-class and semantic tagging as well as syntactic parsing;
- house-keeping tools for corpus maintenance, such as corpus updating and consistency control;
- corpus analysis tools such as WordSmith-style tools and Word Sketch-style tools (see Kilgarriff et al. 2004) for studying word behaviour and collocational patterns.

USERS AND USER SKILLS

Let us not forget the third partner in the interactive process, the translator who uses the new electronic tools and text collections. How can we train the translators so that they are able to improve their performance in translating?

Modern translator competence presupposes an understanding of the potential and limits of modern performance-enhancing tools such as electronic dictionaries, corpora, and corpus tools. These skills should therefore be taught in translator training programs, but first we must ensure that the trainers themselves receive the training and understand the full potential of these new tools (see, e.g., Varantola 2002). In the end, of course, it is still the translators who are responsible for their choices and solutions, but these choices are on a much firmer ground when translators have up-to-date tools at their disposal and when these tools can be found in the same "snap-on" toolbox.

CONCLUSION

Dictionaries and corpora remain essentially different tools. Dictionaries chase a moving target (as Sue Atkins has said), corpora get closer to this moving target, but even they are always slightly behind real time in language use. Dictionary information is elaborated and fully analyzed; corpus information is shakier but more "real" and unrefined, and it leaves a great deal to the user to sort out.

The challenge for us is to find out why translators are looking up particular words or lexical items in dictionaries and corpora, and what they really want to know in different situations. When we know this, we can also make the move from information overload to lexical knowledge management. We will then also be able to incorporate this knowledge into dictionaries and corpus analysis tools and claim that we have really managed to integrate translators into the contextual turn of translating.

NOTE

1 This article is based on a plenary talk given at the Corpus Use and Learning to Translate (CULT 2004) Conference in Barcelona, January 2004.

REFERENCES

Atkins, B.T.S. 1996. "Bilingual Dictionaries: Past, Present, and Future." In *EURALEX '96 Proceedings*, ed. M. Gellerstam et al., 515–46. Göteborg: Göteborg University.

Bernardini, S., and F. Zanettin, eds. 2000. *I corpora nella didattica della traduzione. Corpus Use and Learning to Translate*. Bologna: CLUEB.

Bowker, L., and J. Pearson. 2002. *Working with Specialized Language: A Practical Guide to Using Corpora*. London: Routledge.

Collins Cobuild English Dictionary. 2001. Ed. J. Sinclair. Glasgow: HarperCollins.

Cowie, A.P., ed. 1998. *Phraseology: Theory, Analysis, and Applications*. Oxford: Clarendon Press.

Hanks, P. 2000. "Contributions of Lexicography and Corpus Linguistics to a Theory of Language Performance." In *EURALEX 2000 Proceedings*, vol. 1, ed. U. Heid, S. Evert, E. Lehmann, and C. Rohrer, 3–13. Stuttgart: University of Stuttgart.

———. 2002. "Mapping Meaning onto Use." In *Lexicography and Natural Language Processing: A Festschrift in Honour of B.T.S. Atkins*, ed. Marie-Hélène Corréard, 156–98. Grenoble: EURALEX.

Kilgarriff, A., P. Rychly, P. Smrz, and D. Tugwell. 2004. "The Sketch Engine." In *EURALEX 2004 Proceedings*, ed. G. Williams and S. Vessier, 105–15.

Lorient, France: Faculté des Lettres et des Sciences Humaines, Université de Bretagne Sud.

Laviosa, S., ed. 1998. *The Corpus-Based Approach.* Special issue of *Meta* 43 (4). http://www.erudit.org.revue/meta/.

Macmillan English Dictionary for Advanced Learners. 2002. Ed. Michael Rundell. London: Macmillan.

Meyer, I. 2000. "Computer Words in Our Everyday Lives: How Are They Interesting for Terminography and Lexicography?" In *EURALEX 2000 Proceedings,* ed. U. Heid, S. Evert, E. Lehmann, and C. Rohrer, 39–58. Stuttgart: University of Stuttgart.

Meyer I., K. Mackintosh, and K. Varantola. 1997. "Exploring the Reality of Virtual: On the Lexical Implications of Becoming a Knowledge Society." *Lexicology* 3 (1): 129–63.

The New Oxford Dictionary of English. 1998. Ed. Judy Pearsall. Oxford: Oxford University Press.

Olohan, M. 2004. *Introducing Corpora in Translation Studies.* Abingdon: Routledge.

Rundell, M. 2002. "Good Old-Fashioned Lexicography: Human Judgment and the Limits of Automation." In *Lexicography and Natural Language Processing: A Festschrift in Honour of B.T.S. Atkins,* ed. Marie-Hélène Corréard, 139–55. Grenoble: EURALEX.

Varantola, K. 2002. "Use and Usability of Dictionaries: Common Sense and Context Sensibility?" In *Lexicography and Natural Language Processing: A Festschrift in Honour of B.T.S. Atkins,* ed. Marie-Hélène Corréard, 30–44. Grenoble: EURALEX.

———. 2003. "Translators and Disposable Corpora." In *Corpora in Translator Education,* ed. F. Zanettin, S. Bernardini, and D. Stewart, 55–70. Manchester: St. Jerome Publishing.

WordSmith Tools: http://www.lexically.net/wordsmith/

Zaenen, A. 2002. "Musings about the Impossible Electronic Dictionary." In *Lexicography and Natural Language Processing: A Festschrift in Honour of B.T.S. Atkins,* ed. Marie-Hélène Corréard, 230–44. Grenoble: EURALEX.

Zanettin, F., S. Bernardini, and D. Stewart, eds. 2003. *Corpora in Translator Education.* Manchester: St. Jerome Publishing.

CHAPTER 16

FILM TRANSLATION RESEARCH IN SPAIN: THE DUBBING OF HOLLYWOOD MOVIES INTO SPANISH

JOSÉ-MARÍA BRAVO

INTRODUCTION

In Spain, film translation (FT), as an area of academic study, began to make a modest appearance in university courses from 1994 onward, starting at the University of Valladolid. Then came the first doctoral dissertations (Chaves García on translation for dubbing, 1996; Díaz Cintas on subtitling, 1997). However, it was not until 1999 that the first book about FT in Spanish was published (Agost Canós on dubbing). Yet it is true, as Chaume (2002, 215) has recently pointed out, that, "In the last few years, the study of audiovisual translation has been blossoming in a way which finally makes up for the many years of continual neglect that the field had suffered within translation studies."[1]

The fruits of this new enthusiasm have included several theses,[2] several monographic and a few collective publications,[3] and a string of articles in translation books and journals. Concurrently, there are ever more postgraduate courses and diplomas as well as specialized conferences (starting with the pioneering and historic meeting at the Universidad del País Vasco (UPV) campus in Vitoria in May 1993, Trasvases culturales: Literatura, cine, traducción).[4] As a result of all this, "the complete lack of research on audiovisual translation hitherto" (Chaume 2002, 215) is beginning to be overcome, and concern with this type of translation has become extraordinarily widespread. Proof can be found from day to day in TRAG, the Internet mailing list moderated by Xosé Castro that now has 1,016 subscribers.[5]

MAIN APPROACHES TO THE STUDY OF FILM TRANSLATION

There are several possible approaches to the study of film translation. I will briefly characterize them in the course of attempting to describe, in general terms, the present state of FT in Spain. I will endeavour to do justice to the work done so far while pointing out what remains to be done.

INDUSTRIAL ASPECT

If one is to understand what FT really is, one must first realize that cinema is above all an industry. This means, among other things, that it is governed by the laws of business, the first of which is that the producer is in it to make money.[6] And it has to be big money, because these days the average Hollywood production costs about $60 million (Wasko 2003, 33). Another important fact is that we are dealing with an industry that is overwhelmingly American, whose working language is English and whose archetype is the Hollywood movie.

FT plays an important, though much undervalued, role in the workings of the industry: it helps to globalize the films so that they can reach the largest possible number of markets under the best possible conditions and compete with the local productions of other countries. In this regard, it is worth mentioning that, according to data from the AACCE (the Spanish Academy of Cinematographic Arts and Sciences), about eighty-four percent of all the films released in Spain in the past fifteen years were foreign movies, and more than seventy-five percent of them had been translated from the English language.[7] Yet there has so far been no research, as far as I am aware, dealing even superficially with the repercussions that the essentially industrial nature of filmmaking has had on FT.

WORKINGS OF THE TRADE

A second aspect of study consists of describing the technical processes involved in the various modes of FT. It is common knowledge that the cinema has developed a whole range of FT devices in the course of its history. The two most important ones are of course conventional subtitling and above all dubbing, which have been well researched already.[8] However, the other modes of FT have yet to be described in depth.

TRANSLATION STUDIES ASPECTS

This involves examining problems related to translation itself in the context of conditions that are specific to audiovisual media.

History of FT and the Dubbing versus Subtitling Controversy

Nowadays the history of FT in Spain is fairly well established, having been documented in studies such as Izard (1992), Ávila (1997a, 1997b), Chaves García (2000), Ballester Casado (2001), Díaz Cintas (2003), and Chaume (2004). The topics that have received the most attention to date are the following.

First is the development by the industry, from the very moment that the talkies were invented, of several different systems to solve the problem of conveying the dialogues to audiences who did not know the language that the actors were speaking: dubbing into so-called International Spanish, simultaneously shot foreign-language versions (bilingual or multilingual), conventional dubbing, conventional subtitling, and so on.

Second is the dubbing versus subtitling controversy, a topic that has been written about ad nauseam. The debate has raged around the advantages and disadvantages of each and the alleged reasons why the public prefers one or the other. Furthermore, there has been an important change of direction in the research of recent years. Traditionally, the question was discussed in economic and industrial terms, and it was held that subtitling came on the scene because some of the producers and distributors had concluded that dubbing was too costly, complicated, and slow and were looking for cheaper alternatives (Ivarsson 1992, 16). Recently, however, researchers have been insisting that the phenomenon is more complex than had previously been thought and that ideological factors have played a fundamental role in the way that one method or the other has come to predominate in various parts of the world (see, e.g., Agost Canós 1999, 45; Ballester Casado 2001, 111 ff.).

The Language of the Cinema

While the information in films is conveyed through two channels (images and sounds), which have quite different semiotic statuses, in the end the image must prevail because it carries more information, and the sound can only be a dependent component. Hence, it is commonly said that in films the words are subject to the pictures, and in translation studies the various modes of treating film texts are sometimes grouped together under the label "constrained translation" (see Mayoral et al. 1988). Yet the very important translational implications of the "constriction" have still to be explored in depth. Nobody has gone further than very general and elementary observations, for example the requirement that the words be "perfectly" synchronized with the image or that, in commercial cinema, the dialogue must always be consistent with the images and never be redundant with respect to it. There are descriptions of cases where the constriction has created virtually insoluble translation problems, but they are no more than anecdotal.[9]

It is also commonplace to say that the register of the dialogues in films should be functional and not rhetorical or literary.[10] Likewise, people usually insist on the need for film dialogues to reflect the way that people speak in real life, yet there is a contradiction here because these dialogues, however natural they may seem at times, are texts written by professional authors, and they have usually passed through the studio's writing department, which may rewrite them over and over again—as many times as may be needed to satisfy the production department. To put it in a nutshell, we are in the presence of highly artificial, very intricate texts that are intended to *simulate* spoken language and that do so with more or less success. However, I do not know of any research publication that analyzes carefully the characteristics of what we may call the cinematic oral code and draws the necessary implications for translation studies. Perhaps it is Chaume who has best drawn attention in Spain to the "oral pretence" and the "fabricated spokenness" of audiovisual texts (2001a, 2004, 168 ff.).

General Translation Problems and Core Difficulties

From the beginning, FT has received bad press in Spain—to the point where those who are conducting research in this area have become tired of all the passing references, not to mention whole articles, about its lamentable quality. Such reproaches appear both in the popular media and in specialized publications. The latter in particular ring continually with complaints about the glaring errors committed by film translators, of which there are admittedly many, and the press generalizes from them. One can cite as typical Javier Marías's well-known article "¿Es usted el Santo Fantasma?" ("Are You the Holy Ghost?"). In any case, it is not hard to see why FT has gained this bad reputation. First, few film translators in Spain have been professionals; anybody with the right contacts could do the job. Second, it is inevitable that whenever there are translations there are translation errors. The crux of the matter is that translating is an activity in which it is necessary to make a great number of decisions, and consequently it carries with it a great many opportunities to make mistakes. The risk of error will of course be much greater if the translating has to be done under the pressure of external constraints, as is the case in constrained translation.

Under these conditions, it is not surprising that errors occur, nor is it surprising that they cause loud echoes, because commercial cinema reaches every corner of Spain and receives intensive coverage in all the media.[11] In addition to being of interest to the public, translated films undergo close scrutiny by film critics. This all helps to explain why, for some time, when FT research in Spain was in its infancy, there was much compiling of sporadic errors and a great deal of commentary on them at the anecdotal level; the research publications of the period were largely devoted to them. Then researchers gradually realized that collecting flagrant errors might be very amusing, but it was a dead end, and that, on the other hand, there are certain elements that render film translators particularly prone to making errors and that, therefore, deserve special attention. More specifically, we may say that the main problem areas are the following: (a) microlinguistic problems, especially interferences between the source language and the target language, and difficulties in rendering slang, jokes, taboo expressions, and terms of endearment; (b) cultural problems; (c) accents and dialects; and (d) dependence on the visuals.

In recent times, these problems have begun to claim the attention of researchers. Any one of the above categories would provide sufficient material and scope to fill volumes, but as of October 2004 it is unfortunately still all too easy to take stock of the progress to date. More specifically, there are two sub-areas that have aroused most interest in researchers. The first of these is cross-language interferences. To all intents and purposes, this is tantamount to saying the intrusion of anglicisms into Spanish FTs, because, as everyone knows, English is the dominant language in the film industry. These interferences have been analyzed in studies such as Fontcuberta Gel (1997), Chaume and García (2001), Duro Moreno (2001), Gómez Capuz (2001), and Postigo Martín (2002). The second sub-area is comprised of problems posed by the translation of jokes and other humour. These have been treated notably in Fuentes Luque's doctoral dissertation on *Duck Soup* (2000). As for other language problems, those posed by the translation of slang, taboo expressions, and terms of endearment constitute an area of research in which nothing substantial has yet been published.

Nor has research on cultural difficulties progressed far to date. Today we do at least recognize that film texts do not come out of the blue but are deeply rooted in a particular cultural substrate, which in the case of commercial cinema usually means the popular culture of the United States. We also know that all this connection of the cinema with the real-life context that feeds it and gives it life is something that cannot be left aside when translating. Furthermore, research has shown that any film text may contain references to cultural entities or phenomena that do not exist in the target culture. This is a phenomenon that sometimes presents translators with problems that are very difficult to solve without seriously endangering the film's stylistic equilibrium. As of the end of 2004, we still do not have any substantial publications that deal with this important area of difficulty systematically and in depth, although there are studies that have begun to give some prominence to it, such as Chaves García (2000, 109–10) and Bravo (2002, 204–10).

The situation is even more inadequate with respect to problems due to subordination of word to image. To date, researchers have treated them only anecdotally. The same can be said about the difficulties of transposing accents and dialects, for which no satisfactory solution has yet been found. Yet linguists have shown that these supralingual features are not merely embellishments or exotic touches but also represent a veritable mine of information both in real life and in the cinema. Nevertheless, the practice in FT has traditionally been to smooth over accent and dialect distinctions by replacing them with standard Spanish. (There have been a few exceptions, for instance the notorious use of pseudo-Cuban accents for the dubbing of *Gone with the Wind* [Ávila 1977b, 175]). So far, researchers have scarcely formed any idea of how to handle these important aspects of film texts (Bravo 2002, 208–10).

Ideology and Translation

In contrast, the subject of ideology and translation is an area where there have been studies for a long time, though they have been unsystematic. Mainly, they are studies of censorship in Spain, for example Gubern and Font's (1975) classic *Un cine para el cadalso: 40 años de censura cinematográfica en España* (Cinema on the Scaffold: 40 Years of Film Censorship in Spain). In these studies, there are occasional mentions of censorship-imposed dialogue manipulation by way of the translation, which started with the implementation of the ministerial order of April 23, 1941, which made dubbing compulsory in Spain. Those of us who have been teaching FT studies have been in the habit of making the same kind of observations, and they can also be found scattered throughout some of the monographs in translation studies, for instance Agost Canós (1999, 49, 102–03) and Díaz Cintas (2003, 57–59).

What is really important, however, is that in recent years studies have begun to appear that deal in depth with topics such as the relationships between dubbing, nationalism, and cultural identity; the identification, description, and documentation of the ideological control mechanisms affecting translated films; and the power structure in FT. Among the notable products of this new current are Ávila (1997b), Ballester Casado (2001), and above all the work of the TRACE group from 1994 onward under the leadership of Rosa Rabadán and Raquel Merino. This group has done an enormous amount of work, which has resulted in important achievements such as the DGICYT PB 93-0297 project, Gutiérrez Lanza's 1999 doctoral dissertation, and Rabadán's 2000 monograph—to cite just a few of the most significant.

NEW DIRECTIONS

Currently, the field of FT is in a state of upheaval. Under the circumstances, it is only normal that there should be various emergent lines of investigation. They are opening up new horizons, and we may expect them to produce interesting results over the next few years. Among them, the following are worthy of mention.

FILM GENRES

It is more and more clearly recognized that each genre possesses basic defining characteristics that the films of the genre share and that among them is a particular use of language — and the kind of language used is of course very important when it comes to translating. Thus, one can talk of audiovisual legal language, prison language, cowboy language, and so on. Now people are beginning to investigate the linguistic characteristics of the genres, and the first Spanish doctoral dissertation in the area has already been presented at the University of Zaragoza: it deals specifically with the translation of war films (Gordo Peleato 2003).

AUDIO DESCRIPTION

There is quite a long history of making the speech in audiovisuals accessible to the handicapped, especially the hard of hearing. The first experiments go back to the 1970s in the United States. Much more recently, a new type of transcoding has made its appearance, intended this time for the visually impaired. It is called "audio description" (or AUDESC for short in Spain).[12] The system works basically by exploiting moments of silence in a film in order to describe in voice-over what is going on at the time on the screen; in that way, it does not interfere with the dialogue.

Audio description has been functioning for several years in countries such as the United States, Great Britain, and Japan. In Spain, ONCE (the Spanish national organization for the blind) began developing audio description in 1994, and now over 200 feature films have been processed with it. Furthermore, on December 8, 2001, the TVE1 channel began broadcasting a series of animated cartoons called *Nico* for the very young, using an audio description system for televisions equipped with dual tuners. On October 27, 2002, a feature film was shown with AUDESC, for the first time at a film festival, at the Seminci festival in Valladolid, and slowly this system is starting to be used in movie theatres and on DVDs.

So far, no research on this new mode of translation has been published in Spain. However, it may well turn into a major research topic since it would seem that translation for the handicapped is due for substantial development over the next few years in line with social integration policies.

THE THEORETICAL MODEL

Research at the theoretical level has been very limited so far. For the most part, researchers have not yet moved beyond the stage of collecting data. They have frequently noted the existence of problems and framed questions but without attempting replies and solutions. Hence, on the strictly theoretical level, there is an important knowledge gap that needs filling. For now, we still possess very little theory or research concerning all that is involved specifically in the process of transfer by translation, whether in the audiovisual media in general or in the cinema in particular. If one looks closer, one sees some interesting pieces of descriptive research of the case-study type; however, nobody has yet managed to come up with a well-developed methodology that can be applied generally and that would make it possible to conduct a deeper analysis of those complex artifacts called films. Furthermore, we still seem to be far away from a theoretical model or paradigm.

CONCLUSION

There is no doubt that this area of studies is still in an exploratory phase. My overall assessment of the work published to date is that it has simply served to launch the discussion and to confirm that there is a research gap to be filled.

NOTES

1 All quotations from Spanish have been translated into English by the author of this paper.
2 See Agost Canós (1996), Chaves García (1996), Díaz Cintas (1997), Ballester Casado (1999), Gutiérrez Lanza (1999), Fuentes Luque (2000), Santamaría Guinot (2001), Chaume (2001b), and Gordo Peleato (2003).
3 See Eguiluz et al. (1994), Santamaría et al. (1997), Lorenzo García and Pereira Rodríguez (2000), Sanderson (2001), Chaume and Agost (2001), Duro Moreno (2001), and Pajares et al. (2001).
4 This wide-ranging conference has already been held four times, in 1993, 1997, 2000, and 2004.
5 TRAG (TRAducción de Guiones de películas): http://www.egroups.com/groups/trag (consulted October 14, 2004).
6 Some independent films could be considered an exception to this general rule.
7 See Álvarez Monzoncillo (2002) and Álvarez Monzoncillo and López Villanueva (2003).
8 See, for example, Ávila (1997a, 32–41, 83–92), Castro Roig (2001, 267–87), and Díaz Cintas (2003, 75–87).
9 See, for example, Chaume (1996, 166–69) and Bravo (2002, 195–96).
10 Of course, this does depend to some extent on the type of film in question.
11 The ten foreign films with the highest box-office ratings in Spain in 2002 drew audiences totalling 33 million. See *"El mercado."*

12 Less frequent spelling variants found by Google include *audiodescription* and *AudioDescription*. Apparently, *AUDESC* does not appear in any of the English documentation.

REFERENCES

Agost Canós, R. 1996. "La traducció audiovisual: El doblatge." PhD diss., Universitat Jaume I, Spain.

———. 1999. *Traducción y doblaje: Palabras, voces, e imágenes.* Barcelona: Ariel.

Álvarez Monzoncillo, J.M. 2002. "Informe del Año: El cine español de 2001." *Academia* 31: 150–99.

Álvarez Monzoncillo, J.M., and J. López Villanueva. 2003. "La crisis: Informe del Año: El cine español de 2002." *Academia* 33: 46–89.

Ávila, A. 1997a. *El doblaje.* Madrid: Cátedra.

———. 1997b. *La historia del doblaje cinematográfico.* Barcelona: CIMS.

Ballester Casado, A. 1999. "Traducción y nacionalismo: La recepción del cine americano en España a través del doblaje." PhD diss., Universidad de Granada, Spain.

———. 2001. *Traducción y nacionalismo: La recepción del cine americano en España a través del doblaje (1928–1948).* Granada: Comares.

Bravo, J.M. 2002. "Translating the Film Dialect of Hollywood for Dubbing." In *Nuevas perspectivas de los estudios de traducción,* ed. J.M. Bravo, 187–214. Valladolid: Universidad de Valladolid.

Castro Roig, X. 2001. "El traductor de películas." In *La traducción para el doblaje y la subtitulación,* ed. M. Duro Moreno, 267–98. Madrid: Cátedra.

Chaume, F. 1996. "Algunas consideraciones sobre la construcción de los textos audiovisuales y sus implicaciones en traducción." In *A Spectrum of Translation Studies,* ed. P. Fernández Nistal and J.M. Bravo Gozalo, 161–72. Valladolid: Universidad de Valladolid.

———. 2001a. "La pretendida oralidad de los textos audiovisuales y sus implicaciones en traducción." In *La traducción en los medios audiovisuales,* ed. F. Chaume and R. Agost, 77–88. Castellón: Universitat Jaume I.

———. 2001b. "La traducción audiovisual: Estudio descriptivo y modelo de análisis de los textos audiovisuales para su traducción." PhD diss., Universitat Jaume I, Spain.

———. 2002. "Nuevas líneas de investigación en la traducción audiovisual." In *Nuevas perspectivas de los estudios de traducción,* ed. J.M. Bravo, 215–24. Valladolid: Universidad de Valladolid.

———. 2004. *Cine y traducción.* Madrid: Cátedra.

Chaume, F., and R. Agost, eds. 2001. *La traducción en los medios audiovisuales.* Castelló de la Plana, Spain: Publicacions de la Universitat Jaume I.

Chaume, F., and C. García. 2001. "El doblaje en España: Anglicismos frecuentes en la traducción de textos audiovisuals." *Rivista internazionale di tecnica della traduzione* 6: 119–37.

Chaves García, M.J. 1996. "La traducción cinematográfica: El doblaje." PhD diss., Universidad de Sevilla, Spain.

———. 2000. *La traducción cinematográfica: El doblaje.* Huelva: Universidad de Huelva.

Díaz Cintas, J. 1997. "El subtitulado en tanto que modalidad de traducción fílmica dentro del marco teórico de los estudios sobre traducción (*Misterioso Asesinato en Manhatan*, Woody Allen, 1993)." PhD diss., Universidad de Valencia, Spain.

———. 2003. *Teoría y práctica de la subtitulación inglés-español.* Barcelona: Ariel.

Duro Moreno, M. 2001. "'Eres patético': El español traducido del cine y de la television." In *La traducción para el doblaje y la subtitulación*, ed. M. Duro Moreno, 161–85. Madrid: Cátedra.

Eguiluz, F., et al., eds. 1994. *Transvases culturales: Literatura, cine, traducción.* Vitoria: Evagraf.

"Estudio de Film Interactive: El mercado de la distribución de 2002 en cifras." 2003. *Academia: Revista del cine español* 33: 29–38.

Fontcuberta Gel, J. 1997. "Creatividad en la traducción audiovisual." In *Aproximaciones a los estudios de traducción*, ed. P. Fernández Nistal and J.M. Bravo, 217–30. Valladolid: Universidad de Valladolid.

Fuentes Luque, A. 2000. "La recepción del humor audiovisual traducido: Estudio comparativo de fragmentos de las versiones doblada y subtitulada al español de la película *Duck Soup*, de los Hermanos Marx." PhD diss., Universidad de Granada, Spain.

Gómez Capuz, J. 2001. "Diseño de análisis de la interferencia pragmática en la traducción audiovisual del inglés al español." In *¡Doble o Nada!*, ed. J.D. Sanderson, 59–84. Alicante: Universidad de Alicante.

Gordo Peleato, M.R. 2003. "La traducción para el doblaje del lenguaje militar: Una aproximación desde la teoría de la relevancia." PhD diss., Universidad de Zaragoza, Spain.

Gubern, R., and D. Font. 1975. *Un cine para el cadalso: 40 años de censura cinematográfica en España.* Barcelona: Euros.

Gutiérrez Lanza, M.C. 1999. "Traducción y censura de textos cinematográficos en la España de Franco: Doblaje y subtitulado inglés-español (1951–1975)." PhD diss., Universidad de León, Spain.

Ivarsson, J. 1992. *Subtitling for the Media.* Stockholm: Transedit.

Izard, N. 1992. *La traducció cinematogràfica.* Barcelona: Generalitat de Catalunya.

Lorenzo García, L., and A.M. Pereira Rodríguez, eds. 2000. *Traducción subordinada (I): El doblaje.* Vigo: Universidade de Vigo.

Marías, J. 2001. "¿Es usted el Santo Fantasma?" *El Semanal*, November 25: 10.
Mayoral, R., et al. 1988. "Concept of Constrained Translation: Non-linguistic Perspectives of Translation." *Meta* 33 (3): 356–67.
Pajares, E., et al., eds. 2001. *Trasvases culturales: Literatura, cine, traducción 3*. Vitoria: UPV.
Postigo Martín, M. 2002. "Analysis of Pragmatic Interference in U.S. Films Dubbed into Spanish: *Annie Hall* and *Working Girl*: A Contribution to the Study of Audiovisual Translation, Language Contact, and Language Change." Guided research paper, Universidad de Valladolid.
Rabadán, R., ed. 2000. *Traducción y censura inglés-español: 1939–1985*. León: Universidad de León.
Sanderson, J.D., ed. 2001. *¡Doble o nada! Actas de las I y II Jornadas de doblaje y subtitulación de la Universidad de Alicante*. Alicante: Biblioteca Virtual de Miguel de Cervantes.
Santamaría, J.M., et al., eds. 1997. *Trasvases culturales: Literatura, cine, traducción 2*. Vitoria: Evagraf.
Santamaría Guinot, L. 2001. "Les referències culturals: Aportació informativa i valor expressiu: El subtitulat." PhD diss., Universidad Autónoma de Barcelona, Spain.
Wasko, J. 2003. *How Hollywood Works*. London: Sage.

CONTRIBUTORS

BERYL T. SUE ATKINS was general editor of the original *Collins-Robert French-English Dictionary*, then lexicographic adviser to Oxford University Press, before founding with Adam Kilgarriff and Michael Rundell the Lexicography MasterClass (http://www.lexmasterclass.com/). She originated the idea of the British National Corpus and is currently lexicographic adviser to the FrameNet project at ICSI, Berkeley, California (http://framenet.icsi.berkeley.edu/). In 2002, she was made an honorary life member of EURALEX (the European Association for Lexicography).

CAROLINE BARRIÈRE obtained a PhD in computational linguistics from Simon Fraser University (Canada). Formerly a professor at the School of Information Technology and Engineering at the University of Ottawa, she now works for the National Research Council of Canada as a research officer at the Language Technology Research Centre. She has presented her work at numerous conferences and published a number of articles, including some in the journal *Terminology*. Her research interests include computational terminology and computer-assisted translation.

JACQUELINE BOSSÉ-ANDRIEU, PhD, was a professor at the School of Translation and Interpretation at the University of Ottawa, where she taught translation, comparative stylistics, and French stylistics for thirty-four years until her retirement in 2006. She is the author of *Exercices pratiques de français, Exercices pratiques de style,* and *Abrégé des règles de grammaire et d'orthographe,* and is a key member of the team working on the Bilingual Canadian Dictionary Project.

PIERRETTE BOUILLON obtained a degree in classical philology and a PhD in linguistics from the Université Paris VII. She is now maître de conférence et de recherche (MER) at ETI/TIM/ISSCO, University of Geneva, with a particular interest in lexical semantics (especially generative lexicon theory) and machine translation. She currently heads a Swiss national project called Automatic Spoken Language Translation for Medical Applications.

LYNNE BOWKER, C. Tran., is an associate professor at the School of Translation and Interpretation at the University of Ottawa. She obtained an MA in translation from that institution under the supervision of Ingrid Meyer, and she went on to obtain a PhD in language engineering from the University of Manchester Institute of Science and Technology in the United Kingdom. Her research interests include translation technology, terminology, and corpus linguistics. She is the author of *Computer-Aided Translation Technology* (2002) and a co-author of *Working with Specialized Language: A Practical Guide to Using Corpora* (2002). From 1998 to 2004, she was a co-editor of the *Bibliography of Translation Studies,* and she is currently a member of the editorial board for the journals *Localisation Focus* and *International Journal of Corpus Linguistics.*

JOSÉ-MARÍA BRAVO is a full professor at the University of Valladolid, Spain, where he is currently program director for the MA and the PhD in translation studies as well as director of the ITBYTE Research Institute. His publications include papers and books on screen translation, cross-language interference, corpus linguistics, specialized translation, and translation tools.

M. TERESA CABRÉ CASTELLVÍ obtained a PhD in Romance philology from the University of Barcelona (1977) and is currently a professor of linguistics and terminology at the Universitat Pompeu Fabra (UPF) in Spain as well as a member of the Secció Filològica at the Institute of Catalan Studies, the most important scholarly society in Catalonia. At UPF, she was the founding director of the Applied Linguistics Research Institute (Institut Universitari de Lingüística Aplicada, IULA), which she directed from 1994 to 2004. She was a founding member of the Ibero-American Terminology Network (Riterm), the Pan-Latin

Terminology Network (Realiter), and the European Association for Terminology (EAFT). She is currently president of AETER (Spanish Terminology Association). She is also on the editorial boards of several international journals, including *Terminology*. She has published more than a hundred papers in national and international journals and has authored several books. Originally written in Catalan, *La terminologia: La teoria, els mètodes, les aplicacions* (1992) has since been translated into Spanish (1993), French (1998), and English (1999).

JEAN DELISLE, C. Tr., C. Term., is a professor at the School of Translation and Interpretation at the University of Ottawa, where he has been teaching since 1974. He has authored several books on translation teaching and the history of translation, namely *L'analyse du discours comme méthode de traduction* (1980), *Bridging the Language Solitudes* (1984), *Translation in Canada, 1534–1984* (1987), *The Language Alchemists* (1990), *La traduction raisonnée* (1993; 2nd ed. 2003), and *L'enseignement pratique de la traduction* (2005). He edited *Portraits de traducteurs* (1999), *Portraits de traductrices* (2003), and was co-editor of *Translators through History* (1995), *Enseignement de la traduction et traduction dans l'enseignement* (1998), *Translation Terminology* (1999), and *Traduction: La formation, les spécialisations, et la profession* (2004). He also co-produced a CD-ROM on *The History of Translation*. His work has been translated into Arabic, Chinese, Dutch, English, Finnish, Galician, German, Korean, Italian, Polish, Portuguese, Persian, Romanian, Russian, Spanish, and Turkish.

BARBARA FOLKART was a colleague of Ingrid Meyer at the School of Translation and Interpretation of the University of Ottawa. Her publications include *Le Conflit des énonciations: Traduction et discours rapporté* (1991) and *Second Finding: A Poetics of Translation* (due out this fall from the University of Ottawa Press) as well as critical editions of medieval French texts, and a poetry collection (*Words for Trees*, Vancouver: Beach Holme, 2004), which was a finalist for the 2006 Gerald Lampert Award.

ALINE FRANCOEUR, C. Term., is an associate professor at the School of Translation and Interpretation at the University of Ottawa. She has been involved in various research projects in lexicography since 1994. In 2001, she completed her PhD at the Université de Montréal, where her dissertation addressed the topic of prefatory discourse of French dictionaries. Since then, her research has focused mainly on bilingual dictionaries, especially Guy Miège's *New Dictionary French and English*, published in London in 1677.

FRANCIE GOW has an MA in translation from the University of Ottawa. Her thesis was awarded the 2003 Best Thesis Award from the Localisation Research Centre, based at the University of Limerick in Ireland. She has presented her research results at a conference and published an article in *Localisation Focus*. She is currently employed as a translator at the Translation Bureau of the Government of Canada and is pursuing a law degree at McGill University in Montreal.

BRENDA M. HOSINGTON was a professor of translation history, theory, and literary and comparative translation, as well as English sociolinguistics, in the Département de linguistique et traduction at the Université de Montréal for twenty-eight years before retiring in 2003. She was also an associate research fellow in the Centre for the Study of the Renaissance at the University of Warwick, United Kingdom. It was her great pleasure to have Ingrid as a student in two master's seminars and to have been a member of her master's and PhD thesis juries. She has published widely in North America and Europe on a variety of subjects in translation studies, medieval and Renaissance studies, and neo-Latin literature.

JACYNTHE LANTHIER obtained a BA in translation and writing from the Université du Québec en Outaouais, where she also worked as a research assistant for two years. Working on a terminometric research project with Jean Quirion, she has presented the results at a number of conferences and has co-written an article published in *Actualité langagière*. She is currently pursuing an MA in linguistics at the Université de Montréal.

CLAIRE-HÉLÈNE LAVIGNE obtained a Bachelor of Laws (LLB), as well as a PhD in linguistics with a specialization in translation, from the Université de Montréal. Formerly an assistant professor at the School of Translation and Interpretation at the University of Ottawa, where her teaching and research addressed the history of translation, legal translation, and the theory of law, she currently holds the position of lawyer-reviser in the Montreal office of the Canadian law firm Blake, Cassels and Graydon LLP.

MARIE-CLAUDE L'HOMME obtained a PhD in linguistics from Laval University in 1992, and after working for almost two years in the private sector as a terminologist-documentalist she joined the Université de Montréal, where she has been a faculty member since 1994. She is in charge of courses on terminology and computer tools for translators. She is also a member of the research group Observatoire de linguistique Sens-Texte (OLST), and her research focuses on corpus-based terminology and terminological descriptions based on lexical semantics. She is responsible for the development of a French dictionary of computing, the *DiCoInfo*. She has published papers in *Terminology, International Journal of Lexicography, Cahiers de lexicologie,* and *International Journal of Corpus Linguistics* and has authored *Initiation à la traductique* and *La terminologie: Principes et techniques*. In 2001, she was appointed co-editor of the journal *Terminology*.

KRISTEN MACKINTOSH was at the University of Ottawa for ten years, during most of which she had the pleasure of working with Ingrid Meyer. While completing her MA there, she was a research assistant for Ingrid, conducting research in the fields of lexicography, terminology, and translation. For several years following the completion of her MA thesis on dictionary use in L2-L1 translation, written under Ingrid's supervision, she continued working with Ingrid as a research associate and taught a course on documentary research in the School of Translation and Interpretation. After a three-year sojourn in Geneva, she is now back in Ottawa working as a freelance translator.

ELIZABETH MARSHMAN obtained an MA in translation from the University of Ottawa in 2002, working under the supervision of Ingrid Meyer on discovering knowledge patterns for extracting cause-effect relations from corpora in the field of biopharmaceuticals. She is currently pursuing her doctorate and working at the Observatoire de linguistique Sens-Texte (OLST) at the Université de Montréal. Her thesis focuses on a comparison of the possibilities and difficulties of using knowledge patterns to identify non-hierarchical semantic relations in French and English. She has presented her research at conferences and published in the journal *Terminology*.

JEAN QUIRION, C. Term., is a professor and former head of the Département d'études langagières at the Université du Québec en

Outaouais. He obtained a PhD in linguistics with a specialization in terminology from the Université de Montréal. His research interests include terminology and its implantation, terminometrics, language planning, language technology, and lexicography. He is the author of *La mesure de l'implantation terminologique: Proposition d'un protocole. Étude terminométrique du domaine des transports au Québec* (2003), published as part of the Langues et sociétés collection of the Office québécois de la langue française.

RODA P. ROBERTS, PhD, C. Tran., was a professor at the School of Translation and Interpretation at the University of Ottawa for twenty-seven years until her retirement in 2006. During that time, she was director of the school from 1979 to 1989. She has taught languages, translation, and interpretation at a number of universities in Canada, the United States, and India. In addition, she has trained translation and interpretation trainers in Canada, the United States, and Mexico and has served as curriculum consultant to various educational institutions. She has written numerous articles on translation theory, translator/interpreter training, terminology, and lexicography. She is also the founding director of the Bilingual Canadian Dictionary Project, an interuniversity lexicographic project that has centres at the University of Ottawa, the University of Montreal, and Laval University.

KRISTA VARANTOLA is a professor of English at the School of Modern Languages and Translation Studies at the University of Tampere, Finland. She is currently rector (president) of the university and on leave of absence from her professorship. She has published widely on language for special purposes and on dictionary use in translation. From 2000 to 2002, she was president of EURALEX (the European Association for Lexicography). Her current research interests include the use of electronic text corpora in translation, interactive electronic dictionaries, as well as interactive lexical interfaces to knowledge bases—in other words, the creation of human-driven technology (software) and not technology-driven humans.

SELECT BIBLIOGRAPHY OF WORKS BY INGRID MEYER

This bibliography lists the major works written by Ingrid Meyer and her collaborators. In accordance with the overall organization of this volume, and to reflect the principal areas in which Ingrid carried out research, the works have been grouped into the categories of lexicography, terminology, and translation. Within each category, papers have been organized in reverse chronological order.

LEXICOGRAPHY

1990

Meyer, Ingrid. "Interlingual Meaning-Text Lexicography: Towards a New Type of Dictionary for Translation." In *The Meaning-Text Theory of Language: Linguistics, Lexicography, and Practical Implications,* ed. James Steele, 175–270. Ottawa: University of Ottawa Press.

Meyer, Ingrid, and James Steele. "The Presentation of an Entry and of a Super-Entry in an Explanatory Combinatorial Dictionary." In *The Meaning-Text Theory of Language: Linguistics, Lexicography, and Practical Implications,* ed. James Steele, 63–95. Ottawa: University of Ottawa Press.

Steele, James, and Ingrid Meyer. "Lexical Functions in an Explanatory Combinatorial Dictionary: Kinds and Definitions." In *The Meaning-Text Theory of Language: Linguistics, Lexicography, and Practical Implications,* ed. James Steele, 41–61. Ottawa: University of Ottawa Press.

1988

Meyer, Ingrid. "Pedagogical Lexicography and Translator Training: Teaching Cautious Use of Bilingual Dictionaries." In *Proceedings of the 29th Annual Conference of the American Translators Association,* ed. Deanna Hammond, 277–84. Medford, NJ: Learned Information.

———. "The General Bilingual Dictionary as a Working Tool in *Thème.*" *Meta* 33 (3): 368–76.

1986
Meyer, Ingrid. "Beyond the Book-Bound Barrier: Towards a New Type of Bilingual Dictionary for L1-L2 Use." *Bulletin of the Canadian Association of Applied Linguistics (CAAL)* 8 (2): 111–24.

1985
Meyer, Ingrid. "Translation and the General Bilingual Dictionary." In *Proceedings of the 26th Annual Conference of the American Translators Association*, ed. Patricia E. Newman, 181–86. Medford, NJ: Learned Information.

TERMINOLOGY

2002
Marshman, Elizabeth, Tricia Morgan, and Ingrid Meyer. "French Patterns for Expressing Concept Relations." *Terminology* 8 (2): 1–29.

2001
Meyer, Ingrid. "Extracting Knowledge-Rich Contexts for Terminography: A Conceptual and Methodological Framework." In *Recent Advances in Computational Terminology*, ed. Didier Bourigault, Christian Jacquemin, and Marie-Claude L'Homme, 279–302. Amsterdam: John Benjamins.

2000
Meyer, Ingrid. "Computer Words in Our Everyday Lives: How Are They Interesting for Terminology and Lexicography?" In *Proceedings of EURALEX 2000*, ed. Ulrich Heid, Stefan Evert, Egbert Lehmann, and Christian Rohrer, 39–58. Stuttgart: University of Stuttgart.

Meyer, Ingrid, and Kristen Mackintosh. "'L'étirement' du sens terminologique: Aperçu du phénomène de la déterminologisation." In *Le sens en terminologie*, ed. Henri Béjoint and Philippe Thoiron, 198–217. Lyon: Presses universitaires de Lyon.

———. "When Terms Move into Our Everyday Lives: An Overview of De-Terminologization." *Terminology* 6 (1): 111–38.

1999
Meyer, Ingrid, Kristen Mackintosh, Caroline Barrière, and Tricia Morgan. "Conceptual Sampling for Terminographical Corpus Analysis." In *Proceedings of Terminology and Knowledge Engineering (TKE '99)*, Innsbruck, August 23–27, ed. Peter Sandrini, 256–67. Vienna: TermNet.

1998
Meyer, Ingrid, Kristen Mackintosh, and Krista Varantola. "From Virtual Sex to Virtual Dictionaries: On the Analysis and Description of a De-Terminologized Word." In *Proceedings of EURALEX '98*, vol. 2, ed. Thierry Fontenelle, Philippe Hiligsmann, Archibald Michiels, André Moulin, and Siegfried Theissen, 645–54. Liège: University of Liège.

Meyer, Ingrid, Victoria Zaluski, Kristen Mackintosh, and Clara Foz. "Metaphorical Internet Terminology in English and French." In *Proceedings of EURALEX '98*, vol. 2, ed. Thierry Fontenelle, Philippe Hiligsmann, Archibald Michiels, André Moulin, and Siegfried Theissen, 523–31. Liège: University of Liège.

1997
Meyer, Ingrid, Karen Eck, and Douglas Skuce. "Systematic Representation of Concepts in a Knowledge-Based System." In *Handbook of Terminology Management*, vol. 1, ed. Sue Ellen Wright and Gerhard Budin, 98–118. Amsterdam: John Benjamins.

Meyer, Ingrid, Kristen Mackintosh, and Krista Varantola. "The Reality of *Virtual*: On the Lexical Implications of Becoming a Knowledge Society." *Lexicology* 3 (1): 129–63.

Meyer, Ingrid, Victoria Zaluski, and Kristen Mackintosh. "A Conceptual and Structural Analysis of Metaphorical Internet Terms." *Terminology* 4 (1): 1–33.

1996
Meyer, Ingrid, and Kristen Mackintosh. "Refining the Terminographer's Concept Analysis Methods: How Can Phraseology Help?" *Terminology* 3 (1): 1–26.

———. "The Corpus from a Terminographer's Viewpoint." *International Journal of Corpus Linguistics* 1 (2): 257–85.

1995
Eck, Karen, and Ingrid Meyer. "Bringing Aristotle into the 20th Century: A Tool and Approach for Constructing Definitions within a Terminological Knowledge Base." In *Harmonizing Terminology for Translation and Information Retrieval: Theory and Practice*, ed. Richard A. Strehlow and Sue Ellen Wright, 83–101. Philadelphia: American Society for Testing and Materials.

1994
Meyer, Ingrid. "Linguistic Strategies and Computer Aids for Knowledge Engineering in Terminology." *L'actualité terminologique/Terminology Update* 27 (4): 6–10.

Meyer, Ingrid, and Kristen Mackintosh. "Phraseme Analysis and Concept Analysis: Exploring a Symbiotic Relationship in the Specialized Lexicon." In *Proceedings of EURALEX '94*, ed. Willy Martin, Willem Meijs, Margreet Moerland, Elsemiek ten Pas, Piet van Sterkenburg, and Piek Vossen, 339–48. Amsterdam: Vrije Universiteit Amsterdam.

Meyer, Ingrid, and Bruce McHaffie. "De la focalisation à l'amplification: Nouvelles perspectives dans une base de connaissances terminologique." In *TAO: Recherches de pointe et applications immédiates*, ed. André Clas and Pierrette Bouillon, 425–40. Beirut: FMA.

1993

Meyer, Ingrid. "Concept Management for Terminology: A Knowledge Management Approach." In *Standardizing Terminology for Better Communication: Practice, Applied Theory, and Results*, ed. Richard A. Strehlow and Sue Ellen Wright, 140–51. Philadelphia: American Society for Testing and Materials.

Bowker, Lynne, and Ingrid Meyer. "Beyond 'Textbook' Concept Systems: Handling Multidimensionality in a New Generation of Term Banks." In *Proceedings of the 3rd International Congress on Terminology and Knowledge Engineering (TKE '93)*, ed. Klaus-Dirk Schmitz, 123–37. Frankfurt: Indeks Verlag.

1992

Meyer, Ingrid. "Knowledge Management for Terminology-Intensive Applications: Needs and Tools." In *Lexical Semantics and Knowledge Representation*, ed. James Pustejovsky and Sabine Bergler, 21–37. Berlin: Springer Verlag.

Meyer, Ingrid, Lynne Bowker, and Karen Eck. "COGNITERM: An Experiment in Building a Knowledge-Based Term Bank." In *Proceedings of EURALEX '92*, vol. 1, ed. Hannu Tommola, Krista Varantola, Tarja Salmi-Tolonen, and Jürgen Schopp, 159–72. Tampere: Tampereen Yliopisto.

Meyer, Ingrid, Douglas Skuce, Lynne Bowker, and Karen Eck. "Towards a New Generation of Terminological Resources: An Experiment in Building a Terminological Knowledge Base." In *Proceedings of the 14th International Conference on Computational Linguistics (COLING '92)*, 956–60. Nantes: ICCL.

1991

Meyer, Ingrid, David Miller, and Diane Michaud. "Terminologie et analyse notionnelle assistée par ordinateur." In *Actes du colloque international sur les industries de la langue*, vol. 2, 187–99. Québec: Office de la langue française.

Meyer, Ingrid, and Line Paradis. "Applying Knowledge Engineering Technology to Terminology: A Pilot Project." *L'actualité terminologique/ Terminology Update* 24 (2): 3–8.

1990
Meyer, Ingrid, and Douglas Skuce. "Computer-Assisted Concept Analysis for Terminology: A Framework for Technological and Methodological Research." In *Proceedings of EURALEX '90*, 129–38. Barcelona: Bibliograf.

Skuce, Douglas, and Ingrid Meyer. "Computer-Assisted Concept Analysis: An Essential Component of a Terminologist's Workstation." In *Proceedings of the Second International Congress on Terminology and Knowledge Engineering (TKE '90)*, ed. Hans Czap and Wolfgang Nedobity, 187–99. Frankfurt: Indeks Verlag.

———. "Concept Analysis and Terminology: A Knowledge-Based Approach to Documentation." In *Proceedings of the Thirteenth International Conference on Computational Linguistics (COLING '90)*, ed. Hans Karlgren, 56–58. Helsinki: Helsinki University.

TRANSLATION

1992
Meyer, Ingrid. "Role and Nature of Computer Studies in a Theoretically Oriented Translation Program." *Computers and the Humanities* 25: 297–301.

1990
Nirenburg, Sergei, Lynn Carlson, Ingrid Meyer, and Boyan Onyshkevych. "Lexicons for Knowledge-Based Machine Translation (KBMT)." In *Proceedings of the International Workshop on Electronic Dictionaries*, 107–17. Tokyo: Japan Electronic Dictionary Research Institute.

1989
Meyer, Ingrid. "Facilitation and Expansion of Translation through Computers." In *Proceedings of the 30th Annual Conference of the American Translators Association*, ed. Deanna Hammond, 551–62. Medford, NJ: Learned Information.

———. "A Translation-Specific Writing Program: Justification and Description." In *Translator Training and Foreign Language Pedagogy*, ed. Peter Krawutschke, 119–31. American Translators Association Monograph Series 3. Amsterdam: John Benjamins.

1988
Lambert, Sylvie, and Ingrid Meyer. "Selection Examinations for Student Interpreters at the University of Ottawa, Canada." *Canadian Modern Language Review* 44 (2): 274–84.

Meyer, Ingrid, and Pamela Russell. "The Role and Nature of Specialized Writing in a Translation-Specific Writing Program." *Traduction, Terminologie, Révision (TTR)* 1 (2): 114–24.

1981
Spilka, Irène V., and Ingrid Meyer. "Théories et pratique de la traduction chez Bronislaw Malinowski: Application aux formules incantatoires." *Bulletin of the Canadian Association of Applied Linguistics (CAAL)* 3 (2): 175–82.

INDEX

adgnatorum 6, 133, 135–137, 140
adgnati 6, 133, 135–138, 140
alignment 177, 185, 189
Althusser, Louis 5, 121–130

Barclay, Alexander 6, 145–157
Brant, Sebastian 5, 145–148, 152, 154, 155, 156
Brewster, Ben 122, 125–130,

coherence 167, 176
cohesion 7, 160, 176–177
collocation 5, 27, 30, 69, 76, 121–122, 218, 223, 224, 225
competing terms 5, 109, 111, 112, 113–114, 117
conceptual relationships (see also *semantic relationships* and *terminological relationships*) x, 68, 69, 71, 72, 77, 103, 176
conciseness 5, 16, 111, 112–113, 117
context word 2, 14, 16–17, 27
co-occurrents 3, 69, 73, 74–75, 76
corpus x, 2, 3, 4, 5, 8, 9, 25, 27–31, 70–71, 75, 81–82, 84, 87, 88, 89–90, 94–95, 97, 98, 103, 109–110, 185, 201–203, 210, 212–213, 216–217, 219, 220–222, 223–224
  general corpus (GC) 201, 202–203, 205, 211, 212–213
  linguistic corpus (LC) 201, 202–203, 205, 208, 210, 211, 212–213
  reference corpus 25, 94, 95
corpus-building tool 82, 90
corpus construction, semi-automatic 81–82, 84, 89
Corpus Iuris Civilis 6, 133, 134
cultural shifts 6, 148, 150–152

d'Annebaut, Richard 134, 136–140
Das Narrenschiff 6, 145–146, 154
de la Roche, Guy 134–136
de Lescut, Nicolle 134–140
definition 14, 46–50, 55–59
  intensional definition 16
  morphosemantic definition 15–16, 18
derivative forms 14, 15, 76, 222
  derivative form capability 5, 111, 112, 115, 117
diction 46, 50–52
dictionary x, 2, 8, 13–21, 25–37, 45–60, 94–95, 104, 160–161, 208, 211, 212–213, 216, 217–220, 222, 223, 224–225
  intelligent dictionary 223
dictionary-ese 46, 47–48
disparate 161
disparity 7, 160–169, 181, 185

edit distance 191, 197
englishing 6, 122, 125, 129, 146–157
examples, in dictionaries 2, 3, 46, 52–53, 59, 94, 211, 218

251

film translation 227–235
  audio description 9, 234
  dubbing 9, 227–229, 232, 233
  subtitling 9, 228, 229
formal properties (of terms) 67, 73–74, 75, 76
frame 29, 30
frame element 29, 30, 31
FrameNet 28–30

GENOME Project 4, 100–104

Hollywood movies 228
homogeneity 162, 165
hyperonym 14–16, 68, 73, 75

implantation co-efficient 5, 109–110, 111, 116, 117
Institutes 6, 133, 134, 135

knowledge databases 4, 98–100, 104
knowledge patterns 69–72, 82, 86
knowledge pattern density 4, 82, 86, 88, 89, 90
knowledge-rich contexts x, 69–70, 71, 72, 75, 76, 81, 82, 83, 86
knowledge-rich value 4, 82, 86–89

lexicographic relevance 25, 28
linguistic markers 3, 67–68, 75–76
literal translation 16, 160
Locher, Jacob 6, 145–156

macrostructure 2, 46, 54–55
meaning discrimination 2, 13, 18, 20
meaning potential 176, 219
metalanguage 21, 49, 51
Meyer, Ingrid *ix–xii*, 1, 3, 4, 5, 61fn1, 67, 77, 89, 90fn1, 198fn1, 240, 241, 242, 243, 245–250
Miège, Guy 2, 13–21
multiword term 73–74, 75, 97, 208, 222

noise 70, 71, 83, 87, 88

ontology 99, 100, 102, 103, 104

patriotism 148, 153–156
place names 147, 149, 150
"profspeak" 5, 122, 128

retranslation 6, 127

segment 93, 177–181, 184, 185, 189, 190
semantic features 2, 13, 14, 17, 18
semantic information 2, 14–16, 18–21, 73, 98
semantic prosody 216, 218–220, 223
Semantic Relations in Text software (SeRT) 83, 84, 85, 87, 90
semantic relationships (see also *conceptual relationships* and *terminological relationships*) 3, 73, 74, 76, 81–83, 86, 87, 88, 89, 90, 176
sense indicator 2, 34–37, 40–43
"sentence salad" 181, 183
Shyp of folys 6, 145, 146, 148, 150, 152, 153, 154, 156, 157
social values 2, 45–46, 52–60
subject field 17
synonym 15–16, 18, 34–35, 47, 48, 69, 73, 74, 75, 88, 114, 166, 176, 180, 223
synonymic binomial 136, 139

taboo words 54–55, 231, 232
tagging 96–98, 102, 221, 223–224
tags 71, 87, 96–98
term implantation 4–5, 107–118
terminological data banks 96, 99, 109
terminological knowledge base (TKB) x, 3, 4, 77fn3, 81, 89
terminological relationships (see also *conceptual relationships* and *semantic relationships*) 67–77
  antonymy 34, 69, 74, 223
  cause-effect relationship 68, 71, 72, 75, 99, 101
  co-hyponymy 72, 74
  function relationship 68, 69, 70, 71, 72, 75, 83, 88
  hyperonymy 3, 14–16, 34, 67, 68, 70–76, 81, 83, 88, 99
  meronymy 3, 34, 67, 68, 71, 72, 99, 101
  synonymy 34, 69, 74, 88
terminometrics 4, 5, 108–110, 117,
text banks 94–97, 100–103
translation memory 7, 93, 175–185, 189–198

"wordness" 222

www.ingramcontent.com/pod-product-compliance
Lightning Source LLC
Chambersburg PA
CBHW050437240426
43661CB00055B/2412